If you were born without wings,
do nothing to discourage their growing.

COCO CHANEL

A MEMOIR

FLYING TIGRESS

NORAH O'NEILL

Ascending Journey Press

° SEATTLE °

Ascending Journey Press
4742 42nd Ave. SW #362
Seattle, WA 98116
www.flyingtigressone.com

Cover and text design by Carol Salvin

ISBN 0-9765555-0-6
First printing 2005
Reprinted 2006, 2014, 2016

TABLE OF
CONTENTS

ACKNOWLEDGEMENTS

I want to thank all the Flying Tiger pilots who were alarmed when they heard I was writing a book and told me, "I don't want to be in it." They inspired me to continue to concentrate on and celebrate the good guys. The Tigers who encouraged and helped me include: Bill Helbig, George Gewehr, Dick Crawford, Pete and Gael Okicich, Sandy Donnelly Wiederkehr, Martha Maxham, Sheree Weber, Bob Poindexter, Bob DeArmond, Sheri Laurie, Barbara Ganzkow, Rich Redditt, Dick Rothstein, Frank Campbell, Tom Witts, Jim Booth, Derrel Gibbins, Ron Hall, and Jim Brendel.

People who read the manuscript and offered valuable input that led to changes are: Jimmye Angell, Gayle Hellriegel, Karen Kahn, Gloria Kempton, Mona Maiman, Jean McMackin, Townsend, and Sandy Wiederkehr. (I recommend Karen Kahn's book, *Flight Guide For Success: Tips and Tactics For The Aspiring Airline Pilot*, to readers who want more information on how to become a pilot. It's available from www.AviationCareerCounseling.com.)

The friends who told me that I should write a book and encouraged me to keep at it, word by word, page by page, are: Janet Leigh Brandt, Sheri Hodge, and Sherry Propst.

Gayla Visalli, a patient and extraordinary editor, helped me fine-tune the results.

People who helped me reach the point of sanity and sobriety that allowed me to write a book are: Dr. Steve Juergens, Dr. Gerald Bock, Gabrielle Viethen, Maggie Knowles, Amy Alpine, Char French, Sheri and Craig Laurie, Linda Lloyd, Sueellen Ross, Mary Beth Logsdon, Frances Keir, Lori Patton, Bill Donnelly, John Lenahan, Kelly Dodd, Life Healing Center, and Residence XII.

The West Seattle Library Research Desk was always helpful, as were Fred Epps of Pegasus Books and Gretchen Montgomery of Square One Books. Cynthia Bowles gave me names, addresses, and websites of people in the publishing world. The Pacific Northwest Writers Association, Hugo House, and the Sun Valley Writers Conference were valuable in establishing connections and an encouraging network.

Kevin Johnson, computer guru, persuaded my computer to do what I wanted it to do.

Book designer, Carol Salvin, printing liaison, Van Bagley, and aviation photographer, Mark Garfinkel were helpful and inspiring.

Thank you to all the New York publishers and agents who rejected my manuscript saying, "I like it but it needs work." You forced me to continually revise and improve it.

Thanks, Dad, for ceasing to ask, "When are you going to get a job?" when I said I was going to write a book rather than go to interviews.

I am grateful to Patty Allen, Michelle Luccio, and Terry Ruhl, the first Tiger wives who, after hearing how much their husbands enjoyed flying with me, didn't write hate mail but invited me to dinner. Your acceptance was a blessing.

And thanks always to my Flying Tiger family, the men and women who launched the planes to adventure and held hands during the tough times. Office personnel, crew control, dispatchers, loaders, mechanics, charter representatives, flight attendants, and pilots—you are ever in my heart.

FLYING TIGRESS is dedicated to...

...my parents, Jack and Bertha O'Neill, who turned a blind date in World War II into a 62-year marriage—an incredible act to follow. Their parenting made everything good in my life possible.

...and my children, Cameron and Bren; the joy and privilege of parenting them helped me through the darkest times.

1
MOUNTING MCKINLEY
1973

I didn't believe in love at first sight. Lust at first sight, yes, but not love. Nothing in my experience had prepared me to recognize how I felt when I first looked out a cockpit window.

"Are you kidding? That's our transportation?" I blurted out while looking at the tinfoil hummingbird of a plane parked at the side of a narrow, dusty gravel strip carved into the scraggly trees at the bottom of a mighty mountain in Talkeetna, Alaska.

"I guess so. I don't see another one," replied Wini, the ski-clothing designer who had hired me to fly 10,000 feet up the side of Mount McKinley to model the next season's clothing. She looked daunted and perhaps sought to reassure herself also when she said, "Don Sheldon is Alaska's premier bush pilot. He's had a monopoly on the McKinley business for twenty-five years and he hasn't killed anyone yet."

"Yet?" *Hell. Breathe deep, Norah. If you can jump off cliffs and do somersaults on skis, you can get on that plane.*

Steve and Monica, the other two models for the five-day shoot, got out of the rusted station wagon that had brought us from the lodge and stood side by side, heads tilted back, looking upwards toward the looming mountains we were daring to mount.

"Oh, my," whispered Monica. "They keep getting bigger."

I walked toward our silver bird and poked a finger at the leading edge of a wing, easily reachable from my 5' 10" height. It dented; surely it was too fragile to carry precious human cargo.

"Get away from there! What are you doing?" an angry voice barked. "No one touches my plane but me." Don Sheldon, a man my height in a padded one-piece coverall that outlined his whipcord body, strode toward me. His voice softened. His fortyish face was commanding but not unkind. "You one of the models?" he asked eyeing my tight pants, which certainly weren't designed for rugged climbing. "Get your stuff unloaded. Put it there." He pointed to a patch of dirt a safe 10 feet from his pristine plane. "We have to be out of here in twenty minutes. You're my first load."

Only then did I notice another group of people gathered farther down the strip. Clearly, they were seasoned mountaineers, clad in survival clothing and standing by compact backpacks. They watched us, particularly Monica. I knew why they stared at Monica; I had too when I first met her. I had never seen, outside of the movies, anyone as beautiful as she was. With her tall, slender form in trendy, jewel-toned ski clothes, blonde hair free to her waist, Monica looked like a model. I didn't. I was tall and athletically slender, but my face would not launch ships. Wini had seen me skiing when she was looking for a replacement model, had ascertained that I wore the correct sample size and would work cheaply, and had hired me. This gig was a one-time deal; I was not career-model material.

As we stacked our load beside Don's plane, I was aware that our duffel bags of designer outfits, bags of makeup, and catering that included a whole roast turkey and tossed green salads did not look at all like the climbing party's small-in-volume professional load. They looked at us with disdain and disbelief, not bothering to hide the smirks on their faces. One of the climbers approached me.

"What mountains have you climbed?" he asked. "Oh, none." I laughed. "I'm afraid of heights. I don't even do ladders." He paused, waiting to see if I were joking. "We're here to shoot the winter catalog for a ski company." "On McKinley? You're going to model on McKinley?" The unspoken, "How dare you?" hung between us, obviating the need for further conversation. He backed away.

"What did he want?" Steve asked while walking a pile of sleeping bags toward Don's loading. "He wanted to know what we'd climbed before. He thinks our being here is sacrilegious. I think he decided I was too stupid to talk to."

"Yeah, but he's still looking at you girls. You aren't too stupid for him to allow you in his sleeping bag."

A dusty, road-worn jeep pulled in beside us. A tanned, bearded face poked out and scoffed, "What is this mess? Are you the models?" Ray Genet, McKinley's leading mountain guide had arrived. He had been hired to keep us alive for the duration of our photographic adventure, and he looked as if he might be having second thoughts about his chances for success. His mouth gaped when he saw Monica. It seemed that true mountain men did not include manners in their repertoire. *God, I'm glad I'm not really a model. Does anyone ever treat them with respect?*

Don removed most of the seats from the aircraft and stowed our things in a jigsaw-puzzle order that could be held securely by cargo netting. He took off with the photographer, the designer, and mountain guide extraordinaire. That full load left us models waiting for the next flight.

When Don returned and my time came to be flown up the mountain, a flicker in my consciousness, like the flash of a match in a dark room, made me pause and take a long look around me at the tree-lined runway and mountain peaks beyond. I felt a tension inside, as if my being were a stretched bow drawn back to shoot the arrow of my life at a target. I knew something momentous was about to happen. *Yeah, you're probably about to die. Get moving.*

I got on the plane. After much fussing and shifting of gear and retying of nets, Don told me to lie down in the

13

rear end of the plane. I lay where instructed, as Don packed bags around me and over me, securing a cargo net over it all, and could not see anything but small pieces of the plane's ceiling. I wasn't comfortable with the unexplained noises of engine start and run-up, nor with the roar of takeoff down the bumpy airstrip. I heard the noise of the engine change as we climbed, then change again as we reached altitude. The engine sounds remained the same for a long while, and I was lulled into daydreaming. Suddenly the engine stopped.

I yelled, "What's going on?"

No answer.

I yelled louder. "What happened to the engine? Get me out of here!"

Still no answer.

I could hear metallic clanking noises. Frantic to see what was going on, I tore at the bags over my head and clawed at the cargo tie-down ropes. I started to yell again.

"What are you yowling about?" Don asked, impatience in his tone, as he deftly unhooked the corner of the cargo net and started lifting baggage from around me. "We landed. Of course I shut the engine down." *We landed?*

I had not felt the landing. Don had circled Ruth's Glacier, high on the side of McKinley, and dropped weighted sacks from the plane onto the virgin snow below to give him a visual aid to depth perception. His landing area marked to his satisfaction, he had guided his plane in for an imperceptible landing on deep snow.

The five days on the mountain were full of work and wonder. It *was* work to rise with the sun at 4 a.m. to capture the rosy light that best flattered the colors of our outfits, to slather on makeup, to squeeze into stretchy ski clothes and sit, stand, and crouch in frozen poses. I would much rather have been making ski tracks in snow that no man had ever skied before, which was one reason I had taken this low-paying job. Instead, I smiled prettily, feigned flirtation, and gave a good imitation of actually *wanting* to wear some of the clothing. Having skied sixty days of the previous ski season, I was physically fit enough to do the more grueling action sequences.

Ray Genet showed us how to walk on snowshoes, roped the photographer, the male model, and me together, then led us across the bowl of the Ruth Amphitheater. The glacier that formed the five-mile-wide floor of the natural amphitheater was 10,000 feet in altitude; it was ringed with jagged peaks that soared up another 8,000 feet. We skirted crevasses and avoided finely spun ice bridges. The silence was broken only by the sound of our panting, the crunch of our snowshoe webbing against the snow crust, and the occasional ear-splitting crescendo of avalanching ice and snow. Our group was a mere dot on the mighty mountain.

The spring snow was tumultuously unstable. I watched an avalanche thunder down an escarpment just a mile away and thought, *this place has probably not changed since Creation. I'm so lucky to be here.*

The timing of the photographic shoot was lucky for me also. One month earlier, I had been married to the man I had fallen in love with as a teen-aged college student. We had separated while in a ski resort where we both worked at menial jobs. In a short three-week period, my husband's girlfriend discovered that she was pregnant, he and I filed for divorce, the divorce became final, and he married her. I was shell-shocked at the rapidity of the changes. Two days after my husband's wedding, Wini had offered me the Alaskan job. She said that there might be a lengthy wait in Anchorage because the weather had to be perfect for our ascent.

"You'll have to put your life on hold for a while," she cautioned.

What life? I'd rather be anywhere but here. "No problem. When do you want me there?"

Now on the job, I found that waking to the sky-roofed cathedral formed by Mt. McKinley, Mt. Foraker, and Mt. Hunter towering over the vast whiteness below them was to breathe in splendor—daunting, savage, and incredibly beautiful. Living those days was akin to constant conversations with God.

I insisted on riding in the cockpit on the way down the mountain. I wanted to know what was going on and to not panic as stupidly as I had on the flight up.

As I looked out the cockpit window, I felt curiosity and wonder and fear, but I did not immediately recognize the welling up of need from deep inside me. A need to see the earth from a bird's view; a need to understand how a hollow metal tube could leap into the air and stay there; a need to learn the language of the controls so I could bring the plane down safely; and a need to climb up into the sky again. Those unrecognized needs were born in the first few minutes of that flight.

I was in love.

When I could force my attention back inside the plane, I pestered Don with questions about the instruments and about flying.

"Just how hard is it to learn how to fly?" I wanted to know that at least one part of this incredible experience could be repeated.

"Takes time and work and money and a huge amount of dedication," Don said between mouthfuls of Oreo cookies. "The old pros define flying as hours of boredom interspersed with moments of sheer terror." He looked at me then, really looked at me for perhaps the first time. I'd like to think that he was recognizing the birth of a life-long love affair with flying. But maybe he was thinking it unlikely for a bubble-headed model to drum up the resolve and sacrifice necessary to become a pilot. He didn't say.

I watched through the front windshield while Don guided his plane to a gravel-spraying touchdown in Talkeetna. The rest of my group was going to travel to the lower forty-eight the next day.

I was twenty-three years old and didn't have a home to return to. I didn't know what I was going to do with my life. Those moments looking out the cockpit window were etched in my mind. I had been enrapt, enchanted, and removed from the mundane problems of earth. I wanted to be back in the air soon. I decided that I would stay in Alaska and learn how to fly—whatever that took.

"Thanks, Don, for the great ride," I said, stepping down from his plane. "I'll be seeing you."

2

BOYS-ONLY COUNTRY

1973

I looked for a nighttime job so I could take flight lessons during the day. I was hired for my first nine-to-five job since college—nine at night until five in the morning in Kodiak Island's most popular bar (the one the prostitutes frequented). I lived in the furnace room of an old house and swapped housework for rent. Every cent I earned that was not spent on bare essentials went to flight school.

I walked east from downtown Kodiak on a two-lane blacktop road that turned to gravel a mile before I reached a small runway with a large hangar next to it. There were two small planes to rent for lessons and a grizzled, chain-smoking instructor, Herb, who went with them. Herb had smoke-soaked me for two lessons before he agreed not to smoke in the plane unless he absolutely had to. Once, after an evidently spine-tingling show of flying ineptitude, Herb had had me land on a closed airstrip so he could get out and smoke. In addition to flying, I was spending hours each day studying flight manuals to augment what he was telling me in the air. One day, prior to my tenth lesson, I gave my plane a preflight examination before entering the hanger to drag Herb away from his coffee, his cigarettes, and his well-thumbed *Soldier of Fortune* magazines.

"Hey, Norah. Is our bird ready?" Herb greeted me.

"Yeah, Herb. What a day for it! This is the first time since I've been here that there aren't any clouds. What're we working on next?"

"Let's head out to Port Lyons and practice touch and gos." (pilot lingo for landing and taking off again without stopping)

"Great. My landings are getting better, aren't they?"

"Yeah, they are. You're becoming a pilot, girl. Today, because Port Lyons is a pretty short strip, I want you to be vigilant about getting the throttle full forward just as soon as your wheels hit the runway in the landing. As soon as you have full throttle, retract your flaps. You don't want to have full landing flaps slowing down your next takeoff."

"Yeah, yeah, I know that, Herb."

"I know you know it. I want you to *act* like you do."

"Okay," I humored him. *Why does he keep repeating this really simple stuff?*

We flew fifteen minutes to get to Port Lyons, and I studied the runway as I lined up my plane on the downwind portion of the rectangular pattern I would fly as I practiced. There was no control tower at Port Lyons. It was up to me to study the windsock, the trees, and the water to decide which direction I should land into. I had learned that planes perform better when facing into the wind. I practiced two landings with immediate takeoffs before Herb told me to make the next landing to a full stop. I was surprised that he wanted to stop because I had been performing pretty well. *What have I done to cause him to have a nicotine fit?*

Herb opened his door after we stopped, hopped out, and said, "Okay, girl, You're on your own. I'm going to stand over there." He pointed. "I want you to do two touch and gos and then stop after the third landing and pick me up."

"What? I'm gonna go alone?"

"Yes. You're ready. Just remember the flaps. Go on now." He shut the door and started walking away. I opened my side vent window and screamed over the sound of the engine, "Herb, are you sure, really sure?" He gave me thumbs up and continued walking. *Oh my God. I'm going to solo!*

I taxied back to the end of the runway, read my before-takeoff checklist aloud, lined up the plane with the center of the strip, and pushed the throttles forward. Lightened of Herb's weight, the plane leapt forward faster than usual. *What's wrong? Why's it different?* Then the little plane jumped into the air and rose rapidly, the cliff at the end of the runway falling away into the ocean with stomach churning speed. I made a 90-degree turn to the right, climbing swiftly to my targeted pattern altitude. *Oops, passed it.* I shoved my controls to level off and the force of the change raised me out of the seat. *Come on, Norah, calm down. Be smooth.* I glanced out of my window at Herb's now small, distant figure. *I wonder if he knows that I did that?* As Herb receded further, I realized that I needed to turn again to enter my downwind leg. I jerked the controls into another right turn. *Calm down, Norah; he said you were ready. He should know.*

On downwind, I partially extended my landing flaps and slowed my speed while I began a gentle descent that would gradually bring me from pattern altitude down to the ground. I began reading my prelanding checklist from a plastic-coated card, even though I had already memorized it. Herb insisted that I always use a printed checklist. He explained that many seasoned pilots who had done things by rote in their planes for years, had, in emergencies, forgotten critical items. I was learning that much of flying was developing safe routines.

When I had reached a spot where I could see the runway just behind my right wing, it was time to turn 90 degrees to base leg. On base, I slowed further, extended more flaps and continued my descent. I could now see the runway out of my right window. When the nose of my plane was nearing the right extended edge of the runway, I dipped my right wing into a shallow turn onto final approach. Now, descending down final, I slowed to my landing speed and tried to keep my descent stable so that I would have only 20 feet of altitude left to lose when I passed over the end of the runway. My wings bobbled in the roiled air of trees passing closely under my wheels. My hand clenched on the wheel in response, shallowing my descent. *Keep her coming*

19

down, Norah.

I pushed the plane's nose back down, and just feet above the rapidly rising runway, I pulled the controls back toward me, initiating a flare to ease off the last of the speed and ensure that the main wheels touched down before the nose wheel. The main tires squeaked down, and the nose-gear wheel touched the ground next. I immediately jammed the throttles full forward and guided the plane straight down the center of the runway. In my peripheral vision I saw Herb running down the runway. His arms were in the air and his mouth was open. I leapt into the air again, wondering for a moment what Herb had been doing, and then I sighed with joy. *Oh yeah, oh yeah, who needs Herb?*

But something was wrong. The nose of the plane kept rising, and no matter how strongly I pushed forward on the controls, I couldn't get it down. Because of the nose-up attitude, my speed was bleeding away. It was like a motorcycle doing a wheelie and trying to accelerate down the road at the same time.

I saw the cliffs disappearing below me, now at a sickening angle. *I'm going to stall out if I can't gain speed. What's wrong?* My eyes scanned my instruments, looking for a clue to the problem. I couldn't figure it out and I began to panic. I heard my breath panting and felt my now-moist hands squeezing the controls. I jerked the plane into a turn and started my downwind leg. *Hell. He shouldn't have gotten out. I wasn't ready. Damn you, Herb.* I looked from my window at the speck of Herb by the runway. I knew I wasn't going to make it back to him alive. *Bullshit, Norah. The plane's still flying, isn't it? Just fly. Do it now.* I breathed deep, put my shoulders back, and reached for the checklist. I ticked off the items. My altitude was right but my speed was still too slow, even at maximum power. I reached to extend the flaps and my hand stopped. The flaps were still full down in landing configuration. No wonder the plane was behaving so strangely. No wonder Herb was shouting from the edge of the strip. I corrected the flap setting and concentrated on what I needed to do next. My second landing was not as smooth as the first had been, but I did remember to raise the flaps, and my third takeoff was normal.

I swooped into my next turn with exhilaration growing so huge that I shouted aloud in the cockpit. "Yes! I can fly! I can fly!" I hated to stop even long enough to pick up Herb after my third landing. He crawled back in the plane.

"Damn, girl, what were you thinking on that second takeoff? I thought you were going to stall out."

"Your running down the runway distracted me, Herb. It was all your fault."

"What?"

"I was kidding. Calm down. I didn't stall did I? I looked him in the eye and started laughing. "Oh, Herb, it was so cool! I can do it. I can really do it!"

"Don't let surviving the first round go to your head. We have a lot to work on." He scowled at me and lit a cigarette.

My passion for flying was like my passion for expressing myself in other ways. It was like seeing an image in my mind and being able to paint that image on canvas. It was like feeling an emotion and being able to express it with words that perfectly conveyed that emotion to a reader. It was like looking down a mountainside of moguls and being able to force the skis on my feet to slide down the exact line of descent that would carry me safely to the bottom. When I looked out the window of the cockpit, I had an image in my brain of what the view should continue to look like in order to get my wings safely to the ground. If I coordinated my hands and feet precisely, my dance through the air would touch down upon the earth in exactly the right spot.

Learning to fly was like learning what strokes and movements would give maximum satisfaction to a lover; the pleasure was mutual. The plane was happy, and so was I.

It was difficult *not* to anthropomorphize the plane I flew in that summer. I'd pat its tail as I approached it and say, "Hey, babe, what are we going to do together today?" I was captivated when I was with it. *And* it didn't come with a mother-in-law, emotional baggage, or a desire for blow jobs in the morning.

I became fascinated with previously boring things such as engines, weather, aerodynamics, and navigation. I raced through books about Alaskan bush pilots and the history of aviation. Finally, I had heroes I wanted to emulate. As I earned my wings, I became aware of some realities. Flight lessons cost a lot of money. My $700 share of the marital savings was gone. The more I learned, the more I became aware of the vastness of what I did not know. I thirsted.

However, I was getting burned out working in the smoke-filled darkness of a place where men came to drink until they were senseless. They got rolled out the door at five in the morning only to crawl back in again at nine. It was only the promise of an afternoon's freedom in flight that kept me coming back every night to contribute to humans sinking to such pitiful depths.

I needed to find a way for someone to pay me to fly. I knew that the airlines would not hire women; I didn't even have fantasies about that. There didn't seem to be any women bush pilots in Alaska. The women pilots I had read about, like Amelia Earhart and Jackie Cochran, had been self-financed. The intrepid women pilots from World War II had been unable to get flying jobs once the war was over. Flying jobs were for men.

I had been asking since childhood why men got the best jobs. "Only boys can do that," I was told when I asked if I could be an altar attendant during sixth grade at a parochial school. I was told that only boys could be priests, presidents of the United States, Supreme Court justices, professional basketball players, or race-car drivers.

"Why can't girls do it?" I would ask my dad. His answers never satisfied me.

"I don't want to be any of those things," I told my dad when I came home crying from a career day at my all-girls' high school. The choices presented that day were nun, teacher, nurse, secretary, librarian, and housewife. "Why do boys get all the exciting and important jobs? I'm smart. I work hard. Why not me?"

Here I was again, in Alaska, asking to do what only boys did. But I couldn't stop flying. It was already part of me, as essential as air and water. I knew I would never forgive myself if I did not at least *try* to get someone to hire me. *Maybe*

I could get a job as a flight instructor. Alaska's population had about nine men for every woman. *Maybe a flight school would consider a woman a draw.*

Meanwhile, the winter weather was closing in on Kodiak Island, population 5,000 and home of ten churches and twelve bars. My employers did me the favor of firing me for dropping a tray of drinks over the head of a drunk who had touched my fanny one time too many, and they saved me from the dilemma of making a decisive plan. I asked my parents if I could come to San Diego for a visit. I didn't tell them that I needed a few months of free rent while I got my advanced flying licenses and prepared to ask business owners to allow me to do what they had never before allowed a woman to do.

I was positive that I was not going to like what my dad would have to say about my new assault on boys-only country.

3

WOULD YOU HIRE
THIS WOMAN?

1973

Dad and Mom welcomed me home, though I imagined my dad saying to her, "Oh, Bertha, I wonder what the hell she's up to now. What can we do to help her get on track?"

I had not been their easy child. They had seen their bright and shiny, award-and scholarship-winning daughter drop out of college just a few credits shy of a degree in journalism in order to marry Scott Reynolds three years earlier. I had been too damned young, but of course I didn't know that.

Scott and I had gypsied around the United States, Mexico, and Central America, then shipped out on a sailboat. We didn't have the money for phone calls, and I was stingy with the postage budget. I congratulated myself on being maturely responsible when I wrote my parents a note from Panama saying that Scott and I had been hired to crew on a 50-foot wooden schooner that was leaving the next day to sail to the Galapagos Islands and then on to Hawaii. Scott and I didn't know the people well, and the radio might as well have been nonexistent, considering its range and power, but I was keeping my parents informed. I thought we would be out to sea for perhaps thirty or forty days. "I'll call you from Hawaii. Bye."

I had no idea how worried my parents would be. Mom was sitting home with my younger sister, Peggy, while Dad did another tour as a navy captain in Vietnam. My older brother, John, was also in Vietnam, in the air force.

Scott and I had not been heard from for almost eighty-two days at sea when Dad pulled an oceanic all points bulletin from his ship's telex in the China Sea. It requested aid for a sailboat just northeast of Hawaii with four adults and a dog on board. Dad ripped off the telex and mailed it to Mom with the penciled notation, "I wonder if this is the kids." It was.

That adventure done, Scott and I ran off to be ski bums. Three years into the marriage, Scott, who was ten years older than I was, thought it was time to settle down and have a family. I was not ready. In June of 1973, I wrote to my parents for the first time in two months. They hadn't known that Scott and I were separated. My parents eagerly anticipated my infrequent letters but they probably knew by then that they needed to sit down and pour a stiff drink before they opened them.

"Dear Mom and Dad, I've been really busy. Just want you to know that Scott and I got divorced in April. He got remarried right away, and I took a modeling job in Alaska. Now I'm living on Kodiak Island, rolling drunks and learning how to fly.....Love, Norah"

*W*hen I first got back from Kodiak, Dad said he wanted me to join the military, his family's standard plan for what to do with kids who had potential but no common sense. I pointed out that the U.S. military did not have women pilots yet. A golf buddy of Dad's, who had a connection with the airlines, told Dad that the only good civilian flying job was with the airlines, and airlines were not going to hire women pilots in this century. (We were all wrong. Frontier Airlines had just hired its first woman pilot and the military had just hired theirs. This good news didn't travel fast.) Dad encouraged me to continue flying because I so obviously loved it, but he wanted me to come up with some adult plan for how I was going to earn a living once I was done playing.

I continued taking lessons and checkrides in San Diego's balmy winter skies and headed back to Alaska in the spring. I had met Rex Gray, a military pilot who moonlighted giving flight instruction at San Diego's Brown Field. He had an old Piper Pacer airplane, a hankering for seeing Alaska, and a few weeks of vacation coming. We winged off into an afternoon sun, waggling our wings in a cheery farewell to my parents, who had come to see us off. Mom took pictures. She thought she might never see us again.

Rex and I did the bargain tour of the backwoods dirt strips along our way north. Sometimes we slept under the wings of the plane, nestled in the dirt by its tie-down ropes. The spring rains should have made this miserable, but they did not. We huddled with other young flight-crazed pilots under dripping wings, in sodden sleeping bags, and talked about flying. Flight filled our days and minds and hearts. Such a simple way to be joyous. We flew up the Alcan Highway and over the Canadian wilderness. We met other pilots who were building flight hours flying planes from the lower forty-eight states to their new owners in Alaska and we watched out for each other along the way.

We landed in Fairbanks on a drizzling afternoon and hitchhiked toward town and a cheap motel. Even in anything-goes Alaska, the international airports had rigid views about camping and weenie-roasting fires on their tarmac.

Florence Manville, an 80-year-old pioneering Alaskan, picked us up. She sized us up and took us home with her. She had us bathed and fed before her alarmed children and grandchildren rushed over to see whom Grandma had dragged home this time. Not knowing that she had just promised them the week before to stop picking up hitchhikers, I truthfully answered their questions about how we knew Florence. They berated her. She stubbornly insisted that she had a right to overnight guests of her choice.

I sloshed around the Fairbanks International Airport the next day, handing out resumes and applying for jobs. I met Paul Haggland at the Alaska Central Air hangar, and he seemed to be less scornful than the rest of the potential employers at the idea of a girl flying. He said to call him when I got my flight instructor's certificate.

Rex and I flew on to Anchorage, and he dropped me there. He had to finish his stint in the military, and I had to take my flight instructor's checkride. When I got my certificate, I applied for work at all the flight schools in Anchorage. They were hiring men with fewer qualifications than I had, but no one was interested in employing me. *What if no one ever wants me? What will I do?*

I worried that it wasn't worth the money to pay for a long-distance call to Paul Haggland. But he remembered me and, yes, he did have a place for me in his flight school. He had a charter to Anchorage that day, and I threw my duffel bags into his twin-engine Navajo Chieftain for the return to Fairbanks. He insisted that I fly. I had never flown a multiengine plane before. *Can I do this? How is it different from a single engine? What if I can't fly it very well? Oh my God. Just do it, Norah. Pretend it's a little plane.*

Paul was not easily scared.

I had no money, no place to stay, no car, but I had a flying job! I called Florence, the only person I knew in Fairbanks.

"Florence. It's Norah. I'm back. I got a job! Paul Haggland is taking a chance on me!"

"Well, of course he is. I know his parents. They didn't raise any dummies. Come over and stay with me until you get settled."

I started working as a flight instructor the next day. Florence put me up until she found a rented room for me at her grandson's house.

When I started with Alaska Central Air, Paul said he wanted to give someone who obviously loved flying a chance, just as he had been given his chance at a young age. He admitted that my being an attractive young woman was also a factor in my being hired. I was slightly surprised that he found me pretty. I had developed my own self-image around eighth grade when I was a chunky, flat-chested, hairy-legged (I was the only girl I knew whose dad would not let her shave yet), freckled, carrot top with white eyelashes and white eyebrows. My brother called me the redheaded rooster with the chicken pox. My self-image had not caught up with my having left the poxed rooster behind.

The Alaskan oil pipeline was being built, the economy was booming, and young people had the money to spend on flight lessons. The population was male heavy. Because there were numerous flight schools to choose from, Paul reasoned that his school might be chosen because men would be able to spend time with a woman and fly at the same time. A two-birds-with-one-stone kind of deal.

Being a new flight instructor was an exhilarating, enlightening, and sometimes alarming adventure. I had obtained my flying licenses in the minimum time allowed and had scored a 100 percent on my private license written test, something all my instructors swore they had never seen before. When the FAA designee gave me my private pilot's license checkride, he told my recommending instructor that it was one of the best checkrides he had ever given. Instead of taking that as a head-inflating compliment, I digested that information with mind-boggling alarm. *You mean there are licensed pilots flying out there who know less than I do? There are people licensed to fly who can't even fly as well as I do? Oh my God!*

Flying happened so fast for me that I had not gotten away from the "I am new and don't know anything" mindset. The feeling of being new stayed with me for years. Fortunately, the "new" attitude made me an eager pupil, willing to learn from anyone. Unfortunately, the "new" attitude didn't give me a realistic perception of my growing capabilities.

So when I crawled into a plane with my first flight student, a college kid named Tom, I felt a moment of inadequacy. He looked at me with respect and trust, exactly the way I had looked at my first god-of-flight instructor. *He thinks I can save his life if he screws up in this airplane. He thinks I can teach him to be good and safe. He is putting his life in my hands. What am I doing here?* I breathed deeply, closed the airplane door, and smiled at him with my first orders.

"Take it easy, Tom. We're just going to have fun today.

Let's go bore some holes in that beautiful sky."

I relaxed into my instructing as my CFI hours amassed in the twenty-two hours of daylight in the Alaskan summer. A problem was getting enough sleep. Some students wanted to fly before going to work. I was booked solid between 6 and 9 a.m. Others needed night-flying hours required by the FAA for licensing, but it was dark only between midnight and 2 a.m. I learned to keep food and clothing at the airport as I began to live there, only occasionally visiting the place where I paid rent.

I particularly enjoyed instructing wives whose husbands flew. A number of them decided that if they were going to spend hours flying over barren terrain in small planes, they should learn to be useful. They generally had no interest in getting a pilot's license themselves. They just wanted to learn how to navigate, talk on the radio, do preflight inspections, and land the plane if their husbands were somehow incapacitated in the air.

Pilots dying at the controls were rare, but very newsworthy. In 1973 a new private pilot in Pennsylvania had a heart attack on his first flight with passengers. His wife, in the right seat, and their best friends, a couple in the rear of the four-seater, had never been in a small plane before. Someone had the presence of mind to pick up the radio and ask for help. A flight instructor from a local field flew a small plane beside them and gave the wife her first flight lessons over the radio. I can only imagine the overload her mind was processing. Sitting beside the still-warm body of her newly dead husband, absorbing the panic of the helpless friends strapped into the back seats, that woman learned to fly. Two fright-filled hours later, she landed her plane, and the three of them walked away alive.

Nothing so dramatic ever happened to me as an instructor, but I did get a glimmer of how that Pennsylvania instructor must have felt the first time I soloed a student.

Mike Reid, the first student I had taken from first flight to private license, was an ideal student for me. He was intelligent, coordinated, and motivated. He wanted a flying career. His mother was a licensed pilot, so he had not been

29

stunned to see a woman in a plane.

The clear, calm sunny day came when I thought that Mike could safely fly a plane alone round the traffic pattern at the Fairbanks International Airport. I advised the tower that I would be standing on the infield while Mike did three touch-and-gos. I studied Mike's face as I got out of the plane. He looked concerned (guys guard themselves from showing horrified expressions) and he asked me twice if I were sure he was ready.

I laughed and said, "Hey, babe, you're more than ready. Have fun!" What I was thinking was, *please God, don't let my judgment be so flawed that this guy dies for my ignorance. Why couldn't they have given me a checklist for student readiness for solo in flight instructor school?* Instead of doing what I felt like doing, which was falling to my knees in prayer for Mike's young life, I sauntered off.

Mike taxied to the end of the runway, pushed the single throttle to full power, and roared into the sky. I watched him reach a preset altitude, turn left, and raise his flaps. Then he turned left again to enter his downwind leg. I did not envy him for having to talk to the tower and fly simultaneously. My first solo, at a remote towerless strip, was free of the need to talk and fly at the same time. I could imagine Mike's thoughts—hold altitude, slow down, do prelanding checklist. If I lose my engine now, where can I safely make it to? And, oh, yeah, tower, do I have clearance to land? And can I really do this?

As far as I could tell from the ground, Mike was doing everything well. *How like him*, I thought. He had rarely had to be shown any maneuver twice. He had a wonderful combination of intelligent good sense, deductive powers, daring-do, and a reluctance to push past safe limits.

I watched Mike make his first solo landing in a plane, on centerline, on the numbers, almost perfect except that he accidentally touched the toe brakes as he was using his rudder pedals. His tires squealed smoke, and his plane lurched to the side and headed toward the grass. I saw his face through the windscreen, now heading in my direction, and I saw panic. Then resolve. He straightened the plane's alignment and applied takeoff power and leapt into the air again. I knew then what the phrase "my heart in my throat" meant, though the lump in my throat felt more like lunch about to leave me.

Mike's second approach and landing were not as precisely executed as the first, but certainly acceptable. By his third landing, he had settled in and was doing well. I could see him grinning in his seat. Yes, a love affair was starting: Mike and flight.

"Great job!" I voiced as I climbed back into the cockpit with Mike. "You sure learned quickly to keep your feet on the floor after that first landing."

I don't know why it was not okay for pilots to talk about being insecure or scared. I don't know why a certain coolness was tacitly agreed to be part of the "right stuff" that it took to be a good pilot. I do know that during that first summer of instructing in Fairbanks, I joined the other aviators in perfecting a detached mien. I'd had the ideal childhood training, having been the new kid fifteen times before I had completed high school.

One part of me would always be the six-year-old, fiery-curled, freckle-rusted little girl who was dragged to stand in front of forty-eight first graders after I had transferred midyear. I looked at my feet, bit the inside of my cheek to keep from crying, and mumbled, " My name is Norah. My dad's in the navy. I'm new." I was so scared. I desperately hoped that someone would just talk to me at lunch. Eventually, I learned to stand up straight, put my shoulders back, and smile when I talked to those strangers year after year. It *never* got any easier. Mom had told me that outgoing, laughing people were more likely to make new friends than sad, reserved ones. I learned to present an unneedy visage. My outside rarely matched my inside. I buried fear and just went on.

When I entered the all-male occupation of flying, I already had a lifetime of practice at hiding my feelings. New to flying, I tried mightily not to even *have* the feelings to hide. I didn't know that stuffing my feelings could make me more vulnerable than ever, not less. It would take me many years to learn what a huge price I would have to pay for holding my feelings in.

I knew no women pilots. Some men at work made it clear that they were embarrassed to work for an outfit that would hire a woman. It was rumored that I had gotten my job by having an affair with Paul Haggland.

It was my first bitter taste of male logic. No one in his right mind would turn some incompetent loose with fifty-thousand-dollars worth of machinery that his business and reputation depended upon just because that person had loose morals and a talented tongue. Paul was acknowledged as a good businessman and a great pilot. Why did they also think he could be such an idiot? I learned then of the common male-descriptive phrase of "he's letting his little head do all the thinking for his big head." As far as I could tell, some of my detractors had no access to a big head at all.

4

SHOULD HAVE SENT
A MAN: EXHIBIT ONE

1974

As the hours of summer sunlight waned, so did the number of students. I continued being a student myself by taking the tests and earning the tickets for multiengine planes and seaplanes, instrument flight instructor and ground school instructor. I started lessons for a helicopter rating. I was worried that Paul wouldn't keep me on for the winter, when the flight school closed. I had filled in on charter flights but had not yet flown our larger planes on scheduled mail and passenger service down the Yukon River. I was elated when Paul told me that I was on the fall schedule. I knew I was being tested; it was vitally important that the first flight be trouble free.

It wasn't.

I didn't tell anyone but Paul about the humiliation of my first scheduled passenger flight into Manley Hot Springs. But my passengers were not so discreet. No wonder.

I had flown several charter flights into Manley Hot Springs during the summer. The village borders a winding crook of the Yukon River, and hills curve behind the town. Planes could approach the 900-foot narrow dirt strip from only one direction, over the river, and depart over the river in the opposite direction. Manley didn't have a navigational aid for instruments to home in on, so getting in and out of Manley was by VFR (Visual Flight Rules) only.

My flight was scheduled for a September morning in a six-passenger Cherokee. I looked forward to flying over a lake and river region painted in the fiery colors of autumn.

I awakened to an unseasonable and intensifying snowstorm. Though the cloud ceiling and visibility made it legal to fly to Manley VFR, I was concerned about finding the town if the visibility got any worse. Paul gave me some pointers about how to find Manley and said if I got there and couldn't land safely, to not even try. "Just take them on to Tanana (the next stop), and we'll get them back later." Paul was a terrific employer in that he did not pressure his pilots to get the passengers there no matter what. I was not in a do-or-die scenario. Nevertheless, I didn't want to return to town with a planeload of disgruntled customers. I didn't want to become "Should Have Sent a Man: Exhibit One."

We took off from Fairbanks into the storm. By the time I had dead reckoned that we were near Manley, the forward visibility was decreasing and the solid cloud ceiling was descending. If I didn't find Manley soon, the weather would preclude landing for the rest of the day. I lowered the plane to 1,000 feet above the Yukon and started searching the shoreline to the east. Not much looked familiar; all the S-curves were beginning to look alike. I could not hit anything if I kept the plane directly over the water, but I had no intention of following the river around for hours. I had computed a get-out time for myself, which meant that if I had not found Manley by a certain time, I would have already flown past it. My intention was to climb the plane at that time, activate a back-up instrument flight plan with ATC, and navigate on to Tanana. My viable get-out plan had not taken passenger participation into consideration.

A minute away from pull-the-plug time, I took a deep breath and girded myself for the job of telling my passengers we were not going to make it in. I looked over my shoulder into the passenger cabin and said, "I'm sorry, but the visibility is such that I cannot safely go into Manley. We're all going on to Tanana."

As I was switching my radio to ATC frequency, the man seated behind me said, "Why are you doing that? There's Manley." He pointed a finger toward the right side windows. "Can't you see it? It's right there. You're on a wide right base." With his help, I finally did recognize Manley, though it looked different from any previous viewing. The houses were black dots against white flecks of clearings among sparse trees. The snow-covered airstrip looked like another thin inlet to the river. None of it looked manmade. My passenger, Bob, was correct. I was on a long right base to the landing pattern entry. I methodically prepared my plane for landing: slow down, extend flaps, review before-landing checklist. I turned to my final heading, with the runway straight ahead and my plane configured for landing, thinking that everything was a go. My self-appointed guide did not seem to think so.

"You're too high," he said. "You'll never get her down and stopped." I considered my instruments and decided he was wrong. I continued my descent.

"We're okay," I told him. "I can tell you're a pilot, but perhaps you're unfamiliar with this plane's performance specifications."

"I have 5,000 hours in this plane. You're too high. Go around." His voice was rising. I reassessed. I still thought I was okay but did I want to bet their lives on it? I added power, started to climb, and went around the airport to set up for another approach. The other passengers were getting edgy. They tightened their seatbelts, closed their eyes, and mouthed prayers.

I flew down final a second time. Again, Bob was not pleased.

"You're too high! You're not going to make it," he yelled.

I cringed. *Could he be right?* But the approach looked good to me. *Are you flying this plane, Norah, or is Bob?* I continued down and eased back the controls into a landing flare over the end of the runway. The plane did not settle onto the snow as it should have but continued to float toward a rapidly-nearing wall of snow at the end. *It's too late to go around. You'll never clear the snow bank at the end. Do something.* I reached down and retracted my landing flaps to zero. The plane thumped down into six inches of soft powdery snow, which finally dragged us to a halt. Brakes weren't necessary.

"Man, I didn't think we were going to make it," Bob told me as I was unloading his baggage. "The perspective must be a lot different from the back seat. Nice trick with the flaps. I use that sometimes myself." Bob helped me manually turn the plane for my takeoff to Tanana.

"Thanks for your help," I called to him as I shut the cockpit door. Part of me was glad to have him gone. Part of me wanted him along. I know my Tanana passengers were sorry to see him go.

The rest of that day went as scheduled. I told Paul about the Manley missed approach that night. I knew that if I did not, someone else would. Paul seemed unperturbed about my receiving flight instruction from Bob in front of a load of passengers. "Oh, yeah. Bob would probably try to teach *me* to fly if I'd let him. Never forget who the captain of the plane is, Norah. Good job."

Later, a pilot friend was seated next to an old geezer named Bob on a commercial airline flight. When Bob discovered that his seatmate knew me, he asked how that girl pilot Norah was doing. He told my friend about the snowy day in Manley and how he had saved the planeload of passengers by teaching Norah to fly before she killed them. That's not the way I remember it, though Bob did help me get my passengers home that day and taught me a great lesson: always remember who is flying the plane.

"Geez, did you hear Norah talking this morning? She came in from flying a load of passengers, all bubbly about how she'd just flown an ILS approach with everything all right throughout the entire approach, like it was a miracle or something. She's out there giving herself flying lessons with a bunch of innocent people on board. She's an accident waiting to happen."

"Yeah, I heard her. What a twit."

I had just walked into the coffee-making alcove that was partially partitioned off from the waiting room of Alaska Central Air. I recognized the voices of two of the pilots I worked with. *Oh no. What have I done now? I need to keep my mouth shut.*

During my first months in Fairbanks, I made the mistake of talking to fellow pilots about how my flying was progressing. When they said, "How'd your day go?" I thought they actually wanted to know and told them about mistakes I had made and things I had learned. It was my mother's fault. She was always there when I came home from school and would question me in excruciating detail about my day. *She* really wanted to know.

I learned to shut up about my learning adventures. My first fellow pilots, strongly influenced by a chief pilot who was vocal about his aversion to my hiring, complained about my lack of experience. They ignored the fact that some of them had been hired with as few flight hours as I.

The chief pilot refused to fly with me. He gave all the other pilots their FAA Part 135 checkrides but said he would not be a party to my eventually killing people. He said my becoming a murderer was not a matter of if, but when. Paul Haggland gave me the required FAA tests. I preferred flying with Paul, anyway. His love of flying was infectious and his attitude toward me embodied constructive criticism. Paul's chief pilot eventually quit over me. He said he wouldn't work for a company that would keep a woman like me on the payroll.

Paul's spending extra time with me caused problems with his wife. I was unaware of them until she tried to kill me.

Leaving work one night and driving down a stretch of seldom-driven road on my way home, I scarcely noticed an oncoming large utility vehicle until it swerved into my lane as it passed me. I jerked my steering wheel to the right and hit the gravel just off the edge of the road. *Wow. The drunks are out early tonight.* While fighting my car back onto the road I didn't notice that the vehicle had made a U-turn after it passed me. I saw a car in my rear view mirror, quickly closing the distance between us, but didn't realize it was the same car that had recently passed me in the opposite direction. It zoomed toward me, closing the gap, then veered out to drive beside me. I recognized the car then but couldn't see the driver. *What's he doing? What does he want?* The car didn't pass me, though I slowed to allow that. Instead, it swung toward the side of my car as we were rounding a curve. I swung my steering wheel hard right to avoid a collision. My car headed into the darkness and went airborne. I saw trees rising in the gloom ahead and fought to turn away from them. My car bottomed out in a shallow ditch and stopped. The other car roared off, honking into the night.

After I calmed down, I got out and inspected my car and the slope of the land. I extricated myself without help and continued toward home at a snail's pace, alternating views of the road ahead with the road behind. I thought it was a drunk driver. I could think of no other explanation. I thought of calling the police, but didn't have enough information to make the call worthwhile. I hadn't seen the car's license plates, nor could I say for certain what color it was.

Paul asked me how my car was the next morning. His wife had told him what she had done the night before. She wanted me to leave town—soon. Paul seemed to find the incident funny. The other pilots laughed about it. I was confused. *Am I the only one who thinks that something horrible has happened here?* It was my first lesson in normalizing awful. The practice would be toxic.

*M*y first Christmas in Fairbanks was disillusioning. I had been with Alaska Central Air for nine months and thought the guys were beginning to tolerate me. My logged flight time was growing daily, and, against most expectations, I kept bringing the planes home in one piece. I thought I had earned some respect.

My mom and dad had sent a box of fresh fruit and

vegetables from California, knowing that in Alaskan supermarkets fresh produce was rare and expensive. I decided to throw a Christmas party and share the bounty. I had never given a large party and I worked hard to make sure the food was varied and abundant. I invited everyone from work—pilots, mechanics, office workers, and maintenance men. My landlord, Bill Johnson, flew in from the pipeline to tend bar. On the evening of the party I dressed in a gold-embroidered red velvet Turkish caftan, the most festive gown I owned, and sat with Bill waiting for the guests to arrive. His parents, Shirley and Johnny Johnson, came first.

Shirley, a voluptuous redhead, was swathed in fur and jewels. With her bawdy sense of humor and dancing feet, she could make a party all by herself, which was good because that was what she was finally required to do. About an hour later, one of the mechanics stopped by for a beer. He left quickly. Bill and Johnny and Shirley and I sat for hours waiting for others to arrive. No one did. We pretended that it didn't matter but of course it did. Bill helped me put the food away. I slunk off to bed to cry.

The next morning, Bill announced we were going to forget about the night before and have another party. I wasn't enthused, but we had a refrigerator full of party food, so I agreed to set it out again. Bill, born and raised in Fairbanks, knew where to find party people. He made a circuit of favorite bars and hangouts and invited everyone. The house was filled by 7 p.m., and people continued to come all evening. Dancers spilled into the snow outside. The food was eaten. Bill made an emergency liquor-store run when the bar started getting low. Party animals were still laughing at 3 a.m. For weeks afterward, people thanked us for the grand party.

Bill made sure that people at Alaska Central Air heard about the party they had missed. I pretended that I had not noticed their absence.

There were moments that first winter when the miseries of working with people who did not like me or want me there ate into my joy with flying. Occasionally, I wanted to quit, as if quitting would stop the pain of rejection. *If I quit the bastards will win.* I refused to give up. Who else would hire me if I were a quitter?

I made efforts to fit in with the guys by practicing cussing in front of my bathroom mirror. Having been raised in a home where voices were seldom raised and never in profanity, I needed practice to mouth obscenities without blushing. I learned to smoke cigars without coughing. I learned to up my alcohol intake. Flawed logic led me to believe that if I could just act more like a man, then maybe the guys would think that I could fly like a man.

I buried my alienation by living for flying. Planes gave me back what I gave them. I knew what to expect. I was enthralled with the daily change of experiences and schedules. Exploring vast unsettled portions of the Alaskan wilderness and getting paid to do it felt serendipitous.

My adventures kept me from wallowing overlong in my loneliness. I carried medicine to a village that had an epidemic. I delivered mail and Christmas presents. I dropped supplies for dog sled teams. I flew onto the DEW line and met men who had not seen a woman in months. Everywhere I went, I was invited into homes for coffee and news. Often, I was treated like a queen. I flew injured people from the pipeline to the hospital in town. I looked for downed aircraft, did fire spotting, and rescued stranded hunters.

Many places in Alaska could be reached only by plane, and the people who lived in those places were hardy pioneers, reclusive misfits, and survivors of a battle to make homes for themselves away from the chaos of modern cities. They had fascinating stories. Some were willing to share them while cocooned with me in droning flight.

I met a jade miner, isolated for ten months of the year at the bottom of a mountain. I was flying an empty plane home from a chartered flight when I saw the man signaling from a tiny dirt strip in the middle of nowhere. If my head had been turned the other way for a few seconds I would have left him stranded. His radio was broken, and he was sick. As I flew him to Fairbanks to see a doctor, I learned that he lived with no other human presence and was not lonely. I was surrounded by people and was plagued with loneliness. I had not learned yet that true loneliness was a condition of the soul. It had started inside of me. When I flew him and a planeload of his supplies home the next week, he invited me to tour his mine. My semester of Geology 101 taught me less than he did. I marveled at the life that made him happy and complete. God and work were all he needed.

*F*lying a bishop on a four-day tour of northern Alaskan congregations taught me about functional religion that had no resemblance to my childhood Catholicism. I packed the bishop's personal baggage and boxes of church-bound supplies into a ten-seat Navajo Chieftain before I taxied to the international terminal to meet the man. I had not expected embroidered satin vestments and mitered hat, but I had expected some sign of his rank to show. None did. He wore the ubiquitous clothing of the bush—drab, warm, practical, and styleless. He looked so ordinary—average height, average face, average build, and middle-aged. But his eyes glowed with peace and humor. I was happy to note that his eyes did not flicker with apprehension when he learned that I was his pilot. He insisted on riding in the copilot's seat and he asked knowledgeable questions about the instrument panel. Having established a comfortable repartee with me, he asked, "Would you be insulted if I blessed this plane?"

"Blessed the plane?"

"Yes. Get out, sprinkle holy water on the nose, and ask for God's blessing?"

"Make yourself happy. We have a few minutes to wait for our clearance."

Permission granted, he climbed down the plane's steps and advanced to the nose. He prayed, sprinkled the nose of the plane with liquid from a vial, and made the sign of the cross. I *was* insulted. I was sure he was asking for God's blessing because he was afraid to fly with a woman, but at least blessing the plane was a positive action, certainly better than asking for another pilot. I could live with that. As events unfolded, we might both have survived primarily because he *had* blessed the plane.

We motored on to Ruby, a small, native fishing village two hours west down the Yukon River. I had been there many times before because Alaska Central Air had scheduled passenger and mail service to Ruby, but I had rarely flown a Chieftain there. The settlement's 1,800-foot dirt and gravel strip was better suited to smaller planes that required less runway length. The runway presented challenges other than its minimal length. The prevailing wind was generally off the Yukon, dictating that an approach and landing be flown down a treed hillside and toward the end of the strip that dropped from a sheer cliff to the river. The runway slanted down toward the drop-off, necessitating more than normal brake use. The trees on both sides of the narrow cleared area undulated with the hilly terrain. Any crosswind component was sure to be roiled by its passage through the trees.

On that day the bishop and I bounced just above the treetops on final approach, our extended landing gear barely clearing the trees as I corrected for a crosswind and fought to keep the plane's angle of descent correct for a short field over an obstacle landing. Touchdown correctly firm, I immediately applied full toe brakes. Halfway through our landing roll my feet descended to contact the floor. My brakes had failed.

It was too late to apply full throttle and attempt to take off again. We would plummet off the rapidly approaching cliff and fall into the river with too little airspeed to fly. At the end of the strip I pressed full left rudder and full right throttle in a frantic attempt to turn the plane before it went over the cliff. I expected the gear to collapse under the side load and our broken plane to dive off the runway despite my best efforts. But the plane smoothly swirled to the left and started climbing the uphill slope of the taxiway. It ran out of forward momentum just as it arrived at the wide spot that was our parking area. It stopped on a level patch of grass.

"Neat maneuvering," commented the churchman. "I've never seen anyone do it so smoothly before." I was too psyched-out to respond.

Our brakes repaired, we journeyed on to villages on the

northern slope of Alaska. I was taken into people's homes, welcomed, and fed. Sometimes I slept on the makeshift bed of a church pew. No one asked me what religion I believed in. There was an assumption that anyone who piloted the bush in Alaska must surely pray to some God. I found myself going to church services and enjoying their lack of formality or partisanship. There was no bible thumping nor were there fire and brimstone sermons. Instead, there were people who thought praying was normal. They gathered to help each other with the daily work that survival in the Arctic required. Their joining together in an extended family was the best example of Christian brotherhood I had ever seen.

During our return flight to Fairbanks, the bishop asked if he could take the controls of the plane and fly. A childhood dream of piloting had faded when he answered his call to service, but it had not died. While he flew us, we continued a days-long conversation about literature. He was a mystery buff. I wasn't yet.

A week after our flight, he sent me a book. It was P.D. James' *An Unsuitable Job For a Woman.*

How appropriate.

What I liked best about the bishop and the miner was their liking me. Their acceptance freed me to be just me, a rare luxury.

5

DISAPPEARING
FROM THE RADAR SCREEN

1975

Six feet of dark-haired male, mustached and cocky, swaggered across the room and stopped in front of me. I looked up at him, and the rest of the men in the conference room that housed the flight instructors' seminar faded to background.

"I'm Hayward Evans. I've been hearing your voice on the radio."

"I'm Norah O'Neill."

"Lady, everyone knows who you are. Do you want to have dinner with me tonight?"

I had little time for dating and even less time for macho egotists, but I was hungry. I went.

Hayward was an approach controller. For months, I had been hearing his voice—deep, brisk, and precisely-dictioned, with traces of a southern lilt—give rapid-fire instructions on the radio. I imagined him leaning over a radar screen, assimilating the data pictured by the yellow-green moving blips, then calmly directing those massive airbirds in a choreography of speed and altitude and heading. He would space us just so, line us up for final, and hand us off to tower.

Approach control in Fairbanks in those days of the building of the Alaskan Pipeline was one of the most challenging assignments in the U.S. It commanded a large area that included Fairbanks International Airport, with its three runways, Fort Wainwright, and numerous general aviation strips. The air traffic ranged from 747s to one-seat planes. Their echoes, large to tiny, were painted on Hayward's screen like swarming insects homing in on a honey spill. ATC (Air Traffic Control) was an intense job. Hayward was hot.

I had been told that approach controllers were gods in their own minds, and Hayward did exude confidence. I liked that my notoriety did not intimidate him. I loved that he did not find it odd that a woman wanted to fly. Behind his bravissimo was a gentle, considerate, compassionate, and honest man. Perversely, it was his overbearing self-assurance that lit fires in me. Our yearlong romance was volatile.

Our mutual love of flying seeded the friendship. We could spend hours arguing the relative merits of a particular type of plane or a specific method of teaching. I was intrigued with the peek into piloting from a controller's point of view. I cleaned up my radio work and learned new ways of getting what I wanted or needed from ATC.

When I flew a plane toward Fairbanks and got Hayward as controller, I was thrilled and assured. Thrilled, because I knew the man behind the voice and got tingles knowing I would be in his arms that night; assured, because I knew I would get efficient handling. And if anything started going wrong with my plane, I had someone on the ground I could count on. He had a vested interest in getting my body safely onto the ground. One late-night midair scare led us to devise a code word to be used between us in an emergency.

I was flying an empty single-engine plane back to Fairbanks. As the hours droned on, I combated my fatigue with a paperback thriller. Knowing that reading while flying was a no-no kept me scrupulous about frequently scanning my instrument panel.

Because the plane did not have an autopilot, I had my knees braced under the control wheel. Flying in instrument conditions with my knees was an invigorating challenge and certainly more wakeful than staring blearily into the crystal kaleidoscope of snowflakes rushing past me from the enveloping cloud layer.

Fifteen minutes northwest of Fairbanks, engine and flight instruments just checked, ailerons tweaked into a heading adjustment, and my eyes just back on the printed page, a metallic bang reverberated through the little plane; it shook and veered. *Oh my God, my engine just blew. I'm not going to make it in. I'm over the Chena Hills. Will I break out of the clouds before I impact? I need to be able to see for a few seconds before I deadstick it in.*

My book hit the floor as I grabbed the wheel and prepared to trim the controls for the best engine-out float-down speed. But my speed was still normal and the propeller was still whirring in front of me. The engine instruments read normal. I was on speed, on heading, and on altitude. The engine sounded the same as it had a minute before. *Or did it? Maybe the engine was slowly shedding parts and would not be totally destroyed for a while. What had that noise been?*

The plane was no longer shaking and was on the most direct route to Fairbanks. I picked up my microphone to tell Center that I had a problem. But what was the problem? I should probably declare an emergency while I still had an engine and a radio. But what emergency did I have exactly, aside from being terrified?

"Center, do you have Five Tango Alpha on your screen yet?"

"Yeah we've had you for a while. You can go to approach now. Pretty slow out there tonight, Norah."

"Approach, Five Tango Alpha with you at 5,000." *Let Hayward answer, please. I'm about to lose my wings and I'm not gonna make it if I don't break out before I hit the ground. At least they'll know where the wreckage is. But how can they get a chopper to me in the snow? Please let it be Hay.*

"Evening Five Tango Alpha. Turn right 5 degrees to a heading of 105. Descend to 3,000 feet." It was Hayward.

"Roger, Five Tango Alpha turning to 105 and leaving 5,000 for 3,000. It's a little noisy in my plane tonight." *That's not precise. How can I tell him in professional lingo how scared I am and that I have no idea what is wrong? I can't.*

I flew down toward home, hands white knuckled on the controls and my breathing shallow. The lights of the runway appeared, softened and dimmed by the snow. A sob wrenched out of me when my wheels touched the runway. *I made it.*

Paul Haggland was waiting at the open doors of the hanger. Mine was the last plane in that night. I fueled it near the darkened gas pump area and told Paul about the loud clanking noise, the vibration, the veering. I left out the scared and the book. As we pushed the plane toward the warmth and illumination of the hangar, he called to his twin brother, John, our lead mechanic, that 5TA required an inspection before quitting time. John started a walk-around inspection of the plane as Paul and I walked the hangar doors closed.

"Norah! What happened out there tonight?" he shouted. "Gee. Never seen anything quite like this."

"What? What did you find? There was this big banging, clanking noise and the plane was shuddering and it veered to the left. What is it?"

Paul and I went to John's side as he knelt examining a dent the size of half a basketball in the leading edge of the left wing.

"This happened at 5,000 feet in the clouds?" he asked, shaking his head. "What would a goose be doing in the middle of the night at 5,000 feet in the clouds?"

"A goose? No way."

"Look under the rivets behind the dent, Norah. There's blood all the way back to the trailing edge. And here," he said pointing, "are bits of feathers."

The collision with the lost goose taught me that I needed to be able to communicate distress to ATC without having to declare an emergency if there wasn't one. Hay and I talked over possible solutions to that problem. We agreed to a code word. If I used it in ATC communications, Hay would know that I had trouble of an unspecified kind and needed to get in as directly as possible.

A month later, when I had a real emergency, I wasn't able to use the code word. One of the first signs of impending danger was losing the use of my radio.

FLYING TIGRESS

The day started routinely. I was sipping my first cup of coffee at 6 a.m. and deciding on my fashion statement of the day, mainly choosing the color of turtleneck and scarf I would put on with my long underwear, wool sweater, down vest, padded overalls, and long down parka. Sometimes, I got really zippy and wore rainbow-striped socks under my knee-high mukluks. No one could see them, but I knew they were there.

I started my plane's preflight at 6:30 a.m. and topped off the fuel tanks after checking the weight of the load I would carry to Tanana. It was –40° F., and I was careful to keep my glove liners on when I took off my elbow-length down-and-canvas mittens to unscrew the gas caps. My plane had not made it into the hangar the night before, so I put an electric heater under the instrument panel to heat the instruments to a functioning temperature.

The skies were clear, but the forecast was for snow later that day. I didn't know when I might have to fly solely by reference to my gauges. I'd had midnight medivacs during which the artificial horizon did not erect itself into usefulness until an hour into the flight. I didn't want to experience that problem again.

I sold tickets for my flight at the ticket counter in the terminal and checked in the baggage. "Baggage" in the Alaskan bush was loosely defined. I'd had people check in such things as an unwrapped moose haunch as baggage. Sacks of groceries, brown bags of booze bottles, chemical toilets, and furniture were not uncommon check-ins. If it wasn't dangerous and we could fit it in and hope to deliver it in one piece, we took it. The passengers watched me load the last of the bags as they shuffled out onto the icy ramp. After they strapped in, I hopped into the pilot's seat.

Only one of the six wanted to get out when he saw who his pilot was. That was a good day for me. I explained that I was doing the Tanana run that week, and if he wanted a male pilot, he would have to wait until next week. He decided to stay but complained loudly to the other passengers. "What's the world coming to? Someone should be keeping her in the kitchen where she belongs."

"Sir, if you continue talking so loudly, I am going to be distracted from my work. You want me to be able to concentrate, don't you?" I smiled over my shoulder. He shut up, unwilling to add to the peril of the situation.

That load of people got off in Tanana and more boarded to go further down the Yukon to the village at Ruby and the Air Force Base at Galena. Five hours later, I headed my plane down the snowy runway at Galena and headed home with six adults and one child on board. It was dark then, and the forecast snow had started. Despite having headwinds, I expected to be home in less than three hours.

I settled in and dimmed the cabin lights. Only one passenger kept her reading light illuminated. It was a cozy flight, the steady hum of the engine lulling people to sleep. I wasn't using my radio because I was out of Center's range for that part of the flight. I planned to check back in with them when I was halfway between Tanana and Fairbanks, somewhere over the Minto Lake region.

The first anomaly my scanning of the instruments picked up was my ammeter gauge showing a discharge. That was unusual. The alternator belt, rotating behind the propeller, ran the alternator and usually provided all the juice I needed as well as keeping the battery charged. But gauges were notoriously unreliable in Alaskan winters (I hoped), and there was nothing I could do about a problem with the alternator in flight. I needed to land as soon as possible, but there was nowhere to set down before Fairbanks.

As a precautionary measure, I turned off the cabin lights and got out my two-celled flashlight. I tried my radio. Reception was faint and getting fainter. I broadcast into the blind that I was having electrical problems and would probably arrive in Fairbanks without a radio. I confirmed my estimated time of arrival and hoped that someone in the air would transmit it to Fairbanks. I was going to be arriving incommunicado during a snowstorm, and there were other planes out there.

I turned off my rotating beacon and left my small green and red navigation lights on. I turned off the navigation and communication radios, hoping that I would be able

FLYING TIGRESS

to preserve some charge to use in shooting an instrument approach to Fairbanks. With that thought, I turned off my nav lights.

What instruments would be left to help me find the airport? The magnetic compass was fairly useless, but I could at least bracket a heading with it. *Good old needle-ball turn indicator ought to be okay, or was it electric?* I reviewed which gauges were electric and which ran off the pitot static system. That air-pressurized system should be all right, but I had forgotten the ever-present snow. The heating for the pitot head, placed on the side of the plane's nose, was electric. If the tiny air-intake hole iced over, I'd lose my airspeed indicator. If my static hole iced, I would lose my altimeter. It was as if thinking made that so. I looked up to see my airspeed rising to the redline of overspeed and then peg out at the top of the gauge. My altimeter started to fall. I switched my altimeter source to alternate air. It rose again sluggishly. *I'm going to lose all my instruments. How can I get these people down safely? Stop. Don't think about that. Think about what you do have. Make a plan.*

I was less than an hour out and knew my heading was going to get me near Fairbanks. I also knew the time of my last position point and how many minutes would have to tick by before I was over Fairbanks.

The biggest problem was going to be the descent. Too early, and I would hit the hills. Too late, and I would hit the mountains. With no reliable altimeter and no visibility, I had no assurance that I wouldn't just fly into the ground before I broke out. I lost the readouts from my fuel-quantity gauges but my fuel-pressure gauges still worked, so I knew I had fuel. I still had oil pressure readout. My directional gyro and my artificial horizon operated off a vacuum pump, and they'd be with me until the end.

I was flying now with a flashlight illuminating my gauges. *What if I need both hands? How long could I hold this cold metal tube in my teeth?* I tested that out. The kid in the seat next to mine made no comment about my sucking on my flashlight. I looked at him watching me and grinned around the metal in my mouth.

Someone in back asked what had happened to her reading light. "Precautionary shutdown," I advised. I didn't know how much to tell my passengers, if anything. I didn't want to panic them. What could they do to help? Did they have the right to know we might not make it down safely? I did enlist the aid of the boy in the copilot's seat, just in case. I showed him where to shine the flashlight on the instruments that were most important to me. We made a game of it. I handed him my watch, and he practiced calling out ten-second intervals to me. We laughed.

My passengers were beginning to ask questions, and I was afraid my voice would betray my tension, but I was surprised that I sounded so calm, so bored really. Where did that cool come from?

My calculated descent point arrived. We should be east of Nenana over flat, lake-filled terrain, hopefully near the meandering curves of the Tanana River. I hoped to descend to near the river's surface and follow it east to Fairbanks. If I could find it and stay over it, I could get home without hitting anything.

My eleven-year-old copilot started the timer as I eased the throttles back to the place I knew, from hundreds of hours in this type of plane, to be the spot on the throttle pedestal that I usually set the power for descent. It was rather like driving a familiar car and knowing that just so much foot pressure would give me thirty miles an hour on the flat.

Power set, nose of the plane pushed over to just a hair under the artificial horizon, I trusted that we were sinking at 500 feet per minute at cruise speed. In two minutes, we were a thousand feet lower. I could not see forward or below. Two more minutes, and another thousand feet down. I still couldn't see anything and I couldn't get any further forward in my seat without unbuckling my seat belt.

After another minute of sinking into what was beginning to feel like an abyss, I caught a change in the darkness below. I could see white and black areas that looked like a pinto's back. The white areas unblurred and became rounded, snow-covered frozen lakes. A snow snake curved along their edges—the river.

51

I continued my descent and flew into cottony white. Everything above, below, and in front of me was again obscured in cloud. I didn't know I was holding my breath until we broke out of the clouds again and I heard it panting out. *I can't lose sight of the ground again. I can't descend lower and still hope to break out in time.* I pointed the plane's nose up the river and added power.

I flew through thickening snow flurries but kept the ground in sight. A passenger commented on the close-up view of the river below and the hills rising blackly above our left wing. "Why don't we make this approach more often? It's more fun than higher up." *Why indeed.* The night-lights of Fairbanks glowed through the white in the distance.

Now came another tricky part. Hopefully, an alert air traffic controller had noticed the tiny blip of 5TA disappear from his radar screen just before he was scheduled to hear from it. Hopefully, someone had noticed the return echo of a plane winding its way up the river to the city. Hopefully, he saw the blip approaching and was clearing the runway for it to land.

I saw the lights of Fairbanks International Airport emerge from around a bend in the river. I lined up with the main runway and slowed and did the prelanding checklist while I stared out toward the runway ahead looking for other planes. I was clinching my controls, prepared to turn sharply to avoid a collision.

I landed. The tower gave me light signals for a taxi clearance, and I motored on to park next to the terminal.

The enormity of my physical reaction to an hour of adrenaline rush and fear held in check did not become apparent until I opened the pilot's door to hop out onto the wing and jump to the ground to offload baggage. I swung my legs over the wing, pushed my feet to its surface, grabbed the top of the door for leverage, and tried to stand up. I could not. My knees folded down and I plunked into a pile. The phrase, "My knees gave out," took on a new aspect. *Wow. Now I know what that means.*

My passengers got out by themselves. They waited, stomping in the cold and snow by the baggage compartment door and eyeing my sitting limply on the wing, until one of them finally opened the door himself and heaved the cases onto the ramp.

"Nice flight," one called, turning to the terminal.

"Yeah, thanks," said another.

"I had fun. Thanks for letting me help fly," said my pint-sized copilot.

"Anytime," I called, waving them on. Alone on the wing, I scooched to the edge, swung my legs downward, and clung to the side of the plane as I lowered my weight. I stood, walked back and shut the baggage compartment door, and climbed back in for the taxi to the hangar. I fueled the plane and put it to bed for the night, leaving a note for the mechanics. I could see that my alternator belt was gone.

"Hey, Norah, howzit goin?" asked an arriving office maintenance man.

"Just fine. Long day though," I replied, and walked to my car.

*L*uckily, I did have Hayward to talk to that night. As I debriefed the flight with him, I was grateful to have a boyfriend who understood what I was talking about when I talked about work. Nevertheless, I didn't tell him how fear had disabled my knees.

Hay and I were young and fired up with living on the edge. We must have had some calm, contented moments, but I don't remember them. We partied hard, argued passionately, and tumbled into bed to make up. We flew float planes and ski planes, cross-country skied in the wilderness, danced long, exchanged books, and talked for hours.

Then I made an egregious error and compounded it by lying to Hayward about it. He caught me. I was too proud and childish to admit my mistake and apologize.

Six years passed before I saw him again. He was not easy to replace.

⑥

VERTIGO

1975-76

My second winter in Fairbanks provided a lesson in surviving vertigo, which is deadly in an airplane. Defined as a disorder in which a person or his surroundings seem to whirl about dizzily, from the Latin "a turning around," vertigo has hit pilots with a spatial disorientation so severe that they refused to believe what their instruments told them. Often, they died not knowing up from down. Vertigo was thought to be a major factor in what happened to John F. Kennedy, Jr., when his plane plunged into the water off Martha's Vineyard.

All student pilots have to practice recovering from induced vertigo in order to get a private pilot's license. My first instructor put me under a hood—a long curved piece of white plastic fitted onto my head like a baseball-cap visor. Under the hood I couldn't see out the cockpit windows. I could see only the instrument panel in front of me.

Herb would instruct me to close my eyes and put my head down. Then, with his dual set of controls, he would fly the plane through a series of steep turns and climbs and dives and gut-lurching hard-overs. As soon as he ascertained that I could not possibly know what position the plane was in, he would yell, "You have it!" and take his hands off the controls. I would raise my head, look at primary instruments, and try to return the airplane to flying straight and level. A surge of adrenaline guaranteed a sense of urgency.

Once, Herb handed me the plane after he had induced a spin. I knew going into it that something big was happening because I had heard the blare of the stall warning horn and rat-a-tat of the stick shaker and had felt the airplane rise sharply and fall off on a wing. Or at least I thought that I had felt the nose rise, because it is difficult to tell which direction you're going in when your butt is sliding all over the seat. Hearing the stall warning (a warning that the airflow over the wings has been disturbed and will very soon stop producing lift) was a major hint about what was happening. But looking at the instruments was confusing at first. *Thank God we pilots rarely see what a spin looks like on instruments.* Finally, I managed to do the correct recovery—full opposite rudder and full throttle—but only after I had lost many precious feet of altitude while heading straight for the ground below.

Herb thought I needed more practice, so he had me lower my head and close my eyes again. He launched into the exact same scenario—nose up, stall warning, buffeting of the wings while the nose fell to the left. I was prepared and knew exactly what was happening when I took over the controls. I wasn't going to lose as much altitude this time. I jammed on full throttle and full rudder in the direction opposite of the last turn I had felt. Then I looked at my instruments in order to fine-tune the recovery. I was shocked. Herb had handed me the plane in ordinary straight and level flight. I had "corrected" that to red line airspeed and a wild skidding turn to the right. Herb thought it was hilarious. "Here I hand you a perfectly good airplane and you turn it into a bucking bronco." I got the lesson. Look at your instruments first. Believe your instruments.

55

During my subsequent 20,000 hours of flying, I experienced real-life vertigo only twice. I was lucky that I had some time under my belt before the first incident.

Having taught flying for a while, I had learned to tell if my students were coordinating their turns by whether or not my butt slid in the seat. "Seat-of-the-pants" flying yielded interesting information, but I always backed it up with what my instruments were telling me.

One snowy autumn evening in Fairbanks, I returned to base fatigued by a full day's flying in marginal weather. As I was getting into my car for the drive home, I was tagged for one more flight to Tanana. I wasn't enthused. We had regular scheduled passenger and mail service to Tanana, a village one-and-a-half hours west. It sat in the wilderness beneath the foothills of the Ray Mountains, a short distance from where the Tanana River converged with the mighty Yukon River. Its geography ensured that the air was always turbulent just to the east of it. I hated the descent to the airport through that roiling air. Sometimes I had to fly through it three times a day.

I loaded six passengers and some backlogged cargo onto the last flight to Tanana, cursing my boss's ability to run extra sections as needed. I noticed that I took longer than normal to run through my before-takeoff checklist and was less than courteous in answering my passengers' questions. I ignored those red flags of reduced competency due to fatigue and pressed on. That was my job, to move airplanes whether I felt like it or not.

The scattered snow showers had intensified to a solid wall of decreasing visibility. No problem. Just another all-instrument flight. We took off from Fairbanks, heading west along the Tanana River, the low rise of the Chena Hills solidly off our right wing. I could still pick up our location visually through the front windscreen and could see the ice-clogged river curling below us as well as the unlit gray cliffs. My eyes lingered on the swirling beauty of the funnel of crystal flakes illuminated in our landing lights. I was slow to retract the flaps. I was slow to do the after-takeoff checklist. I was slow.

The seat of my pants started sliding left. That was unusual. The air was calm. We weren't turning. I wondered if my pilot's seat had come unlatched from its tracks. The view from the window was the same—a tunnel of white specks barreling by us. I looked at my instruments. *Holy shit!* We were in a steep turn to the right and descending. Rudder. Ailerons. Elevator. Power. *Oh my God. I almost killed these people.* That surge of adrenaline kept me alert and on the edge of my seat for the rest of the flight.

I did not experience vertigo again for fifteen years. When it visited again, it was mind-bogglingly overwhelming.

*D*uring my second year at Alaska Central, a freelance writer noticed me on the flight line and thought he could sell a story about me. Paul Haggland thought the publicity would be good public relations for his growing company. He arranged for the writer to ride along with me for two days.

While flying the writer around central Alaska, I was careful not to sound like a radical feminist. Bra burning in public places was gathering negative publicity for the Women's Movement.

When the writer asked, "Do you consider yourself to be a women's libber?" I replied that I was a "people's libber." I thought everyone should be able to use their talents to their fullest capabilities.

I don't know if the subsequent story sold some additional tickets at Alaska Central, but it definitely caused problems for me with the men I worked with.

When Paul had approached me with the idea, my first thought was, *Oh, Mom and Dad will be so proud.* And they were. But I had naively not given thought to what the guys would think. Their reactions to the photos and story were demoralizing.

"What makes you think you're so hot?"

"I've done a hell of a lot more for aviation than you'll ever do. Why aren't they writing about me?"

"Good thing they rushed that story out before you crash, burn, and disappear. You're not long for this earth."

"Is there room for your swelled head inside that little cockpit?"

After a couple of weeks of their guff, I removed the magazine from the waiting room table at work and stashed it in the back of my closet at home.

As soon as I logged enough flight hours, I took the tests for my airline transport pilot rating, the highest rating a pilot can earn. Paul Haggland allowed his pilots free aircraft time for the rating because it lowered his insurance costs to have ATP pilots flying his planes.

Alaska Central had contracts with the Alaskan Pipeline—flying mail, personnel, and equipment and providing medical evacuations. Because there were no women in the pipeline camps yet, my flying into them raised concerns for pipeline management. Where would I sleep when I was standing by for medical emergencies? Where would I shower or use a bathroom? Would my mere presence in places where men had not seen women for weeks cause riots? Management's initial stance was not to allow me into the camps at all. That created scheduling problems for Alaska Central.

Paul circumvented the pipeline ban by having me fly copilot for him on a special charter flight for Alaska's first governor, Richard Egan. Egan was campaigning for reelection and had asked Paul to fly him to all the pipeline camps. I was in the news again, standing beside the governor and his plane. The additional flack from my coworkers was outweighed by the positive result of pipeline management seeing that I could visit the camps unscathed. But my being allowed to captain a plane into the camps raised another problem. The pipeline contracts required a copilot, and none of the men at work wanted to fly as my copilot. Nor did the pilots' wives want them to spend the night with me there. Paul called me into his office.

"You're a good pilot and you've done a good job for me, but unless I can find a qualified man who is willing to copilot for you, I'm going to have to let you go. I'd give you a good reference, of course."

"Paul, if you let me go, no one else in Alaska is going to hire me. You know that. How could you fire me?"

"I'm just tired of the headaches and the complicated scheduling. You need to find a copilot."

I was angry and afraid. I went home and was pouring a double drink when my phone rang. It was Rex Gray, my flight-instructor friend from San Diego. He was out of the military and hoping to move to Alaska to get a flying job.

"Do you think I could get a job with Alaska Central?" he asked.

"Would you mind starting as my copilot?" I explained what was going on at work.

"Geez, Norah, that would be great! We could fly together again and get paid for it. What a neat deal."

Rex started working with me that month. After two months of his talking to the boys about how cool it was to fly with me, how I shared the flying equally, how I got invited to all the parties, and how I *never* complained about any of his landings, some of the men started complaining. "How come Rex always gets to fly with Norah?" Rex was promoted to captain soon after, and our flying together ceased, but I no longer had a dearth of copilots.

*O*ne day in a pipeline cafeteria, my copilot said, "There's a guy over there who would really like to talk to you, but he's too shy to approach you. You flew him on an aerial bridge inspection over the Yukon the other day, and he was intrigued."

"Which one is he?" I asked, turning my head to scan the men left in the room after the lunchtime rush. "I have some time to kill here. May as well pass it in intelligent conversation."

My copilot pointed to a man sitting quietly with engineering plans. I stood and walked toward the stranger. We talked for an hour. He was bright and funny and slightly neurotic. *So what if he's slightly different,* I thought, *no one is really himself in the unreal, claustrophobic life of a pipeline camp.* He called me at home that night and started writing letters. I was moved by his engineer's stylized handwriting. I began to ask for more trips to the camp he was stationed in. I had no inkling of how important he would eventually become in my life.

Finally, the pipeline had to allow women to work in the camps. Big money and strong unions saw to that. Most of the female workers did exactly what the men were doing; they worked hard and well in brutal conditions. I was relieved not to be so closely scrutinized as the only woman at lunch with a hundred men. An added bonus was having a woman's bathroom. My copilots no longer had to stand guard outside the door when I showered. The women arriving also sparked an interest in the accouterments for partying.

Alcohol was not allowed in the camps but it was smuggled in. I heard that pilots were approached with cash incentives to not notice a few cases of booze in their planes' cargo compartments when they flew onto the pipeline from Fairbanks. When I was first asked to deal in contraband, I was flying with Jim McSheehy, a furloughed airline pilot who was new to Alaska Central. Jim adroitly settled the issue.

"I *might* consider putting my pilot's license on the line for the right amount of money," Jim drawled, a grin forming on his handsome Black Irish face. I sat forward, intrigued. Jim loved flying. He had just gotten married and moved his wife to Fairbanks. His goal was to retire as a jumbo jet pilot for a major airline. I couldn't imagine any amount of money being enough to separate him from his goal.

"You name it, Jim. We boys are getting mighty thirsty up here," enthused the procurer.

"Well, I figure a few million dollars might just do me if I invested it right. That's about what I would give up if I were stupid enough to break the law in an airplane."

"A few million dollars? You've got to be nuts!"

"Not nuts enough to never be allowed to fly again for any amount of money."

Jim and I were not bothered again by the dry drunks.

Some of the wilder stories about happenings on the Alaskan Pipeline began to trickle down to the lower forty-eight states. Journalists became regular passengers. Jim McSheehy and I were assigned to fly Geraldo Rivera on a tour of pipeline camps. He was filming a special on "Women on the Alaskan Pipeline" for the opening segment of a new television show, *Good Morning America*.

I groaned when Paul Haggland told me about the Geraldo assignment. "No more PR, Paul. I am tired of the guys hating me for it, and I'm not going to volunteer to look stupid in print again. Who is this Geraldo guy, anyway?"

Geraldo was a head turner. He strode toward Jim and me in Fairbanks with his equipment-laden minions following. Oh my God, I silently mouthed to McSheehy. Jim rolled his eyes in response. Geraldo was sporting a black leather flyer's jacket, knee-high polished black leather boots, what looked to be tight, black woolen riding jodhpurs over his muscled thighs, and a long, white silk scarf fluttering back in the slipstream of his passage. His darkly handsome face and high cheekbones were framed in a mass of shoulder-length, curly black hair. He looked just like a Hollywood version of one of the Three Musketeers becoming an early aviation barnstormer.

I steeled myself for an encounter with a prima donna macho man but was surprised to discover a warm and friendly professional. He and his team were excited about being in Alaska and were the perfect audience for our low altitude tour of some of our favorite sightseeing terrain. Jim even gave them his specialty, the "Arctic Circle-Crossing Ride."

As we were flying northward from the Yukon River, Jim pulled our plane into a shallow climb to a higher altitude. When Geraldo expressed dismay that the view was not as good at a greater height, Jim explained that a higher altitude was mandatory for a safe crossing of the Arctic Circle. Jim talked authoritatively about the confluence of air masses, the lowering of the jet stream, the magnetic properties near the North Pole, and myriad other scientific details that caused a mysterious area of turbulence directly over the Arctic Circle. Jim McSheehy was over 6 feet tall; he looked like a young Tom Selleck. His voice was a slow, reassuring baritone, and he had about him an aura of calmness. He was print-ad perfect for the role of airline captain. I believe it was this appearance that allowed him to be so believable, no matter what kind of incredible baloney he was spouting.

As we flew nearer to the dreaded circle, Jim instructed our passengers to tighten their seatbelts and brace themselves. I made sure that they followed instructions. We began a countdown of the seconds until we entered the confluence of air above the circle. And on the count of one, our plane's nose rose sharply, pressing our passengers against their seatbacks. Just as suddenly, our nose pitched back down, levitating us up off our seats and against our belts. We bucked around the sky for another two seconds, then the air smoothed out again. Jim announced, "Made it through again! We were lucky today. It wasn't too bad."

I looked out the side window to hide my smile. Only I could see Jim's hands, low on the controls and in his lap, jerk the elevator to raise the nose then shove the elevator down again to produce the rising in the seats. Jim managed to keep a straight face, though I could see his chest and belly moving with spasms of laughter.

The time with Geraldo and his film crew was mostly hurry up and then wait—the common lot of pilots. On our last day with them, standing on the snow-packed runway at Valdez, the pipeline's terminus, Geraldo asked me if I would mind being interviewed. I told him that I *would* mind. I told him how poorly my coworkers had viewed my previous PR, and how stupid I had sounded in print.

"It's amazing what a difference it can make in meaning to take out just a few words. And some questions just can't be addressed with intelligence. Like, how does it feel to do a man's work? Are you scared all the time? Give me a break." Geraldo laughed and promised he wouldn't make me sound stupid. "Yeah, I can do that all by myself," I responded.

Finally coaxed into it, standing in the cold, hair blowing in the breeze, I answered his questions. They were well thought out and well put. I reassured myself that this was film that probably wouldn't even be aired. Most Alaskan flyers didn't have time to watch television anyway.

I was right in that I never saw the segment, nor did the men I worked with. But I was told that it did air, with my part included, on the opening show of *Good Morning America*. My parents received many phone calls about it.

I picked up the phone in Prudhoe Bay because I was bored and couldn't think of anything better to do and because long distance phone calls from the pipeline were free, one of the perks of the job. In the summer of 1976, the tundra outside the window had thawed enough to hatch forth swarming, black clouds of the unofficial Alaskan state bird, the mosquito. The ragged surface ice of the Arctic Ocean had begun to show watery holes. The wind was blowing at 20 knots. In a few moments the course of my life changed.

Two factors determined the number I dialed that day. One was my relationship with John, the pipeline engineer. He lived with me on his days off from the pipeline. Our feelings were growing in intensity, and I wanted to stay with him and explore where they might go. He was adamant that he didn't want to stay in Alaska after the pipeline was done. I loved flying in the bush and didn't want to leave. John wanted me to get a job with an airline; he said he'd follow me anywhere. *Why can't you just follow me to Fairbanks?*

Because of John, I started asking around about different airlines. I worked with twenty-six men who were regularly updating their applications with airline companies and talking about the pros and cons of each one. I started listening. There was one outfit, the Flying Tiger Line, that was everyone's first choice. It was a grand company, started just after World War II by aces who had flown in Asia with General Chenault's Flying Tigers. The Flying Tiger Line flew only the largest jets all over the world. It had the highest-paid pilots. They went to work and had *adventures*, not just the boring old milk runs of Los Angeles to Fresno to Sacramento to Oakland to Nowhereville and back again. A former flight student of mine had an uncle at Tigers, so I talked to the uncle. I decided that if Tigers would hire me, they would be worth leaving Alaska for.

On the morning of my flight from Fairbanks to Prudhoe Bay, the northern terminus of the pipeline, I had another run-in with my least favorite pilot at work. "Planeboy" made some slighting comments to me before he settled in with his buddies to talk about how to get an interview with Tigers. "They're all professionals at Tigers. I'd never have to work with someone like Norah there."

So I lifted the free phone in Prudhoe Bay, asked information for the number of Flying Tigers in Los Angeles, then asked to speak to the head of personnel. He took my call.

"I've been flying in Alaska for several years and I am interested in working as a pilot for Flying Tigers," I opened our conversation.

"How in the world did you hear that we are hiring? We just made the decision this morning."

"Really? Well, that's good. I'll be flying down to visit my parents in San Diego in a few weeks. Why don't I stop by and talk to you in person?"

"Why don't we talk on the phone first and decide where to go from there?"

We chatted about Alaskan flying and my qualifications. At one point he asked me to please hold on while he went and got my application, so he could have it in front of him as we spoke.

"Well, I haven't applied yet. I thought I would talk to you first and see if there was any reason to fill one out."

"I'll mail you one today. Get it back to me before you come in to see me. When did you say you'd be here? I'll put it on my calendar."

I saw Planeboy back in Fairbanks. When I told him I had an interview with Flying Tigers, the look on his face, as he processed that information, gave me great pleasure.

7

TIGER'S DEN

1976

I was only going to get one chance. I *had* to convince four men that I could do something no woman had been allowed to do before.

I breathed deep, put my shoulders back, and focused on the open office door at the end of the richly paneled hallway. I smoothed my suit skirt and strode forward, but then stumbled. *I shouldn't have worn the heels. I don't remember how to walk in them. What in the hell am I doing here in a major airline's headquarters? They're never going to hire a woman to fly jumbo jets.*

"Hey, are you the girl pilot?"

I turned and saw a California girl in a snug lemon-yellow suit. Her sun-streaked hair was perfectly coifed around her bronzed face. *Oh no. I dressed all wrong. I look like a spinster schoolmarm compared to her. Breathe deep, Norah. They're not interviewing her.*

"Yes, I'm Norah O'Neill. I'm down from Alaska to see about a pilot's job with Flying Tigers."

"Oh, great. We girls have been waiting for you. Tigers has never interviewed a girl pilot before. Lots of the men don't want you here." She laughed. "Time for them to get out of the dark ages. I hope they hire you."

Big smile. "Thanks. I'm so nervous, I can't walk straight. And these heels." I rolled my eyes, and we looked down at my serviceable, chunky-heeled brown shoes. *God, don't let me fall flat on my face.*

"I'll walk you to the door," she offered and squeezed my hand.

"Hey guys, she's here!" she introduced me and gave me a gentle shove through the office door.

Four suit-clad men rose from behind an imposing desk and introduced themselves as Flying Tiger captains Oakley Smith, Dick Stratford, Al Grant, and Dick Keefer. I was glad for my dad's early lessons in the proper way to shake hands. Step forward while extending your hand, always maintaining eye contact; squeeze firmly; break the hold crisply. Three of my interviewers had obviously gotten the same hand-shaking lesson, but the fourth turned our hand clasp into a bone-crushing, macho contest of he who cries out in pain first loses. Luckily, I have a high pain threshold, and our contest appeared to be a draw.

They invited me to be seated. I sank into the too-soft couch, grateful that I was no longer taller than two of the men. (I knew some men had problems with my towering over them, and my heels had raised me to over six feet.) I had wrapped my waist-length bright red hair into a conservative, businesslike, bun. *I should have worn my mukluks and padded overalls and turtleneck. I should have worn my hair down. I'm losing hairpins. What if the bun falls down and I look unprofessional?*

I didn't have a role model, had never even met another woman pilot. I was frantically ad-libbing and feeling like I was coming out of my skin.

I didn't know what kind of questions would be asked, but assumed there would be many technical aviation questions—about engines and aerodynamics, Federal Aviation Administration rules and regulations, licensing, and instrument flying. I was certain they would ask about my hours of flight experience. Because I had acquired many hours in very few years in the Alaskan bush, I thought that my flight time might look like "Parker pen" time to them. I'd heard that some pilots padded their logbooks with fictitious flight time in order to appear more desirable for hiring.

Oakley Smith, Vice President of Flight Operations, carefully explained to me that laws had been passed making it illegal to ask a woman any questions in an interview that were not asked of male applicants. He supposed that I, of course, was aware of this.

I had been in the Alaskan bush for a long time, totally immersed in flying and living, almost literally, in airplanes. I was quietly playing my own part in the Women's Liberation Movement, but I was woefully ignorant of current events.

"That's interesting," I said, "I wasn't aware of that law. But, surely, if you've never interviewed a woman pilot before, you must have some questions about how I might work in an all-male workplace. You have my permission to ask me anything you want." In my youthful naiveté, I had not a clue to the doors I had just given them leave to open.

"Well, thank-you for your understanding," one of the panel said to me with a smile. "Tell me about your periods."

Swallow. Blink. "My periods? What about them?" I was drawing a blank.

"How are your periods?" he elucidated. "How do they affect your reliability at work? How do they affect your flying? I noticed that you took four days of sick leave in the last three years. Were those sick days because of your periods?"

I was definitely *not* following the questioner's logic. My brain raced with the implied math of how many days in my period I had had in the previous three years, at 7 days a month times 12 times 3. Surely if I had had problem periods, I would have missed more than four days of work.

"I have *never* missed work because of my period."

He couldn't let the subject go. I surmised that he was married to someone who must have to take to her bed for days at a time. I had heard of such women and sympathized with them, but I was not one of them.

67

"Can you honestly say that your periods have *never* affected your flying?" he pressed on.

I thought of an incident in Alaska a few months back, flying an empty airplane home to Fairbanks after a long day on a cross-state cargo charter. I was tired and was mildly troubled by menstrual cramps. At the same time, another of Alaska Central Air's pilots was also returning home in an empty plane after a long day of back-to-back medical evacuations on the Alaskan Pipeline. He fell asleep in the cockpit and overflew Fairbanks, his plane heading toward the mountains beyond. What saved his life was one of his engines quitting because of fuel starvation. The subsequent swerving of his plane awakened him just before he would have flown into the side of a mountain.

I thought of that night in Alaska and looked my nagging questioner in the eye. "Oh, yes, my period *has* affected my flying. My cramps have kept me awake on long, boring freight runs."

They asked about my plans for marriage and children. I thought I would do that someday, yes. They wondered if I would quit then to stay home and raise my children.

"Wow," I responded, "have a lot of your pilots done that? I mean, produced a child, then left it up to someone else to feed him and send him to college? It doesn't sound very responsible, and I like to think that I shoulder my obligations better than that."

They asked me whether I liked to party. I wanted to say what they wanted to hear, but I didn't know what that was. In the Alaskan bush, on call twenty-four hours a day, there wasn't much time for going to parties. I had sometimes gone anyway, hoping that the phone would not ring at an inopportune time.

Hoping had not worked out well for me. On one occasion in the previous year, I had been unavailable for a medivac because I was at a party. Even if they had found me, I was in no condition to fly. Fortunately, they did find an able-bodied pilot who successfully flew the injured pipeline worker to the hospital. But I was the one who should have flown, and the plane departed with only one pilot, not the two required by pipeline rules. I made up an elaborate lie about where I had been, a lie so extraordinary that it just might be true. The chief pilot, John Baleski, had said, "Don't insult me by repeating your story, and I won't insult you by calling you a liar. Clean it up, Norah." And clean it up I did. I quit drinking altogether.

I told the interviewers that I liked to party but no longer drank alcohol, so I didn't think going to parties would interfere with my flying.

Oakley Smith wanted to know what I was going to do when someone made a pass at me in the cockpit.

"In the cockpit? Surely there isn't time for that?" I exclaimed.

" It *will* happen," Captain Smith said firmly. "What are you going to do?"

The men all laughed and sat up straighter, awaiting my answer. (In Alaska, if I were on a two-pilot crew, we usually had passengers on board and our cockpit was open to their perusal. We tried to present a professional presence. I was especially conscious of passenger eyes on me because so many of them had expressed open horror that a female was in charge of the plane. One of the main reasons I had applied to Flying Tigers was that they were the world's largest cargo airline, and I never wanted to fly passengers again. I had illusions about what flying for a "real" airline meant. I thought it meant total professionalism and goodbye to many of the problems I had had because I was a "girl" pilot. My education in that area was just leaving grade school and getting ready for junior high.)

These men were waiting for an answer to a question I had not dreamed of being asked. This was not a pilot question but a woman question. I answered as a woman.

"I would handle a pass in the cockpit the same way I would handle one on the ground."

"So what do you do on the ground?" a man asked.

"I say either 'yes, please' or 'no, thank you'."

The men laughed and exchanged glances.

Next, they explored how I had racked up so many flight hours in so short a time. With relief, I produced my logbooks and paystubs. A job-seeking pilot might fabricate flight hours, but no employer would have paid him for them. I think they were relieved to know that I really had flown as much as I said I had.

Dick Stratford said, "Someone with thousands of hours in the Alaskan bush has to be either very, very good or very, very lucky. I hope you're both."

We then swapped stories about flying in Alaska, which several of them had done. This led to the only fun I had in the interview. I got to listen to them "hangar fly," a pilot pastime of sitting safely on the ground and telling stories about how a pilot cheated death by bringing an airplane home against insurmountable odds. I have yet to meet a pilot who can resist hangar flying at any given opportunity.

I listened in fascination as one of them told a story about a Tiger crew flying a World War II vintage C-46 on the northern slope of Alaska during a white out. A "white out" describes visibility commonly encountered during a snow storm when the horizon disappears into unending white above and below it. In that region of very few and very primitive navigational aids, a white out has been deadly for many pilots. Some of the most prominent landmarks on aviation maps for the area are wrecks of old planes.

The Tigers miraculously found the airstrip they were searching for but lost sight of it during their descent and motored on blindly. Noticing their airspeed decreasing, they added power. Their airspeed did not increase but went to zero. It took long moments for them to realize what had happened. They had flown their airplane into the ground. The billowing cushion of snow had prevented them from feeling the ground contact, and their view from the cockpit window had not changed one iota—it was still zero. They had made a good landing by the common pilot's definition—any one you can walk away from is a good landing.

I had flown C-46s out of Fairbanks and was in awe of anyone who could fly them well. They were the most difficult planes to land and park that I had ever been in. While those Tiger pilots talked about captaining the C-46, I wanted more than anything to be able to fly with them one day and to hear more of their stories. For me, they were history come alive.

As the hanger flying abated, one man noted that I had C-46 time and asked me how much fuel a C-46 held. I realized, in a panic, that I did not know. Here I was finally being asked a technical question and I *did not know* the answer. My brief dreams of becoming an airline pilot were flying out the window. I explained, with sinking hope, that the C-46s I had flown were oil tankers and were flown visual flight rules only during the summer in order to replenish the heating-fuel storage tanks of remote villages. We were always at maximum gross weight and fueled the plane with just enough gas to get to the destination. I had never seen the C-46 full of gas.

"I don't know how many gallons of fuel the C-46 holds," I said squaring my shoulders. I was going to take the flunking of this interview like I imagined a man would. I forced a smile and asked the panel of my judges what the correct answer was.

"Captain Smith, you captained the C-46. How much fuel did it hold?"

"Damned if I can remember," he replied. "Do any of you know?"

They did not. I was amazed. How could these gods of Tiger aviation not know the answer to a question they themselves had asked?

The time allotted for my interview was up. They stood to see me out. I didn't have any idea what impression I had made on them. I didn't know that it was not cool to ask, so I did ask.

"Do I have the job?"

They had surprised looks on their faces. "We'll call you if you get the job," they promised.

My mom had flown from San Diego to be with me for the interview process in Los Angeles. We spent two more days together, while I underwent rigorous physical examinations and testing. There were other young pilots at the medical facility who had also had interviews. It seemed hopeful to us that Tigers was paying to have us examined.

I assumed we were all undergoing the same tests until an embarrassed doctor said, "Uhmm. We're not sure what to do here. We have never examined a female pilot before, and there are no spaces on the examination sheet for reporting your, umm, gynecological condition. I should, I guess, do a breast exam. Or, do you, by chance, do your own? Um," he went on, "and I guess I should do a pelvic exam, or do you have regular pap smears done? We could perhaps have your gynecologist send his latest report?"

Poor man. "I'll arrange to have my gynecologist send the paperwork to you."

I returned to work in Alaska and began waiting. Summer was our busiest flying season in Fairbanks, and I was able to forget the waiting while flying almost around the clock.

#

COCKPIT/BOX OFFICE
1976

I passed my 27th birthday in August of 1976 waiting for word from Flying Tigers. September snowed by with still no word.

In October, my phone's ringing at 2 a.m. awakened me. I sat up in bed, a ploy I had discovered helped me further waken and sound lucid for late-night medivac calls.

"Hello. Norah speaking."

"Norah? Norah O'Neill? Howya doin?"

"I'm almost awake here. Who is this?"

"Don't need to know. Don't matter, anyway."

"Who is this? Do I know you?"

I didn't recognize the voice but could hear the sound of music and glasses clinking in the background, unmistakable bar noises. I could barely understand the caller; there seemed to be long-distance crackle on the line. Also, either his speech was slurring or my hearing was not yet as awake as my eyesight.

"I jus want you to know that Tigers is going to hire you. You're gonna be our first woman pilot. I wanna be the first one to tell you."

"Oh my! When do I start? When will I officially hear?"

Click. My anonymous caller was gone.

As the days after the late-night call passed with no written word from Tigers, I began to doubt that the call had even happened. If it had, it might have been a local pilot making a cruel prank call. I never learned who made that call. Weeks later, I received my official notification from the Flying Tiger Line. I had been hired and was to report to ground school in Los Angeles on December 1, 1976.

*O*n one of my last flights for Alaska Central Air, I flew at 11,000 feet southbound to Anchorage in late October 1976. It was clear. The weathermen were calling it 80 miles of visibility.

(I think Anchorage has one of the most beautiful approaches on earth. There are snowy mountains in the north and east and active volcanoes emerging from the horizon in the southwest. Flats and marshes front the volcanoes and circle the lone Sleeping Lady Mountain before rising to another set of mountains beyond. The silver expanse of Cook Inlet divides the mountains. Anchorage is on its shores.)

From the cockpit of my plane, the inlet stretched coldly to the horizon, dotted with oil rigs, ugly water bugs on the shiny surface. A dragonfly-shaped speck of an airplane showed over the water in the distance. I could hear its pilots communicating with air traffic control. It was a Flying Tiger DC-8, four-engine jet. *Oh, wow, I'm going to fly that plane soon. Maybe that very one*

"Hey, Tiger 41, do you know that your cockpit is about to be changed forever?" I recognized the voice on the radio. It was D.G. Creamer, a man who was flying a plane to Anchorage about 10 miles in trail of my plane. *Oh, no. What the hell is D.G. doing?*

"Uh, aircraft calling Tigers, say again," responded the Tiger pilots.

"Tiger 41, you guys just hired a woman pilot," D.G. elaborated over the ATC radio frequency. There was a momentary silence, presumably while the shocked Flying Tiger pilots sucked on their oxygen masks in order to rule out auditory illusions caused by oxygen-starved hypoxia.

"No way!" they asserted.

D.G.'s laughter rang on the airwaves. "Yeah. It's true. She's flying the plane just ahead of mine. She starts December 1. You guys will never be able to call it a cockpit again. It's about to become a box office!"

That was not the way I would have chosen to have the Tiger pilots learn I had been hired. But the news was forever out of my hands. And D.G.'s laughing words were going to follow me for the rest of my career. No matter how hard I tried to be just one of the guys, no matter how much I changed myself in an effort to keep their sacred cockpit the same for them, the fact remained that I was a woman. I could prove that the airplane couldn't tell the difference between the control inputs of a pilot with "inside plumbing" from one with "outside plumbing." But I would learn the hard way that proving my abilities was not enough. I finally had to accept that when I walked in, it was always going to be a box office experience.

9

BAPTISM INTO THE BROTHERHOOD

1976–77

The Los Angeles Airport Hacienda Hotel became my home for the two months in Flying Tigers' ground school. I was studying the innards of the stretched DC-8, four-engine jet in preparation for working as a DC-8 flight engineer.

"Today we are learning about the engines on the DC-8. I'm certain you all know how jets work, so we'll just dive into the particulars of this engine," announced my first instructor. *We do?* I sneaked a peek at the faces of my classmates. They were nodding their heads in agreement. *I'm the only one here who doesn't have a clue about jets and how they produce power? What have I gotten myself into?* I knew I had good study habits but wondered if I was really capable of understanding how a jet engine worked and how jumbos actually made it off the ground.

During my second week in school, a man in Flying Tigers' management called me into his office. He said he had found a discrepancy in my employment application, and I would not have been hired if I had not lied. He said it would be embarrassing to have me fired now, after the publicity about my being Tigers' first woman pilot. So he was offering me a chance, in private, to straighten the matter out. I said I had not lied and would get back-up data to support my position.

He was waiting for me after school that day.

"Hey, Norah, could I give you a ride to your hotel? I'm going in that direction."

"That's okay, the van will be here soon. No reason for you to go out of your way," I said.

"I'd like to talk to you some more about what we were discussing earlier. Come on. Hop in." I was reluctant to do that, but I did. We talked about the rigors of ground school on the short ride to the hotel.

"Let's have a drink so we can talk further," he said.

"No, I have to study."

"I'll walk you to your room."

"That won't be necessary."

"I insist. You never know about safety in hotels." He followed me to my door and as I faced him to say goodbye, he leaned toward me and would have kissed me had I not quickly turned my head. With his face then against my neck, he grabbed my left breast.

"Norah," he murmured against me, "it has probably been a big misunderstanding. You're probably right. Let me come in and talk some more."

"No!" I shoved at him and watched him stumble backwards. "No! You can't come in. There's nothing else to talk about. I'll bring the paperwork to your office as soon as I get it."

I was shaken and embarrassed. I tried to figure out how I had led him to believe that I might be interested in solving problems in bed. My dad had always played the devil's advocate when I brought problems home from school. "What did you do to cause the problem? What could you have done differently?" he would ask. It was second nature for me to assume part of the blame.

I was ashamed to tell anyone about the incident, and I didn't want to call attention to a problem that only a woman pilot could have. I wanted to be one of the guys.

*D*uring that incredibly stressful time of initial groundschool, when we attended classes from eight to five every day and studied every night until we slept in exhaustion, I began to get phone calls and hate mail at the hotel. Some calls and notes were from identifiable sources; many were anonymous.

Pilots who had not been hired in my training class of sixteen were angry that they had been passed over for a "less qualified" minority. I had been identified (incorrectly) as someone hired under a quota system. At first, I tried to reason with these disappointed men, clarifying that I did, indeed, have more flight time than they had. I got calls from wives of unhired men, who asked me what right I had to take a job away from a man who had a family to support. The outpouring of venom depleted me in a time when I needed all my energy just to get through school.

Once, in a burst of frustration (I had been interrupted by a wife in the midst of memorizing the entire electrical system of the DC-8 for a test the next day), I yelled, "He can *have* my job! Tell him to come over and take this test for me!" Into the ensuing silence, I said, "And, of course, you'll have no problem with his sending me a check every month. Someone has to support *me* after I give him *my* paycheck."

My car was repeatedly broken into, but nothing was stolen. After reporting the initial incident to the police and hotel security, I didn't call them again. My room was also broken into, but I could not, at first, discover anything missing. I reported a break-in once, then tried to ignore the other times. People I had never met were angry with me, and I didn't know what to do.

One of my classmates told Tiger management about some of the incidents, and Tigers told me they would send me to another hotel. They indicated that they would do anything I thought necessary to feel safe. I didn't want to leave the hotel where all of my classmates were. We studied together, ate together, and were an intense support system for each other. I reasoned that whoever was harassing me would find me wherever I went.

The most troubling incident was discovering that my underwear drawer had been rifled and some panties were missing. *This is too weird.* I tried to laugh about my underwear being worth stealing.

There was a famous bar in Alaska called the Birdcage. Its walls were covered with signed bras and panties donated by inebriated female customers. There was a pair of bikini panties on a Birdcage wall signed with my name, though I didn't put them there. I suspected that one of my Alaskan Central Air colleagues had. No big deal, really. I tried to view the Hacienda Hotel incident in the same vein. Who knew where my underwear was getting famous now?

My fifteen classmates were my lifelines to sanity. *They* weren't pissed at me for taking their jobs. We had all just gotten our dream jobs. They discovered that I did not mind asking "stupid" questions in class; often they would wait for me to raise my hand, so they wouldn't have to admit their ignorance. Some would even feed me questions to ask. The Flying Tigers instructors made asking questions easy. Their attitude was, "The better you look, the better we look."

John Adcock, a skinny, bespectacled, English-accented, recovering alcoholic and manic, stand-up comedian, was a special favorite of mine. His forte was electrical systems, though he taught many subjects. I knew that if you put a light switch to the ON position, a light should come on somewhere. That's about *all* I knew about electricity. The magic of electricity had, quite frankly, not interested me much before. I had memorized, by rote, what I had to know about the electrical systems, circuit breakers, alternators, and batteries on the smaller planes I had flown in Alaska. But I really didn't understand electricity. Such ignorance was not acceptable in working with huge jets.

On our first day of electrical-systems class, I got so inundated with TRUs, GFRs, GRs, DC, AC, and CSDs, that my notes resembled a scribbled mass of a foreign language. I was delighted when the next slide John Adcock displayed on the projection screen was *not* a tangled, spaghettied mass of wiring but an artist's rendition of what would be the likely result if the coyote of cartoon fame finally caught the roadrunner. The coyote "making love" to the roadrunner was well-timed comic relief.

Later that day, after John had been chewed out by the head of training for not cleaning up his slide show for the lady in his class, John took me aside. He apologized profusely for making me uncomfortable and promised he would try not to do it again.

"You're apologizing for that slide?" I asked with disbelief. "You're not going to show us any more?" I cried with rising voice. "It was the only one I understood *all day!*" John stayed after school with me that day and assessed the depth of my ignorance.

He loaned me a book about basic electronics that was keyed to an elementary-school level. He gave me a booklet about basic jet theory. He tutored me in a way that made it seem I was doing him a favor by needing him, rather than the other way around. He was a gifted teacher.

In sessions alone, he came to know me and my fears of inadequacy. You would think that being an A student in high school and college would have given me the confidence that, with effort, I could learn anything. But my confidence was undermined by years of men telling me I didn't belong and wouldn't fit in and it took "balls" to be a good pilot. John helped to restore my confidence and became a buffer for me from unwanted attention in school.

Our class sessions were interrupted daily by people who came to see the girl. It was bizarre. People would stick their heads in, stare at me, then leave. It was somewhat enlightening to discover how the two-headed snake at the zoo must feel, but it was distracting for everyone and uncomfortable for me. John began answering the knocks on our door with an invitation to come in and teach the class or just stay the hell out.

During that cramming-of-knowledge time, Dick Rothstein became my study mate, mainly because we shared similar study habits and attitude. He had two friends who had instructed on the DC-8, and we called them regularly. Their experience allowed them to explain some puzzling facts or to just say, "Forget it. You don't need to know."

Because our seniority numbers were sequential, Dick and I were also paired together for simulator training. Our classroom studies had ended with a written exam in which any score less than 95 percent was a flunk. This test was followed by a four-hour oral exam with a representative from the Federal Aviation Administration.

My oral exam was scheduled early on a Saturday morning. I barely slept the night before, suffering from extreme "checkitis," a nasty phobia that rendered me barely able to talk coherently, let alone perform well. I had always gotten uptight about flight exams, but the severity had increased rather than decreased with years of taking them. No amount of logic about how well prepared I was alleviated the panic. The Saturday morning of my oral brought out the worst case of jitters I had experienced so far, and it was close to immobilizing.

I was lucky with the FAA examiner assigned to give me my oral; he was patient and kind. He knew I wouldn't have been sent to the oral if I weren't ready to take it. Now, all he had to do was be enormously creative about how to draw some hint of that knowledge from me. I could not answer any of his first ten questions. I was mortified. In an effort to relax me, he said, "Look, Norah, I don't care about the order of the information. Just step up to the picture of the flight engineer's panel and tell me anything you want to about it."

He couldn't have been more accommodating. It didn't help me at all.

After twenty fruitless minutes, he suggested that we postpone the test until later and go out for breakfast. We did. I figured I had failed. Tigers could hardly keep postponing tests until I felt good enough to pass. Over omelets I asked what he thought was going to happen to me. "How bad are you going to tell them I was?" I asked. He ignored the question and asked me about flying in Alaska.

Mid breakfast we were both laughing about trying to make good landings on sandbars sticking up from rapids in the Yukon River. He asked about the electrical sources on the Navajo Chieftains I had flown. We talked about how they compared to those on the DC-8. We talked about the deicing boots on the leading edges of the light twin's wings and how the anti-icing system on the DC-8 was more efficient. We talked about navigation systems in Alaska and how much better inertial navigation systems were going to be. The new instrumentation was so much better than what I had worked with. By the time we had finished our third cups of coffee, I had passed my engineer's oral without knowing I had been taking it.

Oral exams were followed by excruciating weeks in the flight simulator, where Dick and I were drilled in normal, abnormal, and emergency procedures. Midway through those four-hour sessions, I would find myself staring at the clock, mentally trying to move the hands forward so the torture would be over. *Maybe I should just drag my ass back to Alaska where I belong.*

During a break in training for the holidays, I attended my first Tiger employees' Christmas party in Los Angeles—one night, a thousand hands to shake. I drove to the party with Tom and Jinx Cotton. Captain Tom Cotton had allowed me to use his name on my Tiger application, knowing that a captain's name on that paper would ensure it got attention. His nephew had been a flight student of mine in Fairbanks and had arranged the introduction and recommendation. Tom had joked, "I hope you get hired. Just don't take my son's slot." Greg Cotton was in my hiring group, so I remained in Tom's good graces. Jinx, knowing that my classroom wardrobe left me ill prepared for attending a formal function, had raided a friend's closet for evening clothes for me.

I should have been seated at Tom's table and had dinner with him, but I never did sit down or eat. Many people wanted to meet the girl. Many were welcoming. Some were nasty. I was dragged to the head table to meet the bigwigs. The chairman of the board welcomed me publicly but in an aside said, "You had better be good, really good, or we're going to get rid of you. Don't think that being a woman will protect you. You will be closely watched." Other executives echoed his sentiments.

BAPTISM INTO THE BROTHERHOOD

One wife of a senior captain said, "You're not getting near my husband. I told him I would leave him if he ever flew with you. You can't have him." *Whoever he is, I definitely don't want him*, I thought.

"I'm a professional. I have to let you in the cockpit. I have to work with you, but I'll never let you touch the plane," promised several men.

"Who did you fuck to get this job?"

"Couldn't they have found someone uglier? How am I going to be able to think about flying with you in the cockpit?"

"You're going to fill out a uniform right nice."

"When are you going to cut your hair so you can pass the men's hair regulations? You'd better have to have it off your ears and off your collar too. Don't think we're going to let you be any different from anyone else."

"Your tie is going to look good tucked into that cleavage."

"You'll never make it through school. You may have brains, but it takes balls to fly a jet."

"What is the world coming to? What makes you think you can force your way into a man's world? What's wrong with you? Why would you even want this?"

"You don't look like a pilot. I expected someone who looked like a Russian lady wrestler, your being from Alaska and all. You don't look like you can handle a big jet."

Those were some of the comments I heard.

In that glittering ballroom, swelling with big-band music and swirling with jeweled gowns, my confusion and consternation grew, my poise fled, and I despaired of making it through the night with a frozen smile and a hand extended. I escaped to the ladies' room and sat, head between my knees, on a toilet, listening to women I did not know talking about me. *I just want to fly. Is that so wrong?*

I came out of my stall with resolve. They were not going to drive me out. I would not let them get to me. I would study hard. I would do well. I would not give them reason to fire me. I would fly big jets. I would. I put my shoulders back, breathed deep, and walked on.

83

I thanked Tom and Jinx for bringing me and told them I was going home with a classmate. I went in search of someone with a car who would be willing to get me the hell out of there.

On my way to the door I got roped into dancing with a captain I hadn't met before. He was jolly, with a wide smile and a light touch. He told me how happy he was that I was getting to fly jets. He said he could hardly wait to fly with me and thought my efforts would offer hope to young girls that they could fly too. His name was Jim Seymour. I wanted my evening to end on the happy note of our dance.

I fled.

Jim Bailey drove me back to the hotel, where we met other classmates for a nightcap. While slumping into a bar chair and being grateful to not have to smile, I heard my classmates' takes on the evening.

"You sure got the royal treatment. Nobody introduced *me* to the chairman of the board."

"I wish I were a girl. You have it made."

"Has all this attention gone to your head yet?"

I got lucky with my crew on my first solo trip as flight engineer with Flying Tigers in January 1977. Captain Ken Conrad and First Officer John Franzone were my crew that night. They seemed pleased to be with me. Ken had been a professional engineer and had advice to offer on running the pesky air conditioning system; John helped when I got stuck on portions of my paperwork.

We left San Francisco at eleven at night, stopped in Chicago, and landed in New York just after the sun rose. The combination of the long night, my lack of sleep before it started, as well as the stress of doing the job for the first time left me barely ambulatory as we reached our hotel in Manhattan. I was stunned when John called out, "See you in the lobby in fifteen minutes," as we all opened our hotel room doors.

"What will I be doing in the lobby in fifteen minutes?"

"Ken and I are taking you to Cecil's Bar."

"It's seven in the morning! Surely you aren't suggesting that we have a drink?"

"Hey. It's Tiger tradition to end a New York flight at Cecil's. You can't make your first trip without going there."

Mentally shelving my no-alcohol rule, I met them in the lobby and was escorted to a dive that made the lousiest of my Alaskan bars look sophisticated. The bar was full, its clientele ranging from men in three-piece suits, getting a couple of shots before reporting for work, to dirty, disheveled men who looked as if they had spent the night on the sidewalk. John and Ken escorted me to a grungy table and whistled for the bartender.

"We're celebrating this morning! This beautiful woman is Flying Tigers' first woman pilot and she just completed her first flight. Give us champagne!"

The bartender banged around behind the bar then went to a back room. He finally produced an ice-filled mop bucket and a bottle of André wrapped in a soiled bar towel. The inexpert opening of the bottle sprayed us with champagne.

That was my baptism into the band of brothers at Flying Tigers.

10
ESCAPADES
1977

*T*wo weeks after Ken and John introduced me to Cecil's Bar, I returned to New York for a layover with a different crew. They warned me to be careful in our hotel, a major one downtown in which many of the airlines placed their crews.

A flight attendant for another airline had recently checked into a room that smelled bad. She had cranked her window open to the three inches mechanically allowable and had gone to talk to girlfriends while her room aired out. An hour's absence did not dilute the rank odor, so she complained to the front desk and asked for a different room. No other rooms were available.

She showered and dressed for bed but found that being exhausted was not enough to bring on sleep. The odor continued to assail her senses. Finally she gave up and went to sleep in a girlfriend's room. She checked out the next morning without ever returning to her assigned room.

At her flight's first stop in St. Louis, the FBI was waiting for her when the aircraft's door opened to the jetway. The maid who had gone to clean her vacated hotel room had found a decaying, headless female corpse under her bed. The body had been dead too long for the flight attendant to be suspected of having anything to do with its demise, but officials still wanted to question her.

The news about the body passed from crew to crew and airport to airport. My imagination ran with questions. Where did the head go? How could a maid have missed the body or the blood? Had the victim entered the room with the assailant already hidden in the closet? I was in a dither by the time I reached the hotel.

"Miss O'Neill, we have only smoking rooms. Is that okay with you?"

"Yeah, I find a smoking room preferable to the headless-body kind of room."

"I would prefer not to hear that kind of remark."

"I would prefer not to have the grounds for making it."

Key in hand, I dragged my suitcase down a long hallway to the narrow doorway of my room. I leaned my heavy aluminum Halliburton suitcase against the door, propping it open for a quick getaway while I searched under the bed, in the closet, and behind the shower curtain for possible intruders. Relieved at finding only stray dustballs, I was walking to the open doorway to retrieve my suitcase and deadbolt and chain the door, when my phone rang. I grabbed the phone while kicking the case out of the entry, allowing the door to swing shut and click into a latched position.

The phone conversation with another pilot about getting tickets to a Broadway show was lengthy and diverting enough for me to forget the door. I stripped off my uniform as we talked so I would be ready to hop in the shower quickly. We were to meet in the lobby in twenty minutes.

While I was leaning down to shut off the tap, a noise penetrated the rush of water. I couldn't place it but was alert for another sound as I grabbed a large yellow towel and stepped over the tub rim onto the tiled floor. I was facing the bathroom door, which was immediately adjacent to the entry door. As my second foot reached the tile, the room door swung open and a short man in a charcoal business suit and blue tie stepped inside. He was carrying a briefcase.

In the first shocked second, we both did exactly the same thing. I opened my mouth in a silent oh, as my eyes widened and I bunched the towel in front of me. He raised his briefcase to his chest in a protective gesture, as his eyes widened and his mouth formed a silent oh. He moved first. He raised his other hand to hold out a room key and then a babble of words poured from his mouth.

"Oh my God, Ma'am. They gave me this key! This is my room. Don't scream, don't scream; my wife is pregnant too. You don't have to worry about me. I'm so sorry, this is a mistake." He backed out the door and it swung shut behind him before my lips ever formed a word. Then my first thought was, *pregnant? Why did he think I looked pregnant?*

When I had regained a semblance of calm, I bolted and chained my entry door and called the front desk. The answering clerk was bored with my dismay. Clearly he had heard this before.

"Oh yeah," he said, "Simon forgot to mark your room as occupied, so we did check someone else into your room. Happens all the time. Sorry." Click.

It was a cheap lesson in how to properly conduct myself in big-city hotel rooms. I learned that checking a room before I locked myself into it was a good idea, providing I used a buddy system. Leaving my door open while I searched left me vulnerable to a stranger entering from the hall and blocking my retreat. After that, I paid a bellhop to carry my baggage up and stand at the door while I checked the room. When I dismissed him with his tip, I immediately deadbolted and chained the door.

The New York deskman was correct. Hotels did frequently check other people into my room. No room key, however, would undo the deadbolt and the chain. In the future I could listen to someone trying to open my hotel door and call from safety, "This room is occupied. Go yell at the front desk about your inconvenience."

Other useful hotel lessons I learned early in my career were: how to let the maids know that the "Do Not Disturb" sign really meant do not disturb; how to get a room cleaned when you wanted it cleaned; and how to figure out which hotel bar the higher priced ladies of the night worked in, to avoid being confused with one.

Captain Cal Holderman and First Officer Scott Simpson were too senior to have to fly all-night and lower-paid domestic routes. Yet, through a mistake in bidding, they were assigned an excruciating domestic line of time in the spring of 1977. I was their engineer, and they taught me why the DC-8 was known as crew transport between parties. These men took partying to a new level.

Cal discovered that our schedule dictated we fly a plane to New York and then take TWA "home" to San Francisco for two days over Easter. Next, we would take TWA to Cleveland to pick up another plane to fly. Out came his Official Airline Guide and his calculator. He called Jim Ossello, head of Tigers' crew control, and proposed a new routing for his crew. He pointed out that flying us first class from New York to Bermuda for two days and then back to Cleveland was going to be cheaper for the company than putting us up in San Francisco. None of us lived in San Francisco, anyway. Jim agreed. It was imperative that Jim agree because if we did something other than what was scheduled and circumstances prevented us from making the Cleveland flight, we could be fired. If we had permission for a side trip to Bermuda and weather prevented us from getting to Cleveland, then our asses were covered.

Cal made all the arrangements. They included a five-star hotel in Bermuda and airport transportation after a layover in New York, where Cal procured tickets to Liza Minnelli's Tony-award-winning *The Act*. Cal was good at things like that—getting tickets to sold-out shows, getting into the best restaurants, and wearing the most finely tailored clothing. The guys called him "The Gentleman." He went first class or he didn't go. I enjoyed being along for the ride. Out came my best cocktail dress and sheer stockings and spiked heels. I had a man for each arm, and they exchanged turns opening doors for me.

Cal was a 6' 2" prematurely silver-haired debonair man, fine of feature and glib of tongue. Scott "Mr. Hollywood" Simpson had the California bronzed face and sun-touched too-long hair of his Beverly Hills domicile. In the airplane

89

they both had fine-tuned talent as pilots and no bias against women doing men's jobs. They were a sweet deal for me.

Off we flew to Bermuda, sipping champagne through sunny morning skies. The sun faded to gray and then turbulence, and the pounding of rain against the fuselage jostled our fluted glasses. Cal's research into the finer spots in Bermuda had not included the weather reports or the average temperature for that time of year. Neither Scott nor I had bothered to look at a map to see what the latitude of the island resort was. We probably would have gone anyway.

What we learned about Bermuda was little beyond the fact that they don't rent cars there. They do rent motorbikes. After riding in a cab to our hotel along narrow twisting roads in blinding rain while driving on the wrong side of the road, the idea of further exploration on three motorbikes had small appeal. We did see every restaurant and bar in our hotel. The water-blurred view from the windows faded to nothing after about 100 yards. We may as well have been in Cleveland.

Cal's pulling off permission to vacation in Bermuda at company expense, accompanied by the famed player Scott and the girl pilot Norah, had upped by several notches his reputation of being a great guy to fly with. For years afterward, envious guys who had already made up their minds about what we had done there asked me about that layover in Bermuda. My talking about what actually happened was pooh-poohed as a cover up—one further lesson in not letting the truth get in the way of a good story. I learned to roll my eyes, blush a bit, and shrug, "well, you know how things go," and let the guys use their imaginations.

I was both thrilled and terrified when I was called for my first international trip in 1977. Thrilled, because I was on my way to see the world as I had always dreamed of doing, and terrified, because it was a passenger trip to Japan and I was going to work with flight attendants for the first time.

Many pilots had told me that flight attendants were

going to hate me and treat me like shit. They explained that the "girls" would hate me because I made more money than they did and they would treat me like shit because that was those particular pilots' experiences. I wasn't smart enough to consider the source of these remarks—like these guys *were* lazy jerks, were resented for making more money for less work, and were treated abominably because they earned that kind of disrespectful behavior.

I researched the crew I would be flying with, Captain Jack Wibbon and First Officer John Shields; they both got good reviews as being skilled, fair, and fun to be around. I was scheduled to deadhead to Anchorage on one of our DC-8s to pick up the trip and meet the rest of the crew. Shortly before departure from San Francisco, a large man came hurrying out and huffed noisily up the boarding stairs. He plopped his portly bulk down next to me in the two-seated deadhead compartment, squishing me up against the lavatory wall. He proceeded to inspect me thoroughly from head to toe, using no discretion about letting his eyes linger on my breasts and legs. When he spoke, his voice was louder than necessary to be heard over the noise of engine startup.

"I'm Captain Beached-Whale Loudman," he announced, puffing out his chest. *Thank God,* I thought. For a moment I was worried that this might be Jack Wibbon, who had been described as roly-poly and jolly, and that I might have to spend a week flying with a guy who was always mentally undressing me. Plus, this guy stank.

"I'm Norah O'Neill," I said, extending my hand. He mashed it while smiling at my resulting grimace. He sneered more at my efforts to disengage my bruised fingers.

When finally freed, I reached into my flight bag and pulled out a woman's magazine to read. Already, I had ascertained that I wanted as little to do with this man as possible. I didn't want to hear *his* views on anything. He astonished me by ripping the magazine from my hands and throwing it onto the floor.

"You won't be reading any of that trash for this next week," he bellowed.

"Who are *you* to tell me what to do?"

"I'm your captain!"

"Nah. I'm going to fly with Wibbon and Shields."

"No, you're not. I replaced Wibbon on this trip."

"Why didn't they tell me that?" I asked.

"Oh, they never tell crewmembers that they're going to fly with me, because then the guys would just call in sick," he said.

Please, God, let Shields be okay, I prayed. I wanted decent company for the upcoming ordeal.

John Shields was more than okay. He didn't like Loudman any more than I did but was too professional to let that show in the cockpit. However, on layovers I had someone to vent my frustrations with.

I approached the Anchorage terminal for that first passenger flight with trepidation. Though I had been trained to preflight a passenger aircraft with a book and mock-ups, I'd never actually been on a passenger-configured DC-8. I wanted to look confident and knowledgeable to the flight attendants.

A tall, slender, imposing middle-aged woman in a uniform walked up and introduced herself as Lora Direnzo, lead flight attendant. Her uniquely attractive face was surrounded by dark, wildly free hair, and she had an aura of otherworldliness about her in spite of her no-nonsense manner. Later, I came to believe that aura was an extension of her spiritual depth, but at the moment she seemed, well, witchlike and rather scary.

"Have you preflighted the pax oxygen system before?" she asked matter-of-factly.

Ah, shit. It wasn't something I could lie about, though I was tempted to. "No, but I've studied the book and I'm sure I'll be competent," I asserted.

"Come with me," she commanded, taking me by the arm. "I'll show you where the oxygen access doors are. No reason for our first Tigress to run around searching stupidly like all those new baby boys do." *What? Is she on my side?* She walked me through the cabin, showing me where everything was, even some things I had never heard of before. That done, she left me by the cockpit door, assuming that I knew what to do in there. Her parting words were, "If that asshole, Loudman, gives you any trouble, you yell for me. I'll be working first class right outside the cockpit door."

Loudman was every bit as horrible to work with as I had imagined he would be. He seemed incapable of admitting to his own errors and loudly blamed others for them. He was ham fisted on the controls and, though safe, gave the passengers a rougher ride than was necessary.

I was green at working the air-conditioning system with passengers and was surprised when flight attendants came regularly to the cockpit reporting that it was too hot in section one or too cold in section two or too smoky in the tail. They seemed to expect me to fix the problems, when technically there wasn't much I could do about them. For instance, the tail of the plane was the smoking section. Once the flight engineer had all the turbo compressors running and recirculation fans on, there was nothing more to do to thin the cigarette smoke. If the first ten rows of seats were too hot and the second ten rows too cold (while in the same conditioning zone), it was often a matter of flight-attendant perception, rather than actual air temperature. Some of them were standing by the heating ovens, some were in the aisles serving iced drinks, and some were having menopausal hot flashes. With experience, I learned to nod my head with commiseration, flip a few switches on and off, play momentarily with the lollipop-shaped temperature selection handle, and say confidently, "That should do it. Let me know if there is anything else you need." But on that first flight, I was looking through the manual for further instruction and trying fruitless combinations of controls that made no actual difference. Loudman started yelling at me in the cockpit. "What in the hell did they teach you in school? Nothing? Looks like it. I've seen slow pilots before, but I've never seen a man as incompetent as you."

I was mortified and cringing into my seat when the cockpit door slammed open with such force that it bounced off the wall behind it. Lora stomped in, pointed one long finger at Loudman and shook it accusingly.

"Hey you, fatty," she scathingly spit out, "Don't you ever, ever yell at her again. If I hear you raise your voice to her, I'll take care of you after we land. That's a promise!" Then she marched out and slammed the door shut behind her. There was a long silence in the cockpit. I continued to quake, but now I was quaking for Lora, not for myself. How could anyone talk like that to a captain and get away with it? Lora could. She had her own special assertive power, but she also had the power of the flight attendants behind her. I began to catch a glimmer of what that power was.

These women and men (Ken Barton, Tigers' first male flight attendant was also on that trip) were truly a band of sisters and brothers who loved each other and took care of one another. They did some of the most difficult work in the airline industry, all the while reveling in it and taking pride in their work. Whatever it took, they did it. That can-do strength and willingness was coupled with a sense of family that demanded they take care of each other. If someone was weak, she was helped along until she got strong. If he was sick, he was nursed until he healed. If she made mistakes, the group acknowledged them, then covered for her. The esprit de corps was that of an adventurous, cemented team. And what a team those flight attendants were!

One time, a beautiful, voluptuous, young Swedish flight attendant, Barbro, turned down her captain's sexual advances on a layover. The next day, while the crew was beginning to clear customs to enter Japan, the captain whispered to a customs' agent that he thought it was his duty to report one of his crew might be smuggling. He pointed to Barbro.

First, Barbro was given a pat-down inspection, during which several miniature bottles of alcohol were discovered. Then, she was escorted to a back room where she had to submit to a complete orifice inspection. It was hours before a traumatized Barbro was released to rejoin her crew, with a strong admonition to not try smuggling alcohol again. Worse yet, her being detained by customs put a career-long red flag next to her name in customs' computers, ensuring that she would always be examined closely and with suspicion at border crossings.

When Barbro's tattling captain, Frankly Gross, reported to the airplane two days later, he found that his flight bag had been waylaid on the way to the airplane and some persons had repeatedly urinated and defecated on his maps and charts and required flight items. On subsequent flights, Frankly was offered homemade chocolate chip cookies containing chocolate ExLax, coffee that had been laced with Visine, and crew meals that had scrapings from the bathroom floor stirred into them. Frankly Gross finally had to quit flying the passenger trips that his seniority allowed him to fly and captain only domestic cargo all-nighters. The word flew out about Frankly's experiences, and pilots started to give special heed to fair treatment of flight attendants.

Thus, when Lora told Loudman to shut up or he would be taken care of on the next layover, he listened. He didn't yell at me again that day.

*A*fter my first experience with the Tiger flight attendants, I looked forward to flying with them again. One perk was having a larger group of people to select playmates from on layovers. Sandy Ferguson Tanaka was one. She took me under her wing, guiding me around the island of Okinawa. She had met her Japanese husband while climbing Mount Fuji and had become fluent in Japanese by the time I met her. Her fluency allowed us to wander away from tourist spots, and I enjoyed watching the astonished reactions of shopkeepers when they heard a "round-eye" speaking their language.

Flight attendant Ken Barton and I compared notes about coping strategies for handling bigotry. Ken, gay and out of the closet, had been treated abominably at work. Many captains would not allow him in the cockpit. Ken said my arrival had given him a happy new expectation. He anticipated my being captain with an all-woman cockpit crew and his being senior flight attendant in back with an all-male cabin crew.

"Wow, Norah! Can't you just imagine the looks on the

passengers' faces?"

The acceptance and support of the gay male flight attendants was a balm for my ruffled feathers. And it was an overdue awakening for my white middle-class persona to the realities of the barriers being breached by minorities in the 1970s and the problems shared by those pioneers. Once, a captain rudely said to Ken and me, "Women in the cockpit. Men in the cabin. What's next? The world is going nuts."

"Fuck you," Ken responded.

"Fuck you," I echoed. Then I looked at Ken and burst into laughter. "I don't want to fuck him. Do you?"

"Hell no!"

A heterosexual male flight attendant put a new twist on the sexism issue months later. I was flying with two men who were married to Tiger flight attendants. When our flight was delayed, I spent an hour on the ramp talking to Mike, a medical student who had taken time out to refurbish his finances and see the world as a flight attendant. He was fun and interesting but our conversation wasn't flirtatious. I was surprised, then, when Mike came to the flight deck in cruise, knelt on the cockpit floor next to my seat, and formally proposed marriage.

"Why in the world would you propose marriage to a woman you hardly know?" I asked.

"Ah, babe," he answered. "It was love at first sight. And I already know how important it is for you to be one of the guys. I'm giving you a chance to do what all the guys have already done at one time or another—sleep with and support a flight attendant."

I had read *Coffee, Tea or Me* while flying in Alaska. Attending orgies with flight attendants was not a fantasy of mine, but I did wonder how much of that book contained some kernels of truth. I watched the interaction of flight attendants and pilots, waiting for the nonstop partying and pairing off to begin. It didn't happen that way. Sure, there was sizing up among the singles and some dating; there were also affairs, marriages, and divorces. But there was none of the rampant ignoring of ethics that prevailed in *Coffee, Tea or Me*. I worked with many happily and faithfully married pilots and flight attendants.

The exceptions to normal behavior were the ones that got the press. I did meet one female flight attendant whose goal was to have sex with every pilot on the seniority list before she retired. She shared that information with me, when my hiring made it clear that she would never reach her goal. Another female flight attendant, on our first trip together, pulled out her annotated copy of the seniority list and offered its listings to me to "save you time and trouble." She had rated the sexual prowess of all the men she had already slept with. The listing of which crewmembers were in town for what flights she referred to as her "crew menu" and she presumably selected her male de jour from it.

I did work with some men who had problems keeping their pants zipped, but they were a minority. And strangely, it was not the womanizers who came after me. They were either not attracted to me or knew instinctively that I would not put up with their behavior. Indeed, only once did I fall for a player. I thought, of course, he would be different with me. He wasn't. It was an excruciatingly painful experience to be told that I was loved but then be treated like an expendable receptacle.

The most outrageous flight-attendant behavior I witnessed came while I was staying in New York's Midway Hotel, when a rare April snowstorm closed the airport. Some crews from grounded planes didn't have luggage because they expected to be home that night, not stranded in a snowbound city. Area hotels were packed and could not accommodate the reservationless travelers and flight crews. I offered the extra bed in my room to two Tiger flight attendants, asking only that they be quiet because I had an early morning departure. Sleep was difficult; the hotel was overflowing and parties were spilling into the hallways.

At midnight, the noise outside my room increased

considerably, and I stalked into the hallway to ask the revelers to have mercy on those of us who had to work soon. I saw a nude blond woman tearing down the hall, waving a champagne bottle with one hand and holding a hat on her head with the other.

"Caann't catch me!" she challenged over her shoulder to the man following her half a hallway away. He was nude and impeded in his run by a bobbing erection.

"Give me back my hat," he commanded.

"Make me!" she shrieked, while opening a fire escape door and clinging to the edge of a captain's gold-leafed visor. He followed her into the stairwell and I could hear the ensuing giggle of capture and then silences interspersed with rhythmic thumping. Others walked to the door, peered into the landing and then, door still open to the view, began to embrace each other and shed clothing in the hallway.

I returned to my room, inserted earplugs, and pulled the pillow over my head. That allowed me to sleep for an hour before loud copulating noises awakened me again. I foggily deduced that some couple must be having at it against my door for the noises to be so distinct. I was wrong. The couple was in the bed next to mine. A Tiger girl had found some man to be irresistible.

"Get out," I snarled.

"Don't you want to join us? I'll share."

"Get out!" I yelled. I didn't feel any remorse for banishing them to the stairwell for the night.

11

LOVE AFFAIR WITH A FAT LADY

1977–78

At one time, every young pilot's fantasy was to captain a 747 on international routes and retire from a flying career in that seat. For years, my dreams were more modest. I just wanted to sit in the pilot's seat and manipulate the 747 controls while it was airborne. I got a chance to do that in 1977.

I was hitching a ride from San Francisco to Seattle to see my boyfriend, John, and thought I would be riding in the jumpseat of a DC-8. Tigers instead had a new 747 flying empty to Seattle with only check airmen on board. They were accomplishing two tasks: positioning the plane for its first revenue trip and giving line experience to men who would soon be training other pilots to fly the plane.

I crossed the international ramp at Tigers with head and eyes raised to the great height and bulk of the 747. *Wow. I get to see the cockpit. I get to ride in the cockpit and see how it is done. Wow. And these guys I'll be riding with are the most senior Tiger pilots. Air gods. Wow.*

I strapped into a passenger seat located behind the cockpit and separated from it by a low partition that allowed me a serviceable view of the flight deck without getting in the way of the men milling around. As we were reaching our cruising altitude, one of the men walked back and asked if I were *the* lady pilot. When I acknowledged my name and position, he insisted that I enter the cockpit and be introduced to the rest of the 747 pilots there. I let the men know that I had never been in a 747 cockpit before and was thrilled to have the opportunity to see the queen of the fleet up close.

One of them said, "No woman in the world has ever flown a 747. Should we let her in the seat and see if she can keep the plane upright?"

Snorting at the idea, one replied, "I don't want to bet my life on it!" The captain in the left seat was quick to respond, "Hey, I'm good enough to save the plane from her. Let's see what she can do. If she gets out of hand or we get airsick, I'll take over." With that reassurance accepted, he invited me to sit in the right seat and fly.

I get to fly it! I really get to fly it, I thought as I buckled into the copilot's seat. I did not know that hand flying (as opposed to letting the autopilot do the work) at altitude was a tricky experience. High up in thinner air, the plane's balance was more sensitive. I found that keeping that 747 on altitude, on airspeed, and on track was hard work but I loved every second of it. I hand flew the plane to the Seattle area and began the descent before relinquishing the controls to a check airman.

After we parked on the Tiger Seattle ramp, I ran to the nearest pay phone and called my father. My news just couldn't wait until reaching my boyfriend's home. I had just begun an enduring love affair with the fat lady of the fleet.

"Dad! Dad! Guess what I just did?"

"I don't know honey. Where are you calling from?"

"I just flew a 747 to Seattle!"

"That's nice. Will you be there for a few days?"

"Dad, you don't get it. I just *flew* a 747! I wasn't just riding in one. I actually flew it!"

"No! Who let you do that?" I told my Dad about catching a free ride to Seattle and the plane being full of check airmen.

"You mean you really sat in the pilot's seat and actually

flew it?"

"Yes."

"Oh my God. Bertha! Sissy just flew a 747!"

"Yes. And it was sooo cool. It was weird at altitude, but the descent was just like in any other plane, except more stable and more powerful and more fun. It was so cool!"

"Oh my God. They let you make the descent?"

"Yes. It was so exciting."

"Oh my God. They didn't let you land it, did they?"

"Dad! Well, of course they didn't."

The import of that "Of course they didn't" did not occur to me until seventeen years later when I was being inaugurated into the San Diego Aerospace Museum. A new exhibit featuring women airline pilots was opening with press and TV coverage. Many women pilots had flown in for the occasion. My parents, sister, brother, children, and a few close friends were there. The focal point of the display was a glassed enclosure containing two life-sized mannequins. Those dolls were representations of Lynn Rippelmeyer and me wearing the uniforms, hats, and wings that we had made history in. Lynn had been the first woman to fly a revenue trip in the 747 in 1979. I checked out in it two weeks later. Two months later, I became the first woman in the world to fly a planeload of passengers on the 747. Lynn made history again when she became the first woman in the world to captain the 747 for People Express.

My children looked at photos of Mommy when she was young, listened to the speeches, and read all the inscriptions on the walls. They watched me being interviewed for TV.

My daughter, Cammie, ten years old, approached me with a puzzled look on her face.

"Mom, this is all really neat. I'm glad you're being honored and on TV with all your friends, but I don't really get it. You and Lynn were the first women in the world to fly the 747. That's cool. But who taught you to fly it?"

"747 check airmen."

"They were all men?"

"Yes."

"Who taught them to fly it?"

"Check airmen from the Boeing Company."

"Were they all men?"

"Yes."

"Mom, if a whole bunch of boys had already done it, how hard could it have been?" (This from a small-town-girl who was enrolled in gifted-student programs and had yet to meet a boy who was as smart as she was.)

"Oh honey, the plane was easy to learn. They aren't honoring Lynn and me because we learned how to fly this plane. They are honoring us because we had the fortitude to endure what it took to get the opportunity to fly it."

Dad had been surprised that the Tiger check airmen had allowed me to fly the plane in 1977. He had been shocked at the thought of them allowing me to land it. Seventeen years later, he would have been shocked if they had *not* allowed me to land it. Progress.

*T*here were a few Tigers who were legends in the crew force. Cal and Scott were because of their partying. Bob Bax was because of his incredible coolness in emergencies. I was fortunate to fly with all three of them during my first year on the line.

Laid back, laconic Bob Bax, copilot Jim Winterberg, and I were scheduled to fly a Lufthansa charter from New York to Frankfurt, Germany, in the summer of 1977. Maintenance delays had us waiting through the night and finally taxiing out as the sun was rising. Our radio call sign was Lufthansa 12. The JFK controllers had a problem with that because among the planes moving on the ramps and taxiways, none looked like a Lufthansa jet to them.

"Lufthansa 12, which one are you?" they queried.

"Lufthansa 12 is wearing Tiger DC-8 pajamas this morning," Jim replied. Jim was already trying to decide when he could put his own pajamas back on. We were tired.

Once we had flown a curving path up the coast of Canada and over Newfoundland, Bob and Jim got the

INSs (Inertial Navigation Systems) fully programmed for our assigned NATrack. (North Atlantic Track) The North Atlantic is one of the most traveled airspaces in the world, so precise navigation is essential. Deviating from one's assigned course, if not culminating in disaster, can lead to heavy fines for the airline involved. Multiple fines result in an airline's right to fly the Atlantic routes being terminated. I watched the INS loading with fascination.

As engineer, I was responsible for loading the latitude and longitude of the airplane's parking spot. The captain and copilot loaded all subsequent navigational latitudes and longitudes, but only nine sets of numbers could be loaded into the system at one time. When the INS system was hooked up with the autopilot system, the plane automatically flew itself from waypoint one to two, then two to three, three to four, etc. When the plane was flying from waypoint eight to waypoint nine, it was time to load a new set of waypoints.

Early in our established cruise, Jim announced he was going to get some shut-eye. Bob nodded his agreement, and Jim scrunched down in his seat and soon began snoring softly. A half-hour later, Bob asked how I was feeling.

"Oh fine, sir. I'm on top of things," I lied. I was still on probation and didn't think it was okay for me to admit that hanging around a crew room all night during the hours I normally slept and drinking gallons of awful coffee had ill prepared me for spending five hours squinting into the sun over the Atlantic. The Federal Aviation Regulations forbid sleeping in the cockpit. I didn't think it was okay for me to admit that I *really* wanted to break those rules.

However, Captain Bax evidently took my "I'm fine" as his release to shut his eyes. His heavy-lidded eyes looked half asleep anyway, so his descent into slumber was subtle and difficult to detect. His slouching into his seat reminded me of Robert Mitchum slumped in a saddle on the edge of a moving herd of cattle. The slightest change in the sound of their lowing of course jerked him into action. I hoped that was what was happening in the cockpit—Bob just resting his eyes from the glare while still fully vigilant. This was my first trip across the Atlantic as a crewmember, and I did *not* want

103

to be in charge of things.

I watched the fuel gauges on my panel slowly wind down as the fuel gauges on the front panel slowly wound up. I adjusted the throttles to maintain our assigned mach speed. I entered our engine readouts in the engine logbook. I did all the paperwork I could do. I monitored the time and fuel usage and each passing waypoint. This was all dull work, neither engrossing nor intellectually engaging, and the temptation to shut my eyes was growing nearly overwhelming. As our plane was navigating from waypoint eight to nine, I knew that new latitudes and longitudes needed to be loaded soon. I had never loaded the points myself, though I had been trained to do so. Enough captains had told me *not* to touch anything in their cockpit that I did not feel free to touch the INS without specific permission. I began to get nervous about what to do.

Should I awaken Bob or Jim? Should I load the waypoints myself without permission or supervision? My decision making was as slow as the turn our plane started to make as the INS told the autopilot to turn back to America (fly from waypoint nine back to waypoint one). The sun was slowly sliding by our side window as Bob's hand flew to the autopilot control panel and selected a heading that turned us back into the sun.

"Keep us heading to Europe, Norah," he drawled in a quiet tone. I loaded the waypoints and did the necessary checks while Bob slumped back into his saddle. *Wow, he did all that without ever opening his eyes.*

Bob Bax's understated style of hypervigilance and his ability to get to the core of a matter in few words again became apparent as we prepared to fly the approach into Frankfurt. Jim was flying the plane, visibility was low, and the air was turbulent. As we slid down the glideslope and it became more likely that we would have to fly a missed approach, Jim nervously said, "Bob, read that missed-approach procedure to me again!"

Bob said, "Just keep it going straight ahead, Jim, and keep 'er off the ground."

After landing, Bob taxied the plane to the Lufthansa cargo

area and parking spot three. Normally, the engineer calls in on the company radio frequency about twenty minutes before landing, advises the company of the estimated time of arrival, and receives the assigned parking spot. I had made the required call but repeatedly had failed to get a response from Lufthansa.

I explored the possibilities for that lack of response—I had the wrong frequency; my radio was not working; Lufthansa was too busy to answer; their receiver worked but their transmitter did not; they did not understand my English. Captain Bob had become aware of the problem when I asked to borrow his radio to transmit on. I had already borrowed Jim's radio. I knew I had the right frequency because I could hear other Lufthansa flights calling in their arrival times and getting responses. Bob heard a disgruntled German voice saying, "Will the woman using Lufthansa's discreet frequency please quit interrupting and get off the air!"

Bob grabbed the radio from me and transmitted in his deep baritone, "This is the captain of Lufthansa Flight 12. If you want your freight today, you'd best be giving a parking spot assignment to my engineer. *She* has been too patient with you, and *she* has more important things to do than be hassled by you."

"Yes Sir!" was the response.

As Bob nosed our DC-8 into parking bay three, we could see that the ramp was filled with people staring at our plane. They had come to see what woman this captain had allowed to play with his radio. As I finished my postflight checks and walked toward Bob and Jim on the ramp, I was uncomfortably aware of all the eyes on me.

I heard a man in a suit, frustration in his voice and body language, asking Bob, "Who is she really? Who have you allowed on our plane?" Bob, apparently reaching the end of his patience with giving answers that no one believed, said, "Okay, you caught me. I brought my girlfriend along to make coffee. I just gave her one of my old uniforms to play dress-up in."

That was an explanation they *could* believe. (Obviously,

Lufthansa was several years away from contemplating having a woman pilot.)

Bob had flown charters for years. The Tigers' Charter Domicile was created to have a pool of pilots on call for last-minute flights to spots that did not have regular cargo service. Charter pilots were an elite and eccentric bunch who reveled in pushing the limits of the envelope, exploring new territory, and solving unusual problems. Once I learned that Bob liked to tell stories, I plied him with beers and listened.

Bob told me that the night before he was to leave for a place in Africa whose name he had not heard of before or since, an armored car pulled up in front of his house. The driver had a suitcase for Bob that he wanted him to sign for.

"What's in it?" Bob asked.

"$250,000," the man replied. "Just sign here."

"You're kidding!" Bob said. "What's it for?"

"I don't know. Don't you? I'm just the delivery boy."

"What happens if I sign for it?" Bob asked.

"I give it to you. It's yours," the man said.

"Wait here," Bob commanded the driver as he went inside to call Tigers.

He learned that he would be flying to places that would not take credit cards for gas. This money was for fuel. Bob told Tigers that he didn't want responsibility for the money's safekeeping. They explained that, normally, the charter representative accompanying each charter flight would be carrying the money, but he had been delayed en route to the departure point and could not take charge of the money until the next day. With reluctance Bob signed for the money and carried it to the airport the following day, where he relinquished it with relief.

The first stop of their trip was a layover in New York. The pilots, charter rep, and mechanic checked into the hotel together. A number of pilots had had luggage stolen from the lobby of this hotel and all had been advised to keep their baggage with them at all times. Bob was astonished when he saw the charter rep throw the bag full of money behind a potted palm when he went to check in, even though he kept his own suitcase nearby.

"Aren't you going to put that bag in the hotel safe?" he asked.

"Nah," said the rep, explaining that it was his experience that if you acted like you didn't care about it, no one else cared about it either. "If I had that mother chained to my wrist, sure enough, someone would cut off my wrist stealing it. I always pretend that a sack of dirty clothes is the important stuff."

The crew and plane and money arrived in Africa two days later. Upon parking, their DC-8 was surrounded by armed soldiers and tanks.

"What the hell is on this plane?" Bob demanded of the charter rep.

"You don't want to know," was the reply. "Just get us out of here as quickly as you can."

Getting the hell out of Dodge proved to be difficult. After the mystery cargo was offloaded and the plane refueled, the ground controller refused to give them air-traffic-control clearance to leave. Without ATC clearance they couldn't activate their flight plan and couldn't legally take off, let alone safely transit the numerous international boundaries they would have to fly over to get to Italy, their next stop. Bob assessed the situation. He saw more armament arriving, trucks of soldiers on the move, and he thought of what it might take to keep his plane safe while he found transportation for everyone to the nearest hotel, where they would await the snarls being untangled via international phone. And that was assuming that they could find a hotel, arrive there safely, *and* find the phones working.

Bob decided not to assume anything. As he explained to me, "The plane wasn't broken. Seemed like a shame not to take advantage of that."

So Bob pushed up the power, and guards leapt out of the way when the jet started its lumbering taxi roll. The crew hurriedly scanned the horizon looking for possible air traffic. They were going to take off without permission and could hardly ask the tower for vectors around inbound traffic. They did a rolling turn onto the runway only peripherally aware of tanks giving chase behind them. They were, of course, busy finishing all the before-takeoff checklists. Some corners cannot be cut in aviation.

Bob eased the controls back in a max-power takeoff, broke free, and headed north. He kept the plane under 500 feet in the hopes of avoiding radar detection. As Bob made shallow banking turns to avoid rising terrain ahead of them, his crew looked out the windows in wonder at the four sand-filled tornadoing contrails they were leaving behind them on the desert below.

"Look at those!" his copilot said. "We'll probably never see anything like it again. Does it get any better than this?"

Bob eased the plane up to a higher altitude when he figured they were in the airspace of a different country.

"How did you know you were out of the country?" I asked.

"Just guessed," Bob said. "Hell, the navaids didn't work down that low."

*W*hile Bob was flying to Italy, crew control was having a staffing crisis in Los Angeles. They desperately needed a captain to fly a big-revenue trip. One controller called Bob's home at 2 a.m.

"Could I speak with Captain Bax? This is crew control."

"He's not home," replied his wife. "He's out flying."

"Do you know where he is?" asked crew control.

"I don't know where he is and, right now, I don't care where he is. But you should. After all, he's out there somewhere playing with one of your airplanes and your quarter-of-a-million dollars in cash!"

12

FLIGHT CLEARANCE

1978–79

*T*he Tiger boys called him "Santa Claus." I called him my lucky break. Captain Ron Hall was known for being exceedingly fair on pilot checkrides. I *needed* fair on my first checkride as copilot on the DC-8.

When I received my first copilot's bid at the end of my probationary year at Tigers, I was so excited. *I get to fly jets!* That thrilled feeling was abruptly squashed two weeks before I was to report for the upgrade training. A check captain whom I had recently flown with called me at home and asked, "What did you do to piss off Captain 'NoGo'? He's passed the word around the training center that whichever check person gets you in the simulator should make sure that you bust the ride."

"I've never met Captain NoGo."

"You must have. He's hell bent on getting rid of you. I had hoped to train you myself, but I don't want to have to explain to him why you passed."

"I've never met Captain NoGo."

"Why would he be out to ruin you then?"

"Maybe he's a bigot?"

"Nah. He's one of the good guys."

"Doesn't sound like it to me."

I decided to ignore the warning call as an exaggeration and get on with studying. Two days later, another check captain called me at home.

"What's up with you and NoGo? He's trying to get you fired before you get off probation and join the union. Word's out at the training center to bust you in the simulator."

"I don't even know the man. You aren't the first check captain to call and warn me about him."

"You must know him. He wouldn't do this for no reason."

"Maybe it's because I'm a girl?"

"Nah. Who would do something like that just because you are a girl?"

"A male chauvinist pig?"

"Bite your tongue!"

The third call from a concerned check captain had me panicking. I made an appointment to see Captain Lamont Shadowens, new Vice President of Flight Operations, when I reported to Los Angeles for training. I had already flown with him and was taking an aviation history class with him at an Embry Riddle Aeronautical University campus in San Mateo. I might not have gone to management if I had not known Shad. I told him of my predicament. His reaction was as expected.

"The men who called you must have been exaggerating. If management wanted to bust you on a checkride, and I assure you management doesn't do things like that, they certainly wouldn't spread the word around. If NoGo busts you on a ride now, it would be an automatic retake."

"Shad, I don't want to get into the simulator with NoGo. I'm uptight enough about upgrading without stacking the deck against myself."

"Norah, who called you? It must have been a troublemaker."

I gave him the names of the three men who had called me. I could see the puzzlement on his face change to disbelief, then acceptance. The men who had called me were known as straight shooters. They were respected.

"Norah, I promise I will take care of this for you. This

should not have happened. I apologize for NoGo. He will be taken care of. I will personally see that you get a fair ride."

Shad truly made the ride as fair as possible. Captain Ron Hall gave me my copilot's checkride. I was allowed to select the engineer and captain who would fly with me, so I chose Mike Solway as captain and classmate Dick Rothstein as the engineer. I thought if I could not pass a ride with this crew, I shouldn't be an airline pilot.

A standard checkride is slotted for an hour of briefing before the ride, two hours in the simulator, and an hour of debriefing afterwards. In the prebriefing, Ron explained that everyone was going to ask him about this ride later and he wanted to be able to tell them he had given me *everything*.

As it turned out, "everything" included every emergency in the book, including two engines not working on one side of the airplane, with manual reversion of the hydraulic controls. Normally, only candidates for captain were asked to do the two-engines-out work for the practical reason that if a plane lost power on half of its engines in a real-life situation, no sane captain would hand that crippled plane off to a copilot.

"Is that okay with you chicken?" Ron asked my permission, using an endearment he'd borrowed from W.C. Fields.

"Do I have the right of refusal?"

"No, chicken, I know what's best here."

My God, I'm worried about passing the copilot's checkride and now they want me to pass the captain's test? Is there ever going to be an end to the price I have to pay for being the first?

I spent the next torturous three-and-a-half hours in the hot seat. I looked longingly at the clock when it showed the two-hour mark and realized I was not going to get a standard two-hour test.

I'd like to say that I aced the ride. I did not. I was so tense that if I had been poked, I would have twanged. Nothing went perfectly. I was always just a few degrees off heading, a few knots off speed, a few feet off altitude. Not enough for an automatic bust, but not pretty. Mike and Dick did all that they were allowed to do to help, but they couldn't fly it for me.

My first approach with two engines failed on one side of the plane was a roller-coaster ride. I did make the runway, but not in a position to land. I went around. The go around was successful in that we did not crash, but I would hate ever to see a real plane behave like that wildly gyrating simulation.

The second two-engine approach went better simply because I was getting too tired to over control the plane. Ron forced me into a second go around by reducing the visibility to below minimums for landing.

On my third two-engine approach, I knew I was going to have to land it or call it quits. My arms were aching and my left leg was so tired from mashing the left rudder into the floor with all my strength, I was forced to sneak my right leg over to help out. Flying with two feet on one rudder is something I hope never to do again. It didn't occur to me to ask Mike to fly it for me so I could rest. I didn't think that was allowed. As we descended over the runway threshold, Ron (as ATC) called, "Tiger One, there's an elephant on the runway. Go Around."

"Fuck the elephant! This plane is landing!" *Crunch.*

"Park it, Norah. I've seen enough."

A silent crew exited the simulator. Mike and Dick avoided my eyes. I thanked them for their help. I crawled off to receive the bad news behind the closed door of the briefing room. *I will not cry.*

"Well, Captain Hall. Let's get this over with. I'll make it easy for you. I know I didn't make it. You don't have to find a nice way to soften the blow." *Ah, shit!*

"Chicken, you passed. Nice judgment call on the elephant. Let's go have him for dinner."

"I passed? Really?"

"Yeah, of course you did." He looked at me for a long moment. "Chicken, don't ever let anyone tell you that you can't fly. You can."

Gee, Ron, how do I stop them from doing that? And how do I stop myself from believing it?

I was the first woman in the world to fly the DC-8 as an engineer and now I had the opportunity to be the first woman in the world to fly the DC-8 as copilot.

On my first flight as copilot, my captain greeted me with, "I don't approve of your being here. I think you're a dangerous mistake. But I'm a pro. I'll work with you. Just don't touch anything in the cockpit."

Not touching anything in the cockpit made it difficult to do my job. As we were readying for pushback, the captain asked me if I had gotten our departure clearance yet.

"No, sir. To do that I would have to touch the radio."

"You can touch your radio. But don't touch mine."

I got the clearance and we taxied out, reading through the before-takeoff checklist. When he called for me to position the flaps to takeoff configuration, I just sat there.

"Are you deaf?" he snarled.

"May I touch the flaps?" I replied.

After takeoff, I called, "positive rate of climb" and he commanded, "gear up". I just sat there. "Gear up," he repeated.

"Do I have your permission to touch the gear handle?"

"Touch anything that you have to in order to do your job," he replied.

We wallowed on in that kind of atmosphere for two days. He, of course, did not let me actually fly the plane.

A fast-moving weather system in Chicago changed that. I had gone out to the plane to listen to the clearance delivery frequency on the radio. Usually, the clearance we received before pushback was the same as the one printed on our flight plan. All I had to do was memorize the printed routing and listen carefully to see if any of it had changed.

It wasn't unusual for the controller to read a complicated clearance so quickly that no one could possibly write all of it down. Yet we were expected to read it back to him immediately to confirm that we had copied it correctly. Once, I heard a pilot start his readback, hesitate, and then plead, "Say again all after turn left after takeoff. My pencil caught on fire there."

That night in Chicago I knew I was in trouble when the controller started changing everyone's clearance to accommodate moving jets around storm cells. I would not be able to memorize it ahead of time and I knew my captain would be scathing in his criticism if I flubbed my clearance readback. I came up with a plan. I returned to the terminal and reached clearance delivery on a telephone. Explaining that I was a new copilot and flying with an unmerciful captain, I begged him to read my clearance to me slowly when I called him from the plane. He did better than that. He gave me my clearance slowly over the telephone. I memorized it and reported back to the airplane.

When I radioed for our clearance, what emerged from the radio was a streak of gobbledygook that no human could have understood. Anger flashed across the captain's face. He reached for his radio. "He can't do that to you just because you're a girl!" he said.

I smiled, keyed my mike, and read back our flight clearance perfectly.

"Have a safe flight, Tigress," the controller signed off.

"How in the fuck did you do that? I didn't understand a word."

"Oh, experience, sir."

On the way to the runway, the captain said in a softer tone than usual, "Anyone who could get a clearance like that can probably fly. Do you want to do the takeoff and landing tonight?"

*T*hough experiences during my first year were rich with good people, I was still regularly challenged to prove myself to others who had doubts about my being there. Sometimes having a sense of humor was all I needed to get by.

The DC-8 had two large doorknob-shaped metal knobs on the central pedestal between the captain and copilot. These round knobs had two-inch-wide circles cut into their tops, held in place with metal prongs. The circles, which could be removed with fingernails, popped back into their holding clips and became picture frames for artwork clipped from *Playboy* and *Hustler* magazines. The running cockpit joke about these miniature pictures was substituting the examination of them for the preflight check. For instance, if the captain were running late, he would pop off a metal circle, look at the nude female photo inside, and proclaim, "Nice stuff! I guess this plane is ready to fly."

During my first year with Tigers, fellow pilots closely scrutinized me. Many of them later told me that they hoped to torture me enough so I would just quit, and Tigers would not repeat their stupid woman-pilot experiment. Shoving pornographic photos under my nose was just one of their forms of torture.

I didn't mind looking at nude artwork. It was easy to agree that most of it was nice stuff. What I did get tired of was having scrapes on the end of my nose from the guys' enthusiastic sharing of the metal circle. Since I was trying hard to fit in with the men and prove that my presence would not interfere with any of their male cockpit rituals, I decided that complaining would not be effective.

Instead, I bought *Playgirl* magazine for the first time and carefully clipped rounded photos of male genitals. I inserted these photos in the trim-knob covers of all the DC-8s that came through the maintenance base near my apartment.

Not too long after I started my redecorating, I reported for a flight, and, during the cockpit setup, the captain pulled off a trim-knob cover, briefly glimpsed it, and pronounced, "Nice stuff." As he extended his arm to push the photo under my nose, a shocked look appeared on his face as he realized what he had just seen.

"My God! We have a pervert working for us!" he exclaimed. I grabbed his wrist before he could jerk his hand back and took a long look at a tiny flaccid penis.

"Ah," I said, "pretty nice, but pretty small. I wish women wouldn't tell so many lies about how size really doesn't matter."

No one ever shared a trim-knob photo with me again.

Humor also helped when men asked me to be one of the guys in challenging ways. One crew invited me to go to a whorehouse. I said, "Sure, I'd like to go. Does this one have hard-bodied young men to entertain me while you guys are busy?" Another crew asked me to accompany them to a strip

115

joint. When I hesitated in formulating a reply, the captain said, "Come on, O'Neill, when was the last time you saw a really good set of tits?" "When I got dressed this morning, sir. I don't have to pay to see a good female form."

*S*oon after I checked out as copilot, I flew for a month that felt like a year with Captain Dick Andrews. I thought he gave a whole new meaning to the term "dickhead." I was wrong about that, but it would take me several years to figure that out. Dick was shorter than I was and stocky, rough hewn, and stern faced. He was a working farmer on his days off, and that alter ego showed in his earthiness. He was also a good and thorough pilot and ran a tight ship. Though sometimes gruff in the cockpit, he was never abusive. Dick was an honest man, but I thought he was unfair. He was not.

What I brought to our month together were myriad chips on my shoulders and a prickliness that Dick could not assuage, not that he was inclined to try. I flew poorly when it was my turn to fly for the first time. I wanted to do well, but the harder I tried, the worse I performed. That cycle would make me angry and fuel its continuation. Midway through the month, Dick and I spent two hours in the Chicago crew room waiting for our plane to be turned. At one point, as I walked toward him to hand him paperwork to sign, he extended a pack of gum to me with one stick protruding.

"Hey, O'Neill, if you can chew this and walk straight at the same time, I'll let you fly the airplane again." Dick laughed. So did the twenty other pilots in the crew room. I was humiliated.

"I don't chew gum. I wouldn't want to interfere with my ability to get around," I spat out and stomped from the room.

It wasn't congenial in the cockpit for a while after that. I wanted to refuse to fly the legs Dick offered (every other one) because I didn't want to open myself up for criticism. But I knew I needed every leg I could get in order to move beyond being a green newcomer. And there were still many men who would not let me fly at all. So I flew and flew poorly, believing that Dick got mileage out of cackling with the guys about how he had to carry me around the country.

Luckily for both Dick and me, we did not fly together again for a decade. By that time, we had both graduated from the DC-8 to the 747 and I had more time on the Boeing than he did. I was comfortable in the 747; indeed, my love affair with her had led me to fly her very well.

I no longer had chips on my shoulders and had developed a finely tuned sense of when I was encountering sexist bias, experiencing it as tiny currents of hate disturbing the air around feelers on my head. I was amazed at how well this waving of antennae worked, once I trusted my feelings. It was like feeling the hairs on the back of my neck standing on end when someone behind me was staring at me. Sometimes those antennae would wave when I was talking to someone who had given me no visual or verbal cues about how he really felt. The antennae were never wrong.

I did groan when I learned that I had pulled a trip with Dick ten years later. Part of me still blamed him for my never performing well in his presence, as if he had created an atmosphere that was not conducive to getting the job done with polished skill. *But I'm a big girl now,* I reminded myself. *I can be a seasoned professional with him no matter what kind of effort that might take.*

My first surprise was when we greeted each other and my antennae did not wave. Interesting. My second surprise was when he gave me the difficult leg of the evening, saying that he'd had some time off and was not as current as I was in the plane. Being current was useful in flying a nighttime ADF approach over water into a narrow and short runway that neither of us had been to before. The third surprise was that Dick's being in the cockpit did *not* sabotage my work. We rolled into parking at that small military strip in the Carolinas without anyone onboard growing extra gray hair.

The next two hours on the ground changed my opinion of Dick. I was not so naïve as to think he had suddenly become an okay guy in the years since I had seen him. I realized that it was I who had changed and he who had been

117

willing to acknowledge and accept my transformation. I had never really talked to him before and didn't know him at all. Of course I had not *wanted* to before. He told me how proud he was of his wife going back to school and getting an advanced degree in psychology. He also told me that she had given him a lot of flack for the way he had treated me. I found that interesting.

"She told me I was a horse's ass when I offered you that stick of gum. I was just trying to get you to relax."

"Dick, that gum incident was humiliating. You were such a dickhead."

"I guess I was. I didn't mean to be. Can you give me credit for good intentions?"

I could do that. I could also see how frustrating it had been for him to see my performance start off substandard and then deteriorate. He had actually tried to help.

Our new relationship was comfortable, and we worked similarly in the cockpit. Spending time with him on layovers, I was surprised to discover that he had a dry and incisive wit. His standard dress was a plaid shirt, blue jeans, and cowboy boots. He liked to have his after-work cocktail in homey bars that working men frequented. Once, he was seated with a bunch of truckers who were comparing rigs over beers. My rig has twelve wheels and carries 15,000 pounds and so forth. In an effort to get Dick into the conversation, one driver asked him how many wheels his rig had.

"Mine's an eighteen wheeler"

"No shit! Eighteen wheels? What's the payload?"

"Oh, without full fuel, about 200,000 pounds."

"Hell, never heard of one that big. Sure you ain't had too many beers?"

Dick and I had a fun conversation about men's obsessions with comparisons—their cars, their women, their trucks, their planes, their pectorals, their cocks. "Gee," I asked, "why don't you guys just slap your dicks out on the bar at the beginning of the evening, see whose is biggest, and get all the guesswork over with?"

"Yeah, Norah, I can see why you'd like that."

"Like it? Hell, I give up. Be as ridiculous as you want to

be but don't expect me to be your copilot in bars."

"How do you copilot in a bar?" he queried.

"The copilot's most important job is making the captain look good. I'll keep my mouth shut and save my best efforts for the airplane."

Dick laughed. "Perfect. You just shut up and look good, and the guys will think I have a well-trained trophy wife."

*T*wo of the Tiger pilots who had dropped by to stare at me in the classroom in 1976 started a betting pool that year. Whoever slept with me first was to collect the money in the pot. No one told me about the betting then, which is probably for the best, because probationary pilots made very little money. (My take-home pay that first year was $300 a month short of covering my mortgage payment in Alaska, let alone paying for any living expenses.) I might have been tempted to select a likely candidate and split the money with him.

A classmate approached me at the end of our probationary year. We shared our usual warm hug of greeting and recognition of a fellow survivor of an ordeal.

He said, "It's really none of my business, Norah. You have a right to your own personal life, but I am disappointed in your choice of a lover. There are things you don't know about him, and I think you could do much better."

I found out then about the bet and who had just collected the winnings, a guy I had never met. My classmate was astounded that anyone could have told such a lie. He made arrangements to publicly introduce me to the man in the Chicago crew room where we would have a maximum audience of pilots. Most of Tigers' DC-8s transited the Chicago hub every night between midnight and 4 a.m. From that nightly gathering of pilots, planes and gossip dispersed around the earth. If you wanted crewmembers to hear news, it was most efficient to announce it in Chicago.

The night came for the introduction to my phantom lover, Studley. As usual, all eyes were on the girl as I entered the room. When my classmate loudly introduced me to

Studley, it was clear that this was a first meeting. There were witnesses in the room who had just recently handed cash over to him. I told Studley that I expected him to be man enough to hand the money over to me and promised I would personally hand the money over to the "winner" *if* there ever were one. The crew room started buzzing as I exited. Unmanly Studley never did give me the money.

As my probationary year ended I sighed in relief. *I made it. I really am an airline pilot now.* I turned my attention to my personal life, thinking that if I had a more solid base there, relationships at work would be less challenging.

I married my Alaskan Pipeline engineer in late 1977 and moved to Seattle to be with him. I was desperate to have some normalcy in my life, a ring to repel men's advances at work, and a sane and stable haven to come home to. I did not get any of those things but was just applying a marriage-certificate bandage to a terminally ill relationship. Marrying for all the wrong reasons had a large price tag.

13
THE
FOUNDING OF ISA + 21
1978

I was blessed with good chief pilots, but in a way, their very humanity worked against me. They were fair men and could not understand prejudice at a gut level. It was as foreign and inexplicable to them as it was to me. They struggled to find an explanation for why men who had never had a problem with coworkers before had written professionally scathing letters about me.

Dick Wilson, my chief pilot in Seattle, called me into his office one day after I had returned from a two-day trip. I would have described the trip as uneventful. We had flown to Chicago, had a pleasant dinner together, and returned to Seattle the next day. The captain had never said anything to me about my performance. We had parted amicably; yet that night he had written a two-page letter to Dick outlining everything I had done wrong in the plane. The letter concluded, "It's my professional opinion that if I had not been on board that airplane, Miss O'Neill would not have been able to find Chicago, let alone land a plane there. Get rid of her before she kills someone."

Dick said, "Norah, I have received more letters on you than on the entire crew force this year. Most guys finish their careers without a single letter in their file. What is going on?

I have flown with you. You can fly. And certainly after years in the Alaskan bush finding places with no help from navaids, now that you are working with two INSs, two VORs, two ADFs, and three communications radios, you sure as hell can find Chicago. What is this guy so fired up about?"

I didn't know. I told Dick that the captain had never complained to me. Dick was aghast. Standard practice was for captains to correct their copilots. We were all in training to be captains. Only when a copilot refused to correct his mistakes or try things a different way was he written up. Write-ups were rare.

"He didn't say anything to you? Not a thing?" Dick called the engineer and got his version of the events. It matched mine. "That's it," Dick spat out in disgust, "if they don't talk to you, they have no right to write about you." He threw the letter in the trashcan. Still searching for an explanation, he asked, "Why are you protecting this man? Clearly he made a pass at you and you turned him down. This is his childish revenge. Tell me the truth."

The truth was, the man had not made a pass at me. Nor had I done a bad job in the airplane. It would have been easier for me if there had been an obvious explanation. Instead, I was hurt and shaken with mistrust for my colleagues.

That first year a senior captain had said, "Fuck me or I'll get you fired. Captains are gods at Tigers. I can do this."

I cried, "Why would you do this to me? I've done a good job for you. You seemed to like me. Why would you take my career?"

"You don't belong here. You may as well be useful before we get rid of you."

I thought of taking that man to my chief pilot, but I did not. I was aware that part of the entrance admission to the boys club was not tattling. The guys didn't tell tales at the head shed about each other. I was aware that my very presence as a woman had already caused problems for my chief pilots. The problems were not my fault, but I had been the cause for the reactions. I could not change my plumbing. I could not change the bigots. But I could keep from adding to the pile of problems by keeping my mouth shut.

Keeping quiet hurt. The anger and resentment and hurt feelings festered inside of me. Not until I met other women pilots did I finally find a voice. Because I had been questioning whether I was indeed the problem, whether I had picked the wrong career, and whether I just couldn't cut it, I felt huge relief that I was not alone in my experiences.

Flying Tigers hired pilots Karen Dillon in 1977 and Sandra Donnelly in 1978. I met Karen in the training center and hugged her. I nearly slugged Sandy in the eye when I first met her. New on the flight line, Sandy saw me from behind in the Los Angeles crew room. Elbows propped on a flight paperwork counter, I leaned in to talk to the dispatcher, and my rear end wagged in a way that Sandy could not pass by. She gave my rear a resounding slap. I whirled around, fist raised, fire in my eyes. She didn't flinch away.

"You've got to be Norah. I've heard all about you. I've been wanting to meet you."

I had wanted to meet her too. I am no longer the only woman out here. Yay!

What Sandy didn't know when she slapped my behind was that I had just set new boundaries for myself after a month with a touchy-feely captain. He had frequently touched my shoulder and stroked my arms when he talked to me. Cockpit space is confined but not so small as to explain why he brushed against my breasts or hips or fanny any time we were in the cockpit together. I had addressed the problem several times.

"Captain, I am not comfortable with you touching me when we talk or when we are in the cockpit."

"Oh, did I?" he had replied. "I wasn't aware I was doing that."

After two weeks with him, I had had enough and decided to give him a chance to see how I felt. In a crowded Chicago crew room, I was bent over a counter filling out a weight and balance form, when he patted me on the fanny and leaned over my shoulder to view the paperwork. I turned to him, shoved him slightly so he was in clear view of the other pilots in the room, then patted his crotch. He knocked into another pilot as he jumped away from my hand.

123

"I don't believe you did that," he exclaimed.
"Why not? I was just following your example."
He didn't touch me again.

*I*n January 1978, Beverly Bass, an American Airlines pilot, and Stephanie Wallach, a Braniff pilot, spoke to each other about how much they would enjoy meeting other women pilots. They spoke with Claudia Jones, a Continental Airlines pilot, about having a meeting in Las Vegas where Claudia was living. They drafted a letter to the chief pilot at each airline that employed women pilots. Continental became the host airline, and Claudia made the convention and hotel arrangements.

Twenty-one women pilots from ten U.S. airlines met in Las Vegas in May 1978. When I received my invitation to Vegas I was excited. There are other women out there!

I found my way to the appointed meeting room, opened the door, and saw a dozen young women. Some were tall, some short, some thin, some rounded. All of them were speaking with animation. The conversations were about uniforms and schedules and flight history and seat position and pilot contracts and boyfriends and husbands and flying while pregnant. I was overwhelmed with a sense of finally belonging.

The pilots in Vegas that day were Emily Warner (Frontier, date of hire 1/29/73); Stephanie Wallach (Braniff, 12/05/75); Terry London Rinehart (Western, 3/8/76); Valerie Walker (Western, 3/8/76); Mary Bush (Hughes Airwest, 5/11/76); Angela Masson (American, 9/22/76); Beverley Bass (American, 10/24/76); Norah O'Neill (Flying Tigers, 12/01/76); Lynn Rhoades (Western, 1/10/77); Lennie Sorenson (Continental, 2/28/77); Holly Fulton (Braniff, 3/21/77); Claudia Simpson Jones (Continental, 3/21/77); Denise Blankenship (Piedmont, 4/01/77); Karen Kahn (Continental, 7/11/77); Sharon Hilgers Krask (Delta, 9/12/77); Jane Bonny (Braniff, 10/03/77); Maggie Stryker Rose (Piedmont, 10/16/77); Julie Clark (Hughes Airwest, 11/07/77); Gail Gorski (United, 1/09/78); Jean

Haley Harper (United, 1/16/78); and Sandra Donnelly (Flying Tigers, 1/23/78).

We formed the International Society of Women Airline Pilots. Today, ISA + 21 is truly global and numbers over 570 members worldwide from 96 airlines and 36 countries. It unites diverse cultures in the single goal of advancing women in the profession of airline pilot through education and scholarship.

Those pioneering women became my close friends and sounding board. Belonging to ISA was effective group therapy. It helped to keep me sane in the early years at Tigers. Some of the women had few negative experiences with the men they worked with, but some had horrifying and demoralizing ones. I saw for the first time that I had not caused men to do bad things to me. They had acted poorly all by themselves.

The first woman with each airline had taken the heaviest hits. The second and third women entered a more accepting workspace. Some of them were wise enough to recognize that the firsts had made it easier for them. Tigers' third woman pilot, Sandy Donnelly, personally thanked me for being number one.

"I can only imagine what I would have done if some of those things had happened to me," she said. "Thanks for paving the way."

After Karen and Sandy were hired, the Tiger pilots called us C1, C2, and C3. Because "cunt" wasn't a word I'd ever used, it took me time to figure out why they were calling me C1. At a Tiger party, when I was handed a self-adhesive nametag to fill out, I wrote C.U.N.T. 1. Under that I wrote, Carnally Unavailable New Tigress 1. The guys laughed, and I did too.

It became irritating for me, later, when women who were numbers seven and eight at their airlines questioned what the firsts were whining about. None of that nasty stuff ever happened to them; ergo, the firsts must have done something to cause their own problems.

When a leading aviation magazine printed its first article about sexual harassment in the cockpit and its nuances, it asked a female captain to write it. She interviewed me but used none of my stories. She said that my stories were too extreme to use, that they were not indicative of how things really were. She was wrong.

Networking with the other women, we shared coping strategies that worked. I developed the attitude that problems on the flight deck resulted from personality conflicts rather than sexual bias because I could change my personality but not my gender. I grew away from feeling helpless to control a situation.

Sometimes, I pretended I was being paid $105 per hour to baby-sit a talented but spoiled brat. At that price I could put up with almost anything for a few hours.

As the chips fell off my shoulders, I was able to relax and enjoy flying again.

14

PROGRESS
1979

Not all of the Tiger pilots were dundering turkeyheads when it came to women in the cockpit. In fact, a large percentage were neutral or accepting. Later, I would bash myself for feeling put upon and discriminated against much of the time, when actually my good experiences outnumbered the bad.

In that early career atmosphere of walking on eggshells, the generosity and compassion of some men shone brightly through the murk of struggle. Jim Vinson was one who had those qualities.

My crew and I had landed in Philadelphia and were waiting on the ramp for hotel transportation. We watched the Tiger plane following us scud through broken clouds on its approach. Unexpectedly, on final descent, its engines roared with the application of power, its nose lifted, and it climbed back into a solid layer of clouds. We went to the hotel without them.

As I went to meet my crew in the coffee shop, I saw a woman pilot in the hallway. "Oh Norah, I'm so mortified. I didn't get stabilized on the approach, and we had to go around. How am I going to face the guys?" She detailed what had happened. She had not broken any laws or done anything unsafe; she just had not gotten it exactly right. In jets it helps to have it exactly right. So she had done the prudent thing and had taken the plane around and done it better the next time. She was new in the DC-8 copilot's seat, and a go around for a new copilot was not unusual. But she and I held ourselves to strict standards that were sometimes not achievable. So there she was, red with embarrassment.

"Oh, I'm so sorry," I commiserated. I knew how devastating misperforming under scrutiny felt. "I'll go into the restaurant and see how bad it is this time. Wait out here." I had had captains give my flying scathing reviews when they had not even let me fly. I surmised how harsh their critique would be when they actually had a mistake to talk about.

Her captain, Jim Vinson, was being queried about the go around as I got to the table.

"You know how it gets," he said. "We were doing great, then just as we went visual, we hit a low layer of clouds." He shrugged. "What can you do?"

That was the end of that discussion. The way Jim told the story, it sounded as if he had been flying and it was just one of those things. He could have sacrificed his copilot's reputation in order to have one of those they-don't-pay-me-enough-to-keep-saving-the-plane-from-women-drivers bull sessions that other pilots enjoyed. He didn't do that.

What a guy!

Captain Dwight Metcalf earned a place on my good-guy list later that month. He had the sleepy eyes and drawling cowboy voice of Bob Bax and a similar cockpit cool. When I mishandled a crosswind landing on my first leg, he made no comment. As he was flying to our next stop, we learned our destination had a wind across the runway that was close to the maximum allowable crosswind for the plane. *I'm sure glad this is his landing.*

"Well, doll," he said, "I'm not prone to giving flight lessons but I'm a firm believer in getting right back on the horse after you've been thrown. You're making this landing. Let me give you a few pointers." *Ah, shit.*

My landing was on centerline and headed in the right direction. Dwight laughed. "Nice riding, cowgirl. When the guys ask me how you fly, I'm going to enjoy telling them about the second landing."

I thanked Dwight by picking up our dinner tab that night. He taped a red rose to my control wheel the next day. *Kindness and flowers; too bad he's married.*

15

CRYING IN THE COCKPIT

1979

*T*axiing the plane out at Chicago O'Hare, clogged with holiday traffic, I was glad for the clear sky and for knowing it was my last flight for the week. Seattle was our destination and home for me.

As we waited our turn for takeoff, third in a long line of jets, an American Airlines DC-10 started its takeoff roll. We weren't paying much attention as the catastrophe unfolded, but it was impossible to miss the aircraft's shedding metal on the runway and getting airborne slightly cocked with its nose in a lower trajectory than normal. In seconds the huge DC-10 was out of sight. We didn't know what we were seeing, only that it wasn't right. When a billowing cloud of black smoke rose on the horizon, I told myself that it wasn't them, that the smoke was in an industrial area and had nothing to do with a plane going down. That idea was too enormous to take in. I knew all the planes were departing full that day because of the upcoming Labor Day weekend; that meant there had to be more than two-hundred people on board.

"Maybe, maybe they had to touch down in that empty field out there. You know, the one right off the end of the runway? Maybe their wingtip grazed one of those storage tanks out there. Maybe they have a wing on fire, but they're all getting down the slides on the other side?" I tossed these theories at my crew. They looked at me with shock and incredulity. There was no answering hope on their faces.

"They can't all be dead!" I cried. The men just stared at me.

Chicago tower started calling the aircraft waiting for takeoff. We had to be directed to other runways because the metal strewn on our runway precluded its further use. The Air Traffic Control system geared up quickly for a massive changing of departure clearances and rerouting of aircraft. The skill and professionalism of ATC was impressive yet jarring to my senses. Life was *already* going on without the hundreds of people who had died a minute ago. I could not take it in.

I didn't want to take it in.

I repeated our new taxi instructions to the ground controller and wondered if I would be able to get my concentration back in time for our takeoff.

"Norah, are you okay?" my captain asked.

"Well, yeah, I guess so." I didn't think I would be okay to fly the plane myself, but it was his turn to fly and I thought I could probably manage jerking gear and talking on the radio.

"Norah, are you okay enough to fly?" my captain asked again.

"Yeah, I can do my job," I guessed.

"Norah, do you want to go back to the hangar for awhile?" he persisted.

"No, I'm okay," I said with slightly less trepidation. We taxied on toward our new runway and the captain asked how I was about every quarter mile. I finally got the subliminal message.

"Captain, I am *not* okay. I need some time to settle down. I hate to delay our airplane, but you've been right. I'm not okay. I am sorry. I'm so sorry."

We taxied back to the Tiger ramp and parked. The engineer left his seat and threw up in the bathroom. I turned to the captain and saw tears beginning to leak from his eyes. Those tears gave leave to my own. I leaned across the control pedestal and reached out to him. We held each other for a long time in an awkward stretch across the jutting controls. And we cried.

We finally took off an hour later and, as we rose through 500 feet, we passed the crash site. I didn't want to look, but I did. Emergency vehicles ringed the black smoking crater. There was not a single thing in that hole that resembled an airplane or a human—just tiny pieces.

That evening I found a note on the front door of my Bainbridge Island home. There was a neighborhood weenie roast on the beach below our street. I needed to be with people, so I went. It was weird. All these little kids yelling and skipping rocks and sliming marshmallows on their faces. All these well-coupled adults talking and laughing softly while they monitored their children's safety on the rocky beach with the downtown lights of Seattle beginning to show across the darkening Puget Sound. It was as if the horror in Chicago had never happened. They didn't even know about it yet. For them it did not exist.

I stayed on the beach that night for hours after my neighbors went home to bed. I saw car lights on the freeways across the water. Boats motored by. Tiny crabs scuttled by my feet. Life just kept going on.

16

HOW NOT TO BE HUMAN

1979–80

*T*he summer of the Chicago crash was the summer that my second marriage died. We had lived together for only a few months when I came home from a trip and he wasn't there. After a day of phoning friends and family and not finding John, I phoned the police. I thought that John might have had an accident on his motorcycle while not carrying his wallet. After a third phone call to the police, an officer gently said, "Ma'am, has it occurred to you that your husband might have left you?"

No, it hadn't.

Yes, he had.

Evidently, he was frustrated with my being away from home for two weeks a month, earning a living for both of us. He felt sexually deprived and did something about it.

John's leaving was devastating for me. It fed all my deepest insecurities about being unlovable. I beat myself with regrets for things I might have done differently. My traditional coping strategy of walking tall and acting as if nothing was wrong until nothing *was* wrong failed to bring relief. When the pain got too bad on my empty days off, I drank myself to sleep. I recognized the pit I was falling into and quit drinking for the second time.

My family and friends were concerned about my state of mind. Karen Kahn, a Continental pilot and one of the founders of ISA, phoned often and often caught me weeping. Finally she said, "I'm getting you out of that house. Is there anywhere in the world you haven't been that you would like to see?" "Tahiti," I sobbed, "but I've always dreamed of going there with a lover." I was wallowing in self-pity and getting tired of the mire. Karen provided a welcome kick in the butt.

Okay, I have made a bad mistake, or two. Deal with it. Get going.

Karen made all the arrangements. We spent a carefree week, biking and swimming and snorkeling. Karen's intelligence, practicality, compassion, and commiseration were the balms I needed to begin healing the wounds.

I waited almost two years for a divorce court date. I was ashamed at being a two-time loser at marriage. Of course my work was affected.

Chief Pilot Dick Wilson called me into his office to tell me that when he was going through his divorce, he had volunteered to fly as much as was legally allowed. The only place he felt okay about himself was at work in the cockpit. He said he later realized that he had not done the best job he could have and he regretted that. He suggested that I do what he had not done—take time off and spend it getting my life in order.

I thought I had gone through the worst of it and did not take his offer of a personal leave. I should have.

The cloud of my divorce did have a silver lining, however—paying alimony. Having to pay alimony and complaining about it made me one of the boys more than any single thing ever had. One captain who had not let me fly before the divorce finally offered me a leg in the plane.

"Guess you've finally earned it," he said. "Was the fucking you got worth the fucking you got?"

I actually never paid alimony. I just chose not to correct the useful rumors about it. In a community-property state, I had to buy my husband out of his interest in the things we had purchased with my money during our marriage. I thought it was unfair to be penalized for being the more successful of two childless adults. Other pilots felt that way as well.

Another side benefit of the nasty divorce process was that I sought counseling for the first time. Dr. Catherine Feelgood asked me in my first session what I hoped to get out of counseling.

"It's too late for my marriage, but I would like to learn to react less to problems at work. I feel silly for being here. Intellectually, I have a handle on what's happening at work. Men are afraid that I'm not smart enough or coordinated enough to drive heavy machinery. They suspect that I am too emotional and hormonal to keep a clear head in emergencies. They are also afraid that if I do a good job, their images will be tarnished."

"Their images?" Catherine queried.

"Yeah. They present themselves as supermen who can single-handedly carry jumbo jets full of passengers across oceans on their backs. They are heroes. What if someone who looks like their daughter or their girlfriend can do exactly what they do? My very existence hurts their images."

"You think that you threaten them?"

"Yes, and I don't want to."

"What could you do to set them at ease, to reassure them?" Catherine asked.

"Grow a penis?" I laughed. "At least then I wouldn't threaten their free-for-all boys'club atmosphere. Look, I know that for some men I work with all I have to do is show up, do a good job and go home alone, and eventually I'll earn their respect. A big problem for me right now is that I can't keep myself from reacting to the assholes. Then I get uptight and can't perform well; and then I've really given them something to talk about. It makes me so mad."

"What do you want me to help you to learn here?" Catherine asked.

"I want to learn how not to care if they aren't nice to me. I want to learn not to care if they talk about me. I want to learn not to get angry when they say I fly poorly, when they've never even flown with me. I want to learn not to be hurt when they say I fly poorly, even when I *have* flown poorly. I want to learn to disconnect from *any* emotional reaction to them.

"Ah, you want me to teach you how not to be human. Counselors aren't magicians, Norah. I can help you to practice doing healthy things with your anger and hurt, but I can't keep you from feeling them."

"But I feel like such a victim sometimes, and I hate that. I don't want to be a whiny victim."

"Have you considered that perhaps you are in the wrong career?"

Oh, brother, and I'm paying for this? "I'm not in the wrong career. I will not be driven out. I just want to change enough to handle it better. I don't want the price of my success to be so high that I can't be mentally healthy. I'm tired of being unhappy because of what other people do."

At the time, I considered counseling unproductive, but the experience made it easier to ask for help later. Again, I made the decision to fly, whatever it took. The first step was to stop feeling sorry for myself.

17

UNSUITABLE
FOR SWIMMING

1980

*I*n 1980 I blundered into the worst social/cultural error I have ever made. Usually, when I was assigned to fly to a country I had never been to before, I visited my local library and did basic research about local customs, money, food, and historical sights. I memorized "hello, please, thank you, and I am lost" in the appropriate language. However, when I was called to fly to Riyadh, the capital of Saudi Arabia, I got only three hours notice and didn't do my homework.

Our hotel was a welcome five-star relief after a long flight and a limo ride through the 105°F. desert. We often joked about how the most dangerous segment of flying was getting from the airport to the hotel. This ride was no exception. Our driver appeared to think that the dotted yellow line in the center of the road was for straddling, not for demarcating lanes. We looked out our side windows, rather than the terrorizing view of what was happening in front of the car.

When we arrived at the hotel, the air conditioning in my elegant, marble-lined room was malfunctioning. While I was waiting for house maintenance, I saw a swimming pool from my window. *Perfect*, I thought, and slipped into a modest, one-piece, black swimsuit and body-covering, floor-length caftan.

I was the only guest on the pool terrace. Passing a woman's changing room, I selected a lounge to drop my towel and robe on, then dove in. I loved having a pool to myself for laps.

Within minutes, the hotel manager and two of the security staff were beside the pool, calling to me. The manager said I must leave the pool immediately. I was confused and thought there must be some type of joke that I was not getting.

"Why?" I asked.

"Adult women are not allowed to swim in pools in Saudi Arabia!" he responded, his agitation visibly growing.

"But there are women's changing rooms here. What are they for?"

"European women are allowed to sunbathe, but not to go in the water," he explained.

"Who would want to sunbathe in this heat and not go in the water?" I asked, still treading water.

The manager's patience was over. He signaled to the bouncers to go in and get me.

That got my attention; I quickly swam to the side and climbed out under my own power. The situation was graver than I could have guessed. Had I been reported in the pool, the manager could have lost his job and the hotel could have been blackballed.

The three men escorted me to my room. On the way I asked more about local rules, looking for some logic I could follow to stay out of trouble. I knew flight attendants who had dated Saudi princes in Europe. They said that Saudi men shed their inhibitions when they changed their robes for western attire.

I asked the manager, "So it's okay for a Saudi Arabian man to sleep with me but not to swim with me?"

The manager replied, "Perhaps, Miss O'Neill, you should just stay in your room for the rest of your visit." I took his advice. I heard later that they drained the pool.

I fell in love twice in 1980: first, with flying the 747 and becoming the first woman in the world to fly passengers on it; second, with a man. I couldn't stop the falling. I could have stopped the acting on it.

In hindsight I realize that all my life, whenever I judged others' behavior harshly, a cosmic energy created circumstances in which I would repeat their mistakes. If I said, "How could they *do* that?" I created an opportunity to find out how. I got the chance to switch from "What an idiotic, immoral, selfish asshole he/she is!" to "Norah, what an idiotic, immoral, selfish asshole you are!"

That cosmic energy, which I choose to call God, gave me increasingly more difficult lessons to learn when I opted not to learn from others but to just condemn them.

For instance, my first experience with divorce came at age eleven when the couple next door to my parents got divorced. They had four boys, all under age five, three still in diapers. At 35 cents an hour, I was the baby-sitter of choice. Ironically, my parents would still not leave me and my siblings home alone, so John, twelve, and Peggy, six, and I always had baby-sitters when they went out.

All that summer of my eleventh year, I cooked, cleaned, did laundry, and mothered those four boys, though I did none of those things at my own home. The boys' mother, Margaret, was left with the house and children and little money. She was beautiful, smart, talented, and young and she started dating immediately. In the summer of 1960, divorce was still not socially acceptable; a young mother working outside the home was even less so. Margaret's flurry of dating launched vicious rumors in the neighborhood, most specifically that she was hooking for a living. I had only vague ideas about what prostitutes did, anyway, and I didn't judge Margaret, though I did take a troubled view of her making jokes about divorce. I was still a practicing Roman Catholic, and divorcing was just not done. It was a "sin" whose tragic results were visited on the children. Later, when I divorced a first time at an age younger than Margaret had been, I found myself joking about it and was appalled with myself. Margaret had taught me the lesson of laughing at sorrow when you had run out of tears and needed to pull yourself up and go on with life.

I learned, too, that laughter was a way of detaching from my grief when the pain was overwhelming. The downside of that detachment was not feeling what I needed to feel to get through the mourning process.

The worst lesson I learned the hard way was about adultery. I had strong feelings against infidelity in marriage. Clearly, no one wins from that situation, and innocent people get hurt. In my early airline career, I silently condemned fellow pilots who couldn't keep their pants zipped on layovers, often with disastrous results for their families. Closer to home was my experience of having a woman pilot make amatory moves on my second husband during a convention of women airline pilots. I was not silent about judging her, and voila! God allowed me a far-reaching and painful lesson there.

After my second marriage ended in 1979, I spent a year licking my wounds. During that time, I had a brief affair with a friend's husband. I wouldn't have done it if I had been spiritually and mentally fit. I lost the trust and respect and friendship of a woman I loved very much. I lost the love and friendship of her husband. I lost the respect of the people who found out what I had done. (The wife told them; I was certainly too ashamed of my behavior to have told anyone.) I lost my own self-respect, to the extent that it took me almost a decade to forgive myself. During that decade I entered a relationship with an abusive man. Deep down, I thought I did not deserve better, because I had been a liar, a cheat, and a thief.

My daughter asked me, when she was fifteen, what was the worst thing I had ever done; what would I change if I could do it over? I told her that I had had an affair with a married man and that I had stayed too long with an abuser. Both seemed equally horrible and damaging. I believe that if I had not done the first, I would not have done the second.

In the autumn of 1980, Ron "Santa Claus" Hall and I flew a short trip that included a New York to Chicago leg. Tigers had recently bought Seaboard World Airlines, and we were carrying a few Seaboard pilots with us to Chicago. Two mentioned that they had never flown with a woman before, and they spent most of the trip standing in the cockpit and observing.

That day, Chicago airspace was, as usual, crowded, chaotic, and full of adverse weather. Ron and I were familiar with each other's mode of operation. He was a conscientious, by-the-book pilot, but his flying style left room for his wickedly intelligent brand of humor. As I briefed him about what I expected him to do for me on the approach and landing, I added one nonstandard request to the end of my textbook spiel.

"Ron," I said, "as soon as the mains touch down, I would like you to reach up and put all four engines in reverse for me. Those thrust reversers are just *so* hard on my fingernails." I accompanied this request with a wide smile and an airy wave of five, inch-long red-painted acrylic nails. Ron just nodded.

Chicago ATC gave us instructions for a slam-dunk approach, and I turned us to the marker calling for gear down. Often ATC would ask us to turn, descend, slow up, and get aligned in a way that would be easily doable in a jet fighter but almost impossible in a 747.

"Chicken," Ron said turning to me, "do you see what they're doing here? Can you get down and slowed before the marker?"

"Watch me."

After we landed, Ron laughed and shook his head. "Hey Chicken, you didn't let them get to you. Good show." He had, of course, never touched the thrust reversers. Our deadheads thanked us for the ride and left.

Several days later, I received a call from a woman airline pilot whose brother had been on that Chicago flight. He had called and told her that her friend Norah did not deserve to be an airline pilot.

141

"Any woman who would put the condition of her fingernails before her concern for stopping an airplane on the runway does not belong in aviation."

My friend told her brother that she was sure I had been joking. Nevertheless, she called to get my side of the story. I was disgusted. Now, not only did I have to prove that I was okay to my crew but also I was burdened with putting on a show for deadheads.

To hell with them if they don't have a sense of humor.

18

WOMEN DRIVERS
1980–81

I decided that I needed a hiatus from romance in my life while I sorted through my latest errors in relating. I devoted myself to flying, a proven distraction. Flying the 747 around the world was seldom boring.

Flying into Charles DeGaulle Airport just outside of Paris was always an adventure, partly because the airspace was so densely crowded and standard arrival routes so complexly convoluted, and partly because the French air traffic controllers, contrary to international aviation rules, did not speak in English to all aircraft. When they did speak English, it was so heavily accented that it was difficult to understand. I found that being a "girl" pilot in Paris could work to my advantage if I were willing to be humble.

In 1980 I flew to Paris with Captain Ron Burson and Engineer Ken "Salty" Halls. Many airport taxiways were under construction. Though we had studied taxi maps the night before, upon landing we were not clear about where the ground controller wanted us to go or how he wanted us to get there. When Ron asked for clarification, the controller said some words in rapid French that seemed like curse words and then said some words in English that were equally incomprehensible. Having years of experience with controllers treating me condescendingly and speaking to me as if I were an idiot, I instinctively knew that I could be of unique use in this situation.

I keyed my mike and said, "Oh, please monsieur ground controller, I need your help. I've never been to Paris before and I'm afraid I'll get lost. I don't want to cause a traffic jam. Please give me my directions more slowly."

Ron shot me a disbelieving look and said, "I don't believe you did that. Aren't you embarrassed?"

"Yeah, I would be if there was anyone around to identify me by name. Bet it works though." I arched my eyebrows and said, "You men are just lousy at asking for directions."

It did work. The next communication from the ground controller was this, "Ah, mon cheri, put on your brakes slowly now because you have a sharp left turn coming up and you don't want to scruff those big tires, do you?"

Our maps were not required again. That ground controller's instructions were as precise in speed and direction as if he were giving a D.F. steer to a student pilot lost in the clouds.

Ron and Salty wanted to explore Paris during our layover. My body wanted to go to bed and stay there, but they were determined and persuasive men. I bathed and tumbled into bed on that Paris afternoon, awakening to a persistent drumming on my door. I thought it was the maid and that she would just go away if I ignored her. The pounding didn't stop. I blearily stumbled to the door. There were the guys, arms laden with bottles and a picnic basket; they walked by me and settled on the sides of my just-vacated bed.

"You wouldn't go to the park with us, so we brought the picnic to you," Salty said, while he set out bread and cheese and pate and wine glasses. Neither Ron nor Salty paid much attention to the short, lacy orange nightie I was wearing or the hair I had tied in a sleep knot on my head.

Resigned, I crept back under the covers and reached for a flute of champagne. By my second glass, I was awake and joining the party. We did explore Paris that night.

Captain Ron Burson and I flew together again later that month, with Dave Hostvedt as our engineer on a flight into Seoul, Korea. I was flying the approach to Seoul with "no excuses" weather. The visibility was clear and the air calm. If something were to go awry with the landing, it was going to be because I screwed it up. Something did go wrong.

As I started the flare at 30 feet above the ground, the airplane sank abruptly and impacted the ground with a shuddering thud. The oxygen masks in the passenger compartment were knocked from their ceiling mounts and hung dangling over the seats. "Getting the oxygen masks" was pilot lingo for a *really* bad landing. I had not had that experience before and I was mortified. Even more alarming was that I did not know why the bottom had fallen out of my flare. I turned to Ron, an experienced instructor and line check airman, and asked him what he thought had gone wrong. We could not come up with a reasonable explanation other than low-level windshear, which seemed unlikely, given the lack of wind or weather.

My mortification deepened as we parked at the Tiger ramp and the first mechanic up the boarding stairs said, "Who the hell made that godawful landing?!" He and Ron discussed whether a hard landing inspection would be required. (It wasn't.)

I thought the humiliating experience was behind me after a three-day layover in Seoul, but no, I got the chance to further enhance my humility as we met in the Hyatt lobby in preparation for our departure.

I had been swimming laps in the Olympic-sized pool and my hair was still wet as I put on my uniform. I pulled it into horsetails over each ear, and then plaited each section into six braids. I wound the braids into coils over each ear and pinned them in place. This hairdo not only kept my hair off my collar and out of the way of shoulder harnesses and radio headsets but also kept my hair from dripping down my uniform shirt. I thought it a practical solution to several problems but had no idea of its visual impact.

145

As I entered the Hyatt lobby from the elevator, I saw Ron and Dave conversing with six Northwest pilots. They turned toward my smiling arrival, and the Northwest men stared in apparent astonishment.

Holy cow, I thought in self-consciousness, *is my fly open or something?*

Ron made introductions, emphasizing the words, my first officer. I looked to Ron in puzzlement. *What was going on here?*

One of the Northwest captains asked me, while holding eye contact with a no-nonsense, do not lie to me, penetrating gaze, "Did you land that Tiger 747 three days ago?"

Oh no, I thought. *These guys saw the landing. And Ron, that asshole, told them I did it.*

I wished that I didn't like or respect Ron or that I could be sure of never flying with him again, so I could tell these men that Ron had done it. I was painfully aware that I was the only woman in the world flying the 747 at that time, and many men had yet to meet a woman pilot. My landing would make a terrible first impression. I shuddered at the thought of the responsibility and wished, not for the first or last time, that I were a fabulously gifted pilot whose performance was above criticism.

Then I put my shoulders back, smiled broadly, breathed deeply, and choked out, "I regret to tell you that I did make that terrible landing. All I can say in my defense is that we all walked away alive, and the plane was reusable."

Ron and Dave laughed when they told me what had transpired just before I got off the elevator. The pilots, all in identifiable uniforms, had gravitated toward each other and flying conversation as they waited in the lobby for airport transportation. The NWA guys had commented on that days-old landing, thinking that the crash-landing crew had probably already gone. When Ron admitted it had been his plane, they had made jokes about his sleeping at the wheel. He said it had been his first officer's landing, but what had gone wrong was a mini-mystery. Amidst their guffaws, he tried to explain that Norah was really a good pilot and the landing had been unusual for her. At that point, the NWA pilots were convinced that Ron was fabricating an excuse for himself, because they were positive there was no woman pilot in the world senior enough to fly a 747 on international routes. Enter Norah.

"Your stunning entry, six feet tall, gorgeous, and crowned with the Norse goddess hairdo, put those guys into a state of shock!" Ron chortled. "Good job!"

A few months later, I met a woman who didn't need six feet and Norse goddess hair to dominate a room. During a winter ski trip, I accepted a date to a ritzy cocktail party at a millionaire's mansion.

"I've heard about you," my hostess said. "There's another woman here tonight who is making her mark in a man's profession. Let me introduce you." She led me to a conservatively dressed woman with a practical, short graying hairdo. Over a firm handshake, I noted intelligence and humor in her direct gaze and an openness that I was immediately drawn to. She was a judge from Arizona, calmly assured, and certainly not a player of societal one-upmanship in matters of men, money, or fashion. We talked about our jobs and hopes for the future. I confided that I eventually wanted to have children, and she gave me advice, based on how she had meshed her career and parenting. My date and her husband repeatedly tried to drag us away from each other as we talked animatedly in the corner of the room. They succeeded in getting us to leave for dinner only because the party ended.

I saw her on the ski slopes the next day and talked with her again. When I asked to ski with her, my skiing partner was irritated. "Why do you want to ski with her? She'll just slow us down."

"For the conversation on the lift rides," I replied. "To hell with her skiing."

Six months later, I read about her in Time magazine; she had just accepted a new job. Though we had not exchanged addresses and phone numbers, I was sufficiently moved by her promotion to write a note to the place of her new employment. I told her how pleased I was for her and how much more interesting her new job sounded than the one she had talked of pursuing. I didn't know if she would even remember me and certainly didn't expect a reply in that tumultuous time of her relocation.

I was surprised to receive a note from her a month later. Handwritten on her official stationery, it said: "Dear Norah, I enjoyed your letter. Of course, I remember our meeting in Sun Valley. You work on getting more women piloting 747s and I will hope to see more women on the Supreme Court! With best regards, Sandra O'Connor."

What an impressive woman.

19

SEVERE TURBULENCE
1981

On a cold spring night, Captain Tom Frederickson perused the weather data for our flight from New York to Chicago and Anchorage. After noting that the current weather and forecasts for both cities were lousy, he said, "O'Neill, how good a pilot are you? I've heard some bad stories about you, but surely they can't all be true. I'm a weak pilot. I need a good copilot. Do you have much time in the 747?"

Oh, spare me. And I have to spend a week with this guy? "I'm relatively new on the plane, sir, but I'm certainly a competent pilot."

"Good," he replied. "You're going to fly both legs tonight. The weather is beneath my standards. I fly only when it's VFR."

What? I puzzled this over. Was he truly a low-speed pilot who always delegated the tougher flying to his copilot? Or was this a test to see if I were arrogant enough to think I could do better than my captain? Or was he trying to bolster my self-confidence by letting me know that he was relying on my doing a good job? Was I really going to fly both legs?

Chicago weather was as bad as forecast; I flew the leg. After landing, Tom remarked, "Good job. We'll do okay."

We continued onward to Anchorage, where the visibility was acceptable but severe turbulence was forecast. Not too much about weather alarmed me any more except for windshear and turbulence. It was difficult to avoid something you couldn't see.

Professional pilots were expected to avoid any areas that displayed the earmarks of severe weather, yet they were expected to get the plane there on schedule. Even though no sane pilot would knowingly enter severe turbulence, we were supposed to launch the plane on time and hope that the skies would get better during the six hours it was going to take for us to reach our destination.

As we descended into Anchorage, the turbulence came as forecast and worsened as we lost altitude. It was the worst I had ever experienced. I struggled to keep the plane upright. Straight and level was impossible. Striving for it was taking full control inputs in every direction. I was not happy with the choreography of this ballet and asked Tom if we should start considering our alternate airport. He pointed out that other planes were still taking off and landing successfully.

It's hard to explain to a company why you spent thousands of extra dollars in time and fuel going to an unscheduled airport, when other pilots were doing what you were too chicken to do. Shoulders back. Breathe deep. Motor on. (I certainly had no time then to discuss the Tiger aircraft captained by Jack Bliss that had barely survived a windshear encounter at JFK in 1975. Jack had warned the tower of a dangerous windshear on approach and had strongly suggested that the runway be closed. It was not closed. Minutes later, another airline's jet, perhaps reassured by the planes before them making it in, shot the same approach and crashed. One-hundred-and-twelve people died.)

On our downwind leg, we saw a Tiger 747 take off below us. When that plane was stabilized in climb, its captain radioed all aircraft in the vicinity. "Warning. Tigers encountered 20 knots of windshear immediately after takeoff. We almost lost the plane. Watch your asses."

Tom, recognizing the voice of JD Johnson, radioed, "Hey, JD, give us the details. We're next to land."

"It's a bitch down low. Who have you got flying tonight, Tom?"

"Norah's at the wheel."

"Oh, Christ, you can't let her fly it!"

"Why not? She flies better than I do."

"Because she's a woman! Everyone knows that women have lousy depth perception. There's no room for any handicaps tonight."

"Lousy depth perception?"

"Yeah. All of her life she's been told that 6 inches is actually 9 inches. Can't expect her to be able to read scale on maps or judge height with accuracy."

That's one of the things I loved about Tiger pilots. When the going got rough, they started joking. It relieved the tension. I hooted at JD's new take on an old joke and the precision of his timing.

We bounced down final like an autumn leaf falling. Wing up. Wing down. Nose over. Nose up. To hell with airspeed; I could no longer ascertain which numbers the swinging needle was bracketing and couldn't believe that Tom was letting the copilot do this. He was either very stupid or very crafty. Either way, he had balls of steel. We made the runway unscathed, however.

On the way to the hotel, I hung limply in my seat while Tom talked layover plans. I was meeting a girlfriend and wasn't going to be with the rest of the crew.

"What are you and Lisa going to do?"

"Drink champagne and troll for hard bodies."

"Hard bodies?" Tom mulled over the words. He had never heard them before. "What do you mean, hard bodies?"

"You know, young studs with big arms and washboard stomachs," I explained. "Bodies with no flab. Young. Energetic."

He thought about that. "I guess I'm not one. What would you girls call me, soft body?"

"I think I'll stick with Captain Tom."

Lisa and I talked that night about the frightening turbulence and the macho-right-stuff coping mechanism of joking when death was imminent. Part of me was appalled that I would laugh at a penis-length quip during what might be my last moment on earth, but part of me accepted that that is how we pilots did it. To fully experience our feelings at those moments would probably have incapacitated us.

What was not apparent to me at the time was how coping by joking was spilling over into my personal life. Deflecting my feelings by adopting an irreverent attitude kept me from processing the things I needed to process and from making changes in my life that an increasing pain level would have forced me to consider.

Tom and I continued around the world, and the weather remained marginal, so I did all the flying. It was a confidence-boosting time. With the daily practice in the 747, I finally became comfortable with the plane. I almost resented Tom finally flying an approach to Taipei because, he said, "It's sunny. Even I should be able to find the airport."

The weather had regressed to crummy by the time we left Taipei, so I got *my* airplane back. That takeoff, or *attempt to takeoff*, from Taipei was the most hair-raising takeoff of my career. It should have been easy; the wind was 30 knots down the damp runway, and our plane was empty of freight. The broken ceiling of clouds started at 3,000 feet off the ground, so visibility was no problem. I knew that our rudder steering did not become effective until around 80 knots of forward movement, when there was enough air passing our barnside of a tail to ensure left and right directional control. Prior to 80 knots, nose-gear steering with a tiller was used. Usually, lining up with the centerline when entering the runway assured that the slow part of the takeoff roll was on track without having to use the tiller. If the tiller was used at too high a speed, the tires got scuffed, and losing a tire on takeoff was something we wanted to avoid.

"Tigers, cleared into position to hold."

"Roger, position and hold on Runway 5 for Tigers."

"Checklist below the line," I commanded.

"Tigers, cleared for takeoff."

"Cleared for takeoff, Tigers is on the roll," Tom said

I slowly pushed all four throttles forward, with a pause to make sure they were spooling up symmetrically. Tom's hand was behind mine on the backs of the throttles, standard procedure to ensure that he was in position to reject the takeoff if that became required. Reject was a captain's call. The engineer set takeoff power with the power lever extensions on the backs of the throttles. We started our roll looking good, and then everything went to hell.

The nose of the plane started bearing to the right. I corrected with left tiller, and nothing happened. I added left rudder, and nothing happened to stop the turn to the right. I put in full left tiller and full left rudder and started adding more power to the right engines so they would help us turn left. That did not work, and our nose continued to accelerate to the right. *I can't keep it on the runway.* Tom said nothing. *Didn't he realize that I had full everything in and it wasn't working?* No time to ask.

"Reject!" I yelled, and pulled the power back to idle while standing on the brakes. Lots of hands doing lots of things then, and my legs were throbbing with the pressure I was exerting through my toes. We shuddered to a stop with the nose of the plane pointing almost 90 degrees sideways to the runway heading and our nose gear between the runway edge lights. I looked out the window in panting disbelief. We'd missed the tire-blowing lights, and the plane body was still on the runway. *What had gone wrong? Had we lost an outboard engine? No, the engineer would have called that. What had happened to our steering? We didn't even have a crosswind.* The 747s are known to be squirrelly at slow speeds in crosswinds.

"Tiger's rejecting," Tom announced to the tower.

"You want to try that again? You've got the runway," Taipei tower informed us.

"Tell him hell no," I instructed Tom.

"Taipei Tower, we'd like to taxi on the runway to the next exit and hold on the taxiway while we sort things out."

"What happened?" I asked Tom. "I don't want to go anywhere until I know."

We had company mechanics drive out to inspect our tires and brakes. The tires were good and our brakes were cool and the plane was ready to go again, but I wasn't.

I had been stunned by the rapidity of our turn sideways. Literally seconds after the throttles had come up, we had been galloping off the runway.

(One day later Karl Krout, a check airman for Tigers, confirmed that the same thing had happened to him under the same circumstances. Wet runway; empty airplane with an aft center of gravity and gusting winds. The plane had not had enough weight over the nose tires to steer with and the rudder had not become effective yet. The rapid changing of the wind and its velocity against our huge tail had been too great to counteract with our available controls. The only option was to reject, and reject quickly.)

Tom accepted a clearance back onto the runway for another takeoff. He talked me into doing it. "Got to get back on that horse right after you're thrown or you may never have the guts to ride again," he advised.

I was steeled with tension for the next takeoff. It was uneventful.

"You sadist," I berated Tom, "you owe me a couple of beers just for making me do that again."

Instead of collecting a couple of beers, I took great satisfaction in whipping Tom at backgammon. We had had a game ongoing since the beginning of the trip, played at first for a quarter a point and later for flight deck duties like coffee brewing, meal heating, and plotting-chart graphing. I got serious about the bets on the homeward legs. When we landed again in Anchorage, Tom owed Lisa and me champagne and dinner at a restaurant of our choice. (And there were no cheap restaurants in Anchorage.)

While we were in Anchorage, I saw Hayward Evans again. He'd accepted an air traffic control job at Miami Center after the breakup of our relationship in Fairbanks. In 1980 he was seated next to a Tiger pilot in a Florida bar and had asked if the pilot knew me. "Sure, everyone knows Norah." Hay wrote his address and phone number on a cocktail napkin and asked the Tiger pilot to deliver it to me.

I contacted Hayward when I received the napkin. It was as if no time had passed. We still laughed and snarled. He was too much of a gentleman to bring up the ending of our affair. He had married, and we planned to meet in Anchorage when he brought his wife there on vacation.

I waited in front of my hotel and watched Hayward and Mara's taxi pull to the curb. Hay got out and ran to me with open arms. Big hugs, tight and lifting. What impressed me most at first was not how little he had changed on the surface, but how powerfully peaceful he was. Yes, he had matured out of some of his frenetic behavior, but that wasn't it. It was what he had with Mara. Her calm, practical simplicity allowed him to shine on his own while being solidly stable at home.

My meeting Mara was emotional. She had hung back watching us. Concerned that she might not appreciate the warmth of our greeting, I hesitated in moving forward to be introduced to her. She stepped over and enveloped me in a hug as loving as Hayward's.

"Oh, you're just as beautiful as Hayward said you are. I thought he might have been exaggerating because he loves you so." *Good Lord, what had Hay been saying to her? Is this woman for real?* She took my arm and led me back toward the cab that was waiting to drive us to dinner. "Anyone that Hay likes so much I'm sure I'm going to love."

20

FIRE UNDER A WING
1981

The aftermath of an engine fire and a few moments of terror led to a permanent change in the way I handled my job and the hostility of male pilots.

The evening started with the normal routine—a cab ride to the airport in the middle of the night with two sleepy strangers, a ream of boring paperwork, and the preflight inspection of an aircraft before launching over water to an airfield that we hoped would appear in the windscreen as the sun rose.

We didn't see the sun rise over London because as our landing gear rose from the pavement at the end of a storm-soaked JFK runway, we heard the loud clang of a fire-warning bell just as red lights lit up the forward instrument panel. Our lumbering liftoff continued as we entered a cloud layer at 75 feet above ground and our red warning lights reflected eerily back from white clouds outside.

"Ah fuck!"

"Positive rate. Gear up. Engineer's report".

"Fire on number one."

"Out of 1,000 feet. After-takeoff checklist. Fire checklist. Engine-shutdown checklist. Tell the tower that we have to come back."

"Tigers, we see you out of 2,000, contact departure on 128.7," said the tower.

"JFK tower, Tiger 200. We have an engine fire and need to come back."

"Tiger 200, are you declaring an emergency? What is your situation? Maintain 3,000; turn right to 080."

I coordinated the after-takeoff checklist with the engineer and backed him up as he pulled the number-one fire handle and shot the number-one fire bottle and started the engine-fire-and-damage checklist. The captain struggled to get the rudder trim correct with constant throttle changes and adjustments to heading and altitude. He began to paw one-handed through his Jepp manual for a return approach plate. He tried to connect the autopilot several times with no success.

"Tigers, are you still there? Say intentions. Are you declaring an emergency? Did you copy maintain 3,000, heading 080?" called the tower.

"Standby, tower. Tiger 200 maintaining 3,000 and turning to say again the heading?"

"Captain, your call," I said. "Are we declaring an emergency? Do you have a runway request?"

"Norah, you have the plane. Maintain 3,000. Get to the heading, okay? I've got to get the landing plate out. How are we doing on the shut-down checklist?"

Ah hell, I was thinking. The plane was totally out of trim and not on speed, altitude, or heading. My struggle to get those things corrected was interrupted by the captain calling for the in-range and approach checklists and the tower calling with, "Turn further right to 110, expect an approach to Runway 31, and are you declaring an emergency?"

I keyed my mike, "Standby. Tiger 200 turning to 110."

"Captain, we still have the light in the fire handle illuminated. Should I shoot the other bottle?"

"Tiger 200, are you declaring an emergency?" the tower asked again.

"Standby!"

"Yes ma'am. Call us when you want to. Just key your mike if you hear us. You don't have to respond."

I keyed my mike. Click, click went out over the air.

"Tiger 200. We think you want to declare an emergency."

Click, click, I responded.

"Roger the emergency. Maintain 3,000. Do you want the emergency equipment and the fire trucks standing by?" tower asked.

Click, click.

"Sir, they're turning us back over land. Do we want to ask for a holding pattern over water so we can dump fuel?" We had taken off at a maximum takeoff gross weight of 820,000 pounds, and our maximum landing weight was 630,000 pounds. In a "normal" emergency we would dump fuel before going back. We had the complication, however, of still showing an engine fire burning under our wing. Our left-wing fuel tanks contained 100,000 pounds of flammable liquid. How long did we want to sit on this potential funeral pyre waiting for the explosion? Not very long. We chose to land overweight.

"Tigers, turn further right to 270 and descend to 2,000. Cleared for the ILS to runway 31."

Click, click.

We continued motoring around the patch, handing control of the airplane back and forth while we all set up our approach plates, briefed the landing, and finished the checklists. Sometime during that incredible flurry of paper and hands and call outs, we meshed into a seamless team as if our lives depended on it because they did and the red glow of the fire warning light went out.

As we slid our heavy jet down the path of the glideslope, centered on the runway still hidden below smothering clouds, calmness settled over us. The rapid tempo of too much to do in too little time settled temporarily into just monitoring the results of our work. We were on speed, on glideslope, on localizer, and set up for landing and the safety beckoning from the ground. I had time to talk to the tower again, this time in the calm professional voice of a pilot under pressure but on top of things. We did not see the runway at 500 feet, at 400 feet, at 300 feet, at 200 feet. We never saw it at all. At minimums, we were forced to go around. Max power on three engines. Nose up. Gear up. Missed-approach procedure. Plane radically out of trim again. Captain manhandling the controls with muscles stiff from tension.

"Tigers, we observe you executing a missed approach. Maintain heading. Climb to 3,000. Anticipate ILS approach to Runway 4. The ceiling just descended. Right now, Runway 4 is the only one left above minimums and the weather is steadily deteriorating. What is your takeoff alternate? What are your intentions?"

Click, click. After-takeoff checklist. In-range and before-landing checklists. Briefing for Runway 4. My flying so the captain could take a break. Winging our way through the soup for a final try at finding JFK. If we didn't make it in this time, we were off to Philadelphia. I talked to the tower again after everything was set up, so they'd know to direct us to Philly if we missed again.

Sliding down final again. The tower told us the airport had just gone under minimums. We were already inside the marker and could legally continue but knew our chances of seeing the runway in time to land were growing slimmer. We were on the edge of our seats to better position ourselves to see a glimmer of the approach lights passing beneath us. Our altimeters wound down to decision time and 50 feet above "we're outa here." With a fraction of a second remaining until we had to leave, the engineer yelled, "Lights!"

We slammed onto the runway, no finesse left in the captain's fingers or his feet. He stood on the brakes as we roared past the first fire trucks, thrust reversers screaming at full. When we finally trembled to a lurching stop, we watched the fire trucks appear out of the streaming mist and pull under both wings. Men jumped down and hoses unwound. *My God*, I thought. *Had we still been on fire this whole time even though the warning light had finally gone out?* No, but now our brakes were glowing cherry red in the night and our tires were beginning to melt down onto the runway. Our overweight landing and the liberal application of brakes were more than our undercarriage was designed to take. Eventually, we had to be tugged back to the hangar.

Our parking on the runway closed JFK Airport down for an hour that night.

Back in the crew room we were shaken and gladly aware that we no longer had the duty time remaining to fly a plane to Europe, even if they could find an unbroken one for us and the weather would cooperate. We paced and planned what bar we were going to medicate our frazzled nerves in. I could hardly wait.

Meanwhile, Tiger crew controllers and Tiger mechanics were creatively addressing the problem of how to get this 185,000-pound payload to Europe on time. They would not release us to go back to the hotel until they had given up on finding a way to use us to move some plane somewhere. We cursed their skill and adaptability when they announced their plans for us. A Newark reserve crew was being limoed to JFK. The plane they were supposed to fly to Miami was offloaded onto the JFK ramp, and the freight of the sick-engine plane was being loaded onto the Miami plane. That new crew took off east with the night hours before our broken plane was fixed, and we eventually flew south to Miami. So much for seeing London that week. More disappointing was knowing that we would reach Miami after the bars had closed.

In the lobby of the Miami hotel, the captain asked me to his room for a drink. *Yay. He's carrying a flask!* I dumped my bags in my room and ran down the hall, still in uniform, to his room. We had already debriefed the emergency in New York. (The captain had thanked us profusely for doing such a good job. We had patted ourselves on the backs for our good work before we settled into breaking down the aborted flight minute by minute and critiquing where we might have done something differently to streamline the confusion. Pilots are generally their own best critics; we found fault with our own performances and discussed them.) I didn't expect to talk about the fire again so I didn't see a red flag when Captain Rat steered the conversation to a personal vein as we sipped our drinks. Red flags waved when he said that sex was much better than drinking for calming nerves.

I stood to leave, and Rat shoved me onto the bed and jumped on top of me. I said, "Get off of me. You're a married man and I can't do this." Inside of me, the panic button had been pushed.

Rat started slobbering on my neck and telling me how much I really wanted this. I started struggling, and my uniform shirt ripped. When he got more forceful, I became less diplomatic.

"I'm in love with another man. I can't be unfaithful."

Rat said, "Don't worry, we aren't going to have an affair. This will just be one night and you don't have to tell him about just one night."

"Rat, get off of me right *now* or I'm going to scream."

He rolled off. "Well Jeez, you could have just said no."

"I did say no! You weren't listening." I crawled off the bed and headed for the door, pulling my shirt together. Hand on the knob, I said, "I'm going to try to forget that this happened so we can fly together for the next few days as a crew that is still talking to each other."

"That reminds me," he rejoined, "I have to say that your performance during the emergency was substandard and I may have to write a letter to your chief pilot about giving you some extra training."

Those unjustified words freed me from five years of feeling hurt by sexism to being able to feel outraged.

"You just do that, Rat! You tell the chief pilot how incompetent I am. It won't be my first letter. It'll go into a file full of buddies—all equally worthless. And I promise you that I am going to write a letter too. It will document my version of the emergency *and* it will tell what happened in this room tonight. It will make clear what you have to do to get laid. And I'm not just making one copy of my letter. I'm making 1,500 copies. Because I am going to send one to the chief pilot and to each pilot on the line, and I am going to send one to each flight attendant on the line, and I am going to send one to your wife!"

Exit. Slam.

Rat was congenial on the flight deck the next day. He never sent his letter, and I never sent mine. But I saved it.

161

Years later, I would thank Rat for his mauling and his threats because after that night, I would never let the assholes get to me in the same way again. Getting angry and setting boundaries felt much better than getting hurt. I was beginning to learn that when someone does awful things around me, it says a lot more about the state of his humanity than it does about mine.

21

SUN VALLEY ROMANCE

1982

*T*wo years of commuting from an island in Washington state to a base in New York for the privilege of flying the 747 was beginning to erode my health. The weariness and disorientation of jet lag never completely went away. I awoke one morning in my own bed and didn't immediately know where I was, the ceiling of my bedroom being less familiar than that of the New York hotel. *Oh yeah, I'm home packing for my annual vacation. Thank you, God.*

I longed to put down roots. Despite my dispiriting marital failures, I still wanted a chance at what my parents had and I wanted children. While packing, I considered looking for a man again. I thought of the qualities he should have. *Bright, funny, hard-working in a field he likes, no ego problems, honest, responsible, faithful, not jealous. Looks don't really matter, but it would help if he had baby-sitting experience, could cook, and could keep a house clean.* I laughed aloud. *What I'm looking for is a wife. I've already become the husband I want to have.* I didn't think of the qualities of nurturing and having an even temper. I should have.

I always took my vacation on the ski slopes of Sun Valley, Idaho. In January 1982, I strapped on my skis and opened my season with a warm-up down the side of College Run. I picked up speed on Flying Squirrel and lingered on the cat track at the bottom of Limelight to watch the mountain's best skiers show off. I wove through the beginners on Lower Warm Springs to reach the chair for another ride up. Shooting through the singles line, I recognized the fellow in line ahead of me and hopped on the chairlift with him.

Rebel and I had both learned to ski in Sun Valley in 1970. I had ski bummed for a few winters and then learned to fly. Rebel had stayed. He was satisfied with the odd jobs the resort town offered and augmented his income with modeling and performing in adult movies. He had a wild reputation with women and was, reputedly, a world class stud. I had rarely seen him without a woman in tow. Since I had no desire to wait in line outside of some guy's bedroom door, Rebel and I had maintained a ski-buddies-only relationship.

We skied together that day, and he invited me to helicopter ski with him the next day. *Yes!* I had always wanted to have a helicopter fly me to distant, untouched powder, but my timing and the weather had always been slightly off. Not that year.

We met at the helicopter pad the next morning. I was nervous. He was protective and reassuring. The ski patroller loading the chopper raised an eyebrow when he saw me. "Sure you're up for this, Norah? How many days have you skied this year?"

"Only one," I replied.

He addressed Rebel, a regular heli-ski customer. "It's tricky up there today. Are you going to be responsible for her?" "Yeah, Carl. If she can't make it out on her own, I'll carry her out."

The baby-sitting thus assigned, we climbed on board. The pilot recognized me as a fellow flyer and invited me up front. The view from the bubble window was exhilarating once we started whump, whump, whumping our way through the winding canyons behind the resort. It reminded me of my first plane ride down the sides of Mount McKinley, with slopes that suddenly fell away into a 1,000-foot drop of descending cliff. The area was inaccessible to all but the hardiest trekkers and we moneyed interlopers with hired wings. My excitement mounted, adrenaline rushed. I was on the edge of fulfilling a fantasy and I knew it.

We flew low over side hills that had been dynamited for avalanche control that morning and saw the blue-shadowed tracks of the ski guides' testing runs. We finally settled onto a ridge top amidst a blinding cyclone of disturbed snow. Head bent to be safely below the still driving blades, I hopped down to run clear and fell forward onto my face in the hip-high snow. Not a great start, but I churned my way forward without help and watched the guides offload our equipment. Skiers pushed off over the edge and gave whoops of joy as they flew through the light snow, leaving their essing tracks as marks of their passage in the wilderness. I poled to the edge and stopped. The descent was much steeper than it had looked from the air. Was I really up for this?

"Go babe. I'm right behind you," Rebel urged. And he was. He sacrificed the skier's delight of first tracks by navigating through my chopped-snow wake. If I fell, he was going to be uphill in a position to ski down and dig me out.

I was stiff and clumsy with the first few turns, testing my balance against the weight of the snow and the gravity pull of the incline. By turn five, I had a rhythm. By turn six, I stopped trying to check my speed and swooped straight downhill. Halfway down the first 1,000 feet, I stopped hearing Rebel behind me. I was unaware of anything beyond my legs lifting and turning below me, my eyes focused on the crystal white ahead, and my hair billowing in my own slipstream. I was so totally into that reverie of sliding oneness with the mountain that the looming white and silver of the helicopter appearing in front of me was startling. I was at the bottom. I turned uphill and stood with my arms stretched skyward in triumph and yelled, "Yes!" to Rebel's fast approach. I looked beyond him to see our tracks, perfect descending ellipses of blue energy. He skied into my arms.

"Thank-you, thank-you," I said against his neck as I hugged him. He tilted his head back and laughed.

"I knew you'd love it. It's flying without the noise." We climbed back into the helicopter for another ascent—again and again. I wanted to go on forever. We went until I could no longer stand.

Rebel carried me to his car in the parking lot of the helicopter service. He drove to a house with a hot-springs-fed river rock pool carved against the mountainside. He lay me beside it and started gently removing my boots. I murmured a protest when he began to peel down my clothes.

"Shh. Shh. Trust me. I know what you need." I allowed him to minister to me and lift me into the steaming soothingness of the water. I melted into it, eyes closed. A change in the lapping of the water against my chin had me struggling to open my eyes. Rebel was beside me with a bottle of Dom Perignon. We toasted a perfect day.

Rebel had a ladylove he had to meet for dinner that night. I saw him again the next day when he dragged me to an after-ski party and introduced me to Scott. I was not impressed. Scott appeared to be my height, though it was difficult to tell because he slumped so badly. He was dressed unbecomingly in tattered, ill-fitting jeans and a threadbare, faded plaid flannel shirt. His voice was grating and loud. He seemed to have no social grace, and he clearly thought he was the greatest skier of his generation. Within the first few sentences of our try at a conversation, he had become so offensive that I blurted out, "You're the biggest asshole I've met in years." He laughed at that, and I turned away. I saw friends and made arrangements to meet them for dinner. As I was leaving, Scott cornered me and said, "What did I say that was so offensive to you? I'd like to know so I can use it again. Women never notice me when I'm being a nice guy." I was astounded. "You're sick," I said in parting.

I was stood up on dates three times in the next four days. I couldn't figure it out. Why did they ask me out if they weren't going to show up? I was skiing from the opening of the lifts until closing. Skiing had, after all, never let me down. I had resolved not to even consider another date, when I encountered Scott again while walking to my favorite after-ski watering hole. I didn't recognize him at first. The man walking near me was dressed in a fire-engine-red jumpsuit and was limping badly.

"Did you get hurt falling on the slopes today?" I commiserated.

"I didn't fall down," he replied. "I had a childhood disease that left one leg shorter than the other." *Oops, definitely off on the wrong foot here.*

"I'm sorry. I hope I haven't made you self conscious."

"Nah. It doesn't bother my skiing. That's all I care about." I looked at his face then. *Hell, that asshole, Scott.*

"I see you've finally recognized me. Met any other assholes lately?" I burst out laughing. "As a matter of fact, I have." I told him about how many times I had been stood up and began railing about men in general. He jumped right in on that topic, and soon we were laughing together. I was surprised that he was quite sharp. By the time we reached the bar, I was taken with his ability to keep me laughing and asked if he had any plans for the evening.

"Why do you want to know?" he asked. "Are you looking for someone *you* can stand up?"

"No. I just like to laugh, and we seem to be able to do that together. And I already know you're an asshole so I can't possibly be disappointed. I'm forewarned." We agreed that he would pick me up at seven for dinner.

I didn't bother to get ready for dinner, as I didn't really think Scott would show up. When he knocked on the door at seven, I was in a bathrobe reading a book in front of the fire. I expressed surprise that he had taken the date idea seriously. Nevertheless, I threw on clothes, and he asked where I wanted to eat.

"Anywhere but Sun Valley. I don't want to be seen in public with you. Let's drive to Hailey." I thawed enough over dinner to agree to have an after-dinner drink with him in Sun Valley at a place where we could play backgammon. I looked forward to fleecing him. I was surprised that two different women interrupted my cleaning his pockets at the game board. They were blatantly flirtatious and fawning. *What's going on here? What do they see in this creep that I haven't noticed?*

I started taking a closer look at him. He was smart. He was funny. He wasn't bad looking if you ignored the way

FLYING TIGRESS

he dressed. He was a college-educated farmer from Eastern Washington and was part of a successful family operation. The farm owned a condominium in Sun Valley where the whole family spent their winters skiing. He believed in hard work and hard play. We agreed on politics and religion, money and sex and in-laws.

Scott and I skied together every day for the rest of my vacation. By the time I flew out of town, we were lovers. He called me and wrote to me and visited me on the island where I lived. I wrote to him from Europe and Iceland and New York. When I got sick with mononucleosis in the spring of 1982, he asked me to come to his farm so he could take care of me. I went for a visit.

It was my first experience with small-town living and I liked it. I had never settled into one place but I wanted to. I liked that Scott was tied to the land and would always be there to take care of things when I traveled. Our careers meshed well. My visit turned into a permanent move.

When he first asked me to marry him, I said no. I was afraid to marry again and risk having another promising relationship collapse. Scott finally gave me an ultimatum. He didn't want to continue in a relationship with a woman who was incapable of making a commitment.

"Marry me or I'm out of here."

I married Scott in 1983.

Modeling ski clothes on Mount McKinley, Alaska, 1973. L–R: me (in the pink jacket,) John Terence Turner, photographer, Wini Jones, designer, and Ray Genet, mountain guide. The flight down the mountain with Don Sheldon lit my love affair with flying. Photo credit: John Terence Turner

Rex Gray, his Piper Pacer, and me on our quest to Alaska in 1973. He was simply seeking adventure; I wanted someone to hire me so I could continue flying.

Flying planes that had skis instead of wheels was especially challenging because there were no brakes.

My first Tiger trip as DC-8 engineer, 1977. L-R: Ken Conrad, me, and John Franzone.

Alaska Central Air snow removal was accomplished by pilots with brooms and ropes.

Ron Hall, a line pilot and flight instructor for Tigers, was an early mentor who helped to level the playing field for me.

Dwight Metcalf, shod in cowboy boots, nitpicked my performance for good things to talk to other pilots about. His support inspired hate mail to me from his wife.

Bob Bax, a Tiger legend, was known for his laid-back humor and coolness in emergencies. He forced a German airline staff, who didn't believe I could possibly be a jumbo jet pilot, to work with me.

Photo credit: Mark Devereaux

ISA + 21 founders, 1978. This band of sisters offered career-long group support. Front row: (L-R) Claudia Jones, Jean Haley Harper, Beverly Bass, Mary Bush, Angela Masson, Stephanie Wallach, Holly Fulton Back row: Denise Blankenship, Maggie Rose, Gail Gorski, Karen Kahn, Sharon Hilgers, Terry London Rinehart, Lennie Sorenson, Norah O'Neill, Sandra Donnelly, Jane Bonny, Lynn Rhodes.

The founders of ISA + 21 on its twentieth anniversary in 1998. Front row: Sharon Hilgers Krask, Karen Kahn, Sandra Wiederkehr, Emily Howell Warner, Jean Haley Harper, Julie Clark, Lynn Rhodes Back row: Denise Blankenship, Angela Masson, Norah O'Neill, Stephanie Wallach, Beverly Bass, Maggie Rose, Claudia Jones, Terry Rinehart. Note the proud display of four captain's stripes. We'd come a long way.

A snapshot of me in Ocho Rios, Jamaica, in 1983, before motherhood retired my bikini bathing suits.

The famous photo of me as a pregnant "captain" in 1984.

Bren, Cameron, and I standing in front of my mannequin in the exhibit about women airline pilots, which opened in 1994 at the San Diego Aerospace Museum.

Cameron, age 2, displaying her general attitude towards life's challenges. Photo credit: Glenn Dodge

Bren, age 6, is grinning because he has just received his first "big boy" haircut.

Dick Maxey, the legendary deadhead, filled my life with laughter for a special eight-month period.
Photo credit: Mark Devereaux

Derrel Gibbins was "struck blind" while flying with me, much to Maxey's dismay.

Jim Bailey, a classmate who coached me in handling prejudice and regularly beat me at backgammon.

Dick Rothstein, my initial training partner at Tigers and a supportive colleague after I returned to work in 2002.

Gary Stearns, the chief pilot who was creative in helping me sidestep outdated pregnant-pilot rules, carried my pregnant "captain" photo in his flight bag.

Larry and Patty Allen. While I was flying with her husband for the second month in a row, Patty saw a photo of me and said, "Larry, I think I need to meet this woman. Invite her home for dinner." After I passed her inspection, I was okayed to fly with Larry again.

Karen Kahn, a Continental pilot who decided that a week in Tahiti would cure my divorce blues, Deborah Lawrie, the first Australian woman airline pilot and godmother to my daughter, and me at ISA + 21's twentieth-anniversary reunion, 1998.

Captain Ron Burson, who kindly demonstrated that landings could get worse than my Korean cruncher, was able to fly his last trip before retirement with his son as his copilot.

Dick Crawford, wearing his girl's tie and Tiger Circle T cowboy boots, and Barbara Ganzkow, during the month we operated an "undermanned" 747.

Jim Brendel, seldom seen without his leg-flattering hot pants, poses briefly in his captain's cloud suit.

George Gewehr, who tied for first in the best-lines contest and the kissing contest.

Jim Booth, calm captain and
master of CRM, swam with
me in a tropical paradise
and showed me what happily
married could look like.

Janis Skliar, the first female captain
I flew with, gave a new meaning to
blonde jokes.

Sandy (Donnelly)
Wiederkehr, Tigers' third
woman pilot and first
woman captain, visited
me frequently while I
was out of work and
accompanied me to the
2001 Flying Tigers'
reunion.

Bill Helbig, hugging me
on the day I regained my
Airman's Medical in 2001.

Rich Redditt, fearless ex-navy-carrier pilot, was my check captain on my around-the-world final segment of training in 2002

Craig and Sheri Laurie, a Tiger couple who invited me to live with them after my stay at the trauma treatment center. Their home was an oasis for me.

Swimming with a dolphin in the Abacos Islands.

Bob DeArmond, a Tiger pilot upgrading to captain, was paired with me in my return-to-work training. We smiled with relief when we graduated from the MD-11 simulator in September, 2002.

22

MOTHERHOOD
1983–86

I did my last bit of public relations for Tigers in 1983. They had requested that I do PR for them when they hired me in 1976. I was not enthused. I did some radio and print work that got predictably mixed reactions from my coworkers. *Cosmopolitan* magazine interviewed me for a 1983 article on women in aviation. After pouring out my guts to their writer, telling him of traumatic events, he said, "We like to stick with the upbeat stuff."

"Upbeat?" I grimaced at him, "like all men think I'm wonderful?"

I was disgusted to see that the opening to my section of the article was a quote from me. " 'All men think I'm wonderful,' said statuesque ex-model Norah O'Neill." That article made it onto bulletin boards all over the Tiger system. Somebody wrote in red marker over it, "*I* don't think she's so wonderful."

My disappointment with the Cosmo article and dealing with the adverse reactions was quickly dispersed by my great joy in discovering I was pregnant with my first child.

I was the first woman pilot at Tigers to take a pregnancy leave. Chief Pilot Gary Stearns and I tested the parameters of the newly written pregnancy clause together.

In May 1984 I had my husband take a photo of me in my uniform when I was thirty-four years old and nine months pregnant. Of course, the pants didn't fit, so I substituted a black bikini bottom that nearly disappeared under the huge outhanging of my belly. I thought that view of me pregnant in uniform was pretty amusing.

I sent Gary a copy of the photo with a letter saying, "Dear Captain Stearns, I have been divorced and paid alimony, I have gray hairs, and now I have a pot belly. I believe that I have finally completed the prerequisites for captain. Just mail me my fourth stripe." Gary mailed me a glue-on fourth stripe and carried the photo in his flight bag, showing it to the people he flew with. Not everyone thought it was funny, including my father, who thought the photo was embarrassing. Women in his day did not have seminude pregnancy photos taken and shown around the world.

My daughter, Cameron O'Neill, was born May 14, 1984, after two-and-a-half days of excruciating on-and-off labor. I was so physically exhausted right before she emerged, I could no longer push and just lay there mewling like a dying animal and praying that God would allow me to live long enough to see the baby I was dying to bring into the world. As they lay my bloody daughter across my chest, she kicked me in the face, and my last thought before I passed out was, *Oh, fuck, she inherited my weird long feet!*

During my pregnancy, a girlfriend had described childbirth to me as "pretty painful, kind of like trying to poop out something the size of a basketball; but don't worry, you'll forget the pain afterwards." Later, I berated her for hedging on the truth. Childbirth could more accurately be described as akin to having a giant cram his arm into your vagina, grab a fistful of internal organs and then slowly, over a period of hours, twist and yank them from your body. That's what it felt like to me, and I never forgot that agony afterwards. My daughter was worth the torment of childbirth, but the joy of having her never gave me amnesia.

In order to return to work after Cammie's birth, I had to find a live-in nanny. This was difficult to do in a small farming community where people expressed shock that I would even consider letting another woman raise my child. None of the few big-city nanny services was interested in placing their workers so far from civilization, so I advertised locally and started interviewing. We were lucky to eventually find Vicky, who lived with us for three years before she got married in our back yard and quit to make a home of her own.

Living with a nanny in the house was a major adjustment, rather like having a third person in our marriage. Scott and I spent many dollars in the offices of marriage counselors working through our problems with Vicky and the women who followed her.

Two years later, in 1986, I flew until I was five months pregnant with my son. The FAA thought it was okay to fly pregnant, but our contract's pregnancy clause said I was supposed to quit flying as soon as I found out I was pregnant. I didn't have morning sickness or dizzy spells and I wanted to work until I couldn't hide it anymore. I outgrew my uniform shirts two months into the pregnancy and wore baggy sweaters over their unbuttoned fronts. One man said, "I'm disappointed in you. I didn't think you were the kind of woman who would have breast enlargements."

"I didn't have implants put in, though I don't see anything wrong with women doing that if they want to."

"I can't believe you would lie to me about it."

"I'm not lying."

I was hampered in explaining myself by the knowledge that I was violating the contract, though I was not doing anything unsafe or illegal. If I told people about my pregnancy, they would be coconspirators. So I kept quiet and let the guys think I had had cosmetic surgery and was getting fat. I quit flying after I saw a friend, Del, in Hong Kong. He hugged me hello and whispered, "When is the baby due?"

"Oh my God, is it that obvious?"

"No, Norah, but my wife, Julie, is about five months along, and you two are in exactly the same shape. Normally, both of you are slender."

I called Chief Pilot Gary as soon as I got home from

171

Hong Kong. "Hey, Gary, I just saw my doctor today and I'm pregnant again."

"Congratulations, Norah. When is the baby due?"

"About three months from now."

"You want me to believe that you're six months pregnant and just found out today?"

"Well, Gary, I thought of calling you the night the diaphragm broke, but I thought I'd wait and be sure."

"Right answer, babe. Call me if you need anything."

*M*y son, Bren Maxey, was born on August 8, 1986. My daughter had weighed 8 pounds 9 ounces at birth; Bren was a walloping 10 pounds 9 ounces. I sat up on the delivery table and said, "That's it for me. Just tie my tubes off now. I've squished out 8.9. I've squished out 10.9. I absolutely refuse to squish out 12.9."

Bren was a fat and contented baby in some respects, but his calorie-low light was continuously flashing. I kept track once and found I was spending a total of eight hours a day with Bren attached to my chest. I definitely liked breastfeeding, but having to feed, burp, transfer to the other side, then feed, burp, and change diapers once every two hours became totally exhausting. My longest period of sleep in those days was four hours, if I were lucky enough to have Bren sleep from midnight to 4 a.m.

Cammie's reaction to her new brother added to my stress and sleeplessness. I had done all the preparatory things parenting books had instructed me to do. Cammie saw Bren's ultrasound wiggling. She liked to put her ear and hands on my stomach and sense the baby. She seemed fascinated by the books that delineated the stages of fetal development. "Mommy, the baby is growing fingernails this week." Bren brought her presents from the hospital. My girlfriends never brought a new-baby present without a present for Cammie too. I had Vicky take Bren for two hours a day so Cammie and I would have our own undisturbed special time. I read to her while I was breastfeeding Bren. Despite our best efforts, Cammie did not like having any competition for her exclusive space.

One afternoon, I left Bren lying under his mobile in a bassinet in the living room and Cammie coloring in the kitchen while I went to the bathroom. Shortly, I heard an odd thud-thud-thud sound.

"Cammie, what's that noise?" I called from the bathroom, which was near the living room. I could hear Cammie but could not see either her or Bren.

"What noise?" replied Cammie. The thump, thump, thump continued.

"That thumping," I called as I rose and prepared to go see for myself. Bren was not in his bassinet. Cammie was no longer at the kitchen table. I turned the corner to the kitchen and saw Cammie dragging Bren by one of his legs across the tiled floor, his little head thudding like a cantaloupe across the grouting in the tiles. He was smiling and waving his arms, quite happy with just about everything as long as he wasn't hungry.

"What are you doing with the baby?" I was proud of how calm I sounded. I knew I was tired in those days and I was bitchy when I was tired. I tried to protect Cammie from that, but she was pushing all my limits of control. She, six-months potty trained, had already reverted to dropping her panties and peeing and pooping in odd corners. She would then call me and tell me she had had an accident. Her "accidents" never inconvenienced her by fouling her clothes. I didn't berate her for the poop scooping, but this baby dragging was an altogether different issue.

"What are you doing with the baby?" I asked again.

"I'm going to put him in the oven, cook him, and eat him all gone," explained my angelic-faced, smiling two-and-a-half-year-old as she continued onward toward the microwave.

"We don't eat babies," I explained as I grabbed Bren and backed away from the monstrous cannibal I seemed to have raised.

"I would. I want him gone," she cried.

That disaster averted, I called a child psychologist I had met in a parenting class at the local junior college and told him what had just happened in the kitchen.

"Oh, good," he said. "Cammie is not bottling up her feelings. She is expressing how she feels. That's good."

"That's good?" I shrilled, voice rising. "That's normal? She's trying to kill her brother! Just what am I supposed to do?"

"Don't ever, ever leave her alone with him," he advised me.

I didn't go to the bathroom alone for the next year.

Days after Cammie had tried to cook her brother, my parents arrived for a visit. Dad and Mom helping out were a relief for me, though no one could help me feed Bren.

Dad was always an early riser, as was Cammie. He sat alone with her in the breakfast nook that first morning and poured cereal for her. Cammie's giggling broke the peaceful silence of their companionably spooning up cereal together. Dad looked up from the paper and saw her laughter fade back into concentration on her bowl. Soon she broke out in laughter again.

"What's so funny?" he asked.

"I just thought of a new big no-no to do," she replied grinning. She knew that there were unpleasant consequences if she did things she had been told not to do. Her circumvention was to dream up things that were not very nice but that she had not been specifically warned about yet.

Dad told me about Cammie when I crawled out of bed an hour later. "Bertha and I always hoped you'd have one just like you. Looks like we got our wish."

By the time Bren was two-and-a-half-months old, I had been pushed past my limits. Both my obstetrician and Bren's pediatrician were concerned about the ever-present dark rings under my eyes, my shuffling gait, and my tendency to cry about everything. Bren's doctor suggested that with Bren's appetite, his getting a meal or two a day from a bottle would not threaten my milk supply. He suggested that my husband take over the night feedings for a few days a week so

I could get a full night's sleep. I was ecstatic at the prospect.

I had formula already measured into bottles when Scott got home that night. I told him what the doctor had said about allowing him to help me feed Bren. I was stunned by his refusal. "When you go out and farm for me, I'll feed the baby for you," was his logic. It didn't matter that I was bringing in more money than he while on paid leave or that he had many hired hands on the farm. It was a matter of principle he said. To me, it was a lack of willingness.

The next morning, after waking up yet again on the floor next to Bren's crib, where I had passed out after the last early-morning feeding, I mumbled, "I just can't do this anymore." I stretched out my cold, cramped arms, untangled a wet diaper from my hair, and crawled off to the nearest phone. I punched in my chief pilot's office phone number.

"Gary, this is Norah. Get me a hotel room."

"A hotel room? You mean here in Los Angeles?"

"I don't care, Gary. Anywhere."

"Ah, Norah, does this mean you're ready to train for returning to work?"

"I don't know, Gary. I am so tired, I just can't think straight."

"When are you planning on coming to L.A.?"

"I don't know. I haven't thought that far. My husband won't feed the baby, and the baby's so huge he needs to eat all the time, and my daughter is trying to kill him, and I can't go to the bathroom alone, and I just can't handle it anymore. Just let me sleep one night," I sobbed.

"Norah, it's going to be all right. I'll take care of you. I'll call you back in a few minutes."

I woke again to the ringing of the phone.

"Norah, it's Gary. Grab a pencil. You have plane reservations to L.A. for this Friday. You're booked at the LAX Sheraton. You start ground school on Monday. If two days of sleep is not enough, just stay in the hotel until you are rested. See you then, babe. Welcome back."

I called a girlfriend to help me pack. My doctor gave me pills to dry up my breast milk. Both Bren and I were going to go cold turkey. I called the nanny who was to start work full-time with my departure.

Then I stumbled off to L.A. and slept the weekend through. I did show up for work on Monday and went by Gary's office to thank him.

"Oh Gary, I'm so embarrassed. I must have sounded like an idiot."

"Yes, but you sound like yourself now. I'm glad I could be there for you."

I returned home three weeks later. The nanny, who had not had a night's sleep since I departed and Scott moved the crib into her room, ran out the back door to her car. Clearly, she was not going to be available at all when I was home. As Scott and I prepared for bed that evening, I noted that neither of us had prepared bottles for night feedings.

"Is Bren sleeping through the night already?"

"Nah, Vicki said that she still had to feed him twice during the night."

"Well, maybe you should get a couple of bottles ready. It'll save time at midnight."

"Why me? Aren't you going to feed him?"

"No, I'm not. When you fly for me, I'll feed the baby for you."

He prepared the bottles and fed the baby for the next three nights. I showed mercy on day four when I found him sleeping in his truck. It was 10 a.m. and his idling truck was parked on a farm road. I suggested that we alternate nights of feedings so that neither of us would get to the point where we were no longer functioning. He agreed.

*B*ecoming a mother dramatically changed my career plans. I passed up my first chance to be a captain and instead opted for being a senior engineer with first choice of days off and vacation slots. My first trip back on the line after Cammie's birth in 1984 was also my first trip as a 747 engineer and my first trip with two women on the crew.

When the captain reported in, he complained that he would have gone on sick leave if he had known he was going to fly with two women. Copilot Sandy Donnelly and I rolled our eyes at each other and got on with the paperwork.

The trip was scheduled to be two short, daylight legs out of JFK and a two-hour return by limousine. What should have been an easy day was complicated by the captain's not trusting his crew and trying to do everything himself. Morning on the Eastern Seaboard was no time to be short crewed on a jumbo jet. When we finally made it to our crew transportation, Sandy and I settled in for a chat. We discussed childbirth, Lamaze Method, breast-feeding versus bottle, infant colic, potty training, diaper brands, how to get the baby to sleep all night, and sex after childbirth. Then we got into how to lose the pregnancy weight, what to do about stretch marks, and whether breasts would ever return to normal after breast-feeding. Having exhausted those topics and being caught in traffic, we had time to get into other things of interest such as current events, vacation destinations, jewelry, and our favorite chick flicks.

When our limo stopped in front of the hangar at JFK, the captain fell out of his door in his haste to leave. Sandy was laughing so hard, she had to lean on the limo to stand.

"Oh Norah, I have wanted for so long to do that! To bore one of the guys the way they have bored me with baseball scores and endless talk of sports and cars."

"Yeah, Sandy, and we couldn't have picked a more deserving guy to do it to," I chortled.

We learned later that the captain had told everyone that he'd had to solo a 747.

When I became a mother I resolved to set a good example at home and leave the swearing at work. I wasn't always successful. However, a frightening experience when Cammie was two years old forever changed my view of profanity. Cammie and I were driving through town on a summer morning, doing errands before having lunch with my husband and his mother, Beth. Cammie was singing in her car seat, which was strapped into the passenger seat beside me.

FLYING TIGRESS

She already talked well, with a large vocabulary, but she had trouble pronouncing the letter F. Her fingers were her "dingers." When she had a good time, she was having "dun." When she was hungry, she asked for "dood." As we sang together on that summer morning, I drove into an intersection and saw, in my peripheral vision, a car racing toward us from the right. I could see that he was not going to stop for his red light. His present trajectory would have him impacting our car at Cammie's door. Doing everything I could to avoid the crash, I ended up stalled on the Main Street sidewalk. We were unscratched. I saw a policeman pursue and stop the drunk driver who had run the light.

When I had calmed down, Cammie and I continued our drive together singing.

As I sat across from my lovely and genteel mother-in-law at lunch, I heard her ask Cammie, "What did the two of you do today?"

My daughter replied, "Mommy and I had so much dun! We parked on the sidewalk and Mommy got out and yelled at a ducking asshole." I never said "duck" at home again, and began to clean up my language on the line.

*L*eaving my children to go flying was never easy. I would have liked to take several years off, but long leaves were not granted at that time. If I had quit, I would never have been hired as an airline pilot again. I was not ready to quit flying, nor was I ready to be totally dependent on Scott financially. There were already serious problems in our marriage. I felt great guilt when my children began begging me not to leave while clinging to my suitcases as I was going out the door.

Once, when Scott was going on a ski trip with his friends, Cammie clung, crying, to his suitcase at the front door. I held her and in an attempt at consolation said, "Just pretend he's going off flying. You don't cry when I leave anymore."

"But, Mom," she sobbed, "Mommies are *supposed* to be gone half of the month. Daddies are supposed to be home every night."

My piloting sometimes gave my children a skewed sense of how things were in the "real" world. Cammie and Bren accompanied me to annual ISA + 21 meetings, where they met my flying girlfriends. Our husbands had their own club called H.A.L.P. (Husbands of Airline Pilots).

When another Tiger pilot, Larry Allen, stopped by my home, I introduced him to Cammie.

"Honey, this is Larry Allen. He and I have flown together several times."

"You flew with him at work?" she asked.

"Yes. He flies for Tigers too."

Her eyes widened. "They let boys fly? I thought only girls could fly."

"Norah, what are you teaching this kid?" Larry sputtered.

My daughter was still waiting for an answer to her question. "Oh, Cammie. Boys can fly too." I grinned at Larry and, for his benefit, said, "If boys are really good, we let them fly too."

When Cammie was eight, her teacher asked her if she wanted to grow up to be a pilot just like Mommy. Cammie said, "Oh, no. I'll get a pilot's license because flying is fun, but I don't want to work as a pilot. Airline pilots spend too much time away from their families."

I know that for a time I appeared to some as a woman who "had it all." I had a solid husband and two glorious children and a glamorous career. I was living on green acres in a dream house we'd built together. We were all healthy and we had enough money. The truth was, my marriage was becoming abusive. The truth was, the marriage would have ended sooner if it were not for the children and the job that took me away just long enough each month for me to con myself into thinking that things were not as bad as they seemed. The truth was, I was just barely holding on to my sanity.

23

MAXEY, THE LEGENDARY DEADHEAD

1977–85

Dick Maxey was a legend at Tigers. I'd heard lots about him before we met. His dry, acerbic wit was so well known that he was often quoted in the cockpit. "Have you heard the latest Maxeyism?" they'd say.

I heard how he had dealt with a letter on the bulletin board from a new chief pilot. Maxey thought the chief pilot's letters to the crews were overzealous, banal, and too frequent. One day, he removed the latest missive from the bulletin board, carried it to the chief's office, laid it on the desk and opined, "John, you need to do something about this. Some idiot has been writing stupid memos, forging your signature, and hanging them in crew rooms. He's making you look bad."

I heard how Maxey had come back from a trip, taken his paperwork in to drop it off, and had seen two of Tigers' most flagrant and notorious lotharios in the crew room. Both were check captains who had had affairs with other pilot's wives while the husbands were out flying. Maxey harrumphed and said, "I guess my wife isn't getting laid today."

I heard how he had come home from a long trip in a lusty mood and banged open the front door of his house, calling, "I know someone who is going to get bedded today!" He entered to find himself in the center of an all-female bridge party. The embarrassed women left early.

Maxey and I met at my first meeting of the Airline Pilots Association in San Francisco in 1977. I was the only woman there, self-conscious and rightfully so. A buzz always started when I entered a room full of pilots. "It's her, the girl."

A guest speaker, the manager of Tigers' San Francisco terminal who had been on the job for six months, was talking about his accomplishments such as beefed up security, less theft, and better parking. The international pilots were being asked to park away from the terminal in a distant dirt lot so their parking for a ten-day trip would not take up customer parking spaces near the terminal. (I longed for international flying to exotic places, but was still only a lowly three-nights-out-and-back domestic flyer.) I listened to the senior pilots' complaints about wading through knee-deep, water-filled potholes to get to their cars during a rainy winter. The new manager acknowledged that their parking lot was "kinda rough" and needed some improvements but pointed out that his new patrolled security system had reduced the car break-in/theft reports to zero in the last three months. Maxey stood up and said, "Hell, all you've proven is that thieves can't swim."

I asked for an introduction to him and liked that he barely paid attention to me. To be ignored in those days was a welcome relief.

A year later, Maxey deadheaded with my crew. I was a new DC-8 copilot, struggling with men's changed attitudes toward me. As an engineer, I had sat in the back of the cockpit where I ran and monitored systems and basically could do no damage. (I later learned that engineers could be creative in screwing up a flight; indeed, could even cause or prevent a disaster.) But when I moved up to copilot, I went from being a fun accessory to a potential danger and was getting a lot of flack. I wanted to do a good job with Maxey on board because, for some reason, his respect was already important to me.

When I tried really hard to fly well, I undermined myself. I couldn't attain that mix of hypervigilance and deep-breathing relaxation that is required to get a good performance from a pilot, no matter what his level of experience and skill. Flying an approach to Detroit with winds gusting across the runway, I worked so hard trying to keep the DC-8 on the runway centerline that I was breathing heavily and my arms were aching.

No particular control input seemed to work well; I was constantly changing it and fighting to even out the changes. Thankfully, the landing wasn't a beer landing (as in, "I owe you two beers for the damage I just did to your lower parts.") and we all walked away from it.

Maxey, eyes twinkling, started laughing and said to the crew, "Not bad, considering she created her own crosswind all the way down." He advised me to brief the engineer to watch the throttle alignment for me. The engineer could keep my little finger from pushing too far forward on the #1 throttle and creating an artificial right crosswind for myself. I was embarrassed not to have noticed what I had been doing. He kindly said, "How do you think I knew to look for that glitch? I've done it myself."

Not long after, when we had our first trip together, an all-night two-legger, I was surprised to find Maxey quiet; no bon mots that night. We were all tired. As we shook hands goodbye after the flight, he said, "You're disappointed in me aren't you? You expected me to keep you entertained all night. Those funny stories you heard about me took thirty years to compile. I'm not a comic all the time."

My real adventures with Maxey covered an eight-month period in 1983. He was #1 captain on the DC-8 and I was #1 engineer. I had met my farmer husband and had bid back from 747 copilot to DC-8 engineer in order to have the seniority to get the schedule I wanted. Because there was a reduction in DC-8 flying then, invariably, there was only one good schedule, and Maxey and I got it. For eight sequential months, we were paired with either of the two most senior copilots, both of them eccentric characters. We had fun.

His captain's briefing was, "If you see me deviating from standard procedures, it is *not* because I think I am hot shit and have found a way to improve upon the manual, and it is *not* because I am too dumb to know the book; it *is* because I am screwing up and haven't caught it yet, so yell it out loud and clear!" That invitation to tell him his mistakes helped to solidify his crew. He knew he wasn't perfect and didn't expect us to be either. He made it clear that he was counting on us as much as we were counting on him. I wish other captains could have espoused his healthy crew concept. His knowledge of his own limitations was one of the factors that made him an excellent captain.

I enjoyed watching him try to straighten out our copilots in a tactful way. Tact was not his long suit. The copilot seat is a difficult one, and these two men had been in the copilot's seat for too long. Generally, copilots had to fly the captain's pet way on every flight, resulting in their learning an ever-increasing repertoire of "right" ways to do things. After a while, they forgot how they would have planned on flying if they had ever had a chance to fly without interference. I was sympathetic to their dilemma, having recently stepped out of the hot seat myself. I was also enjoying a lack of performance pressure for the first time in my career. No longer on probation nor the only woman pilot at Tigers, I was also no longer intimidated by four-engine jets. I knew the DC-8 engineer's job well and, from this comfortable position, I decided to participate in Maxey's copilot training.

When I suggested to him, in private, that Bob would do better if he were just left alone, Maxey was truly surprised. He didn't want to "ride" his crew and suggested that I call him on it if I saw him doing that. This agreement led me to discreetly pass notes to Maxey in the cockpit. The notes, printed in capitals in felt tip pen, were used over and over again because Maxey seemed to require the same communication over and over again. They said:

SHUT UP!
NOT AGAIN.
HE ALREADY HEARD THAT.
SIT ON YOUR HANDS!
HE IS NOT BREAKING THE F.A.R.S.
HE IS NOT DANGEROUS. LET HIM GO.
I enjoyed watching Maxey actually sitting on his hands

and biting his lips together to keep from speaking. Maxey's sense of humor and mine meshed well, and our verbal barbs often went over others' heads. Sometimes we would make comments at another's expense and then snort together when we got away with it.

Maxey was looking older than God then, a combination of prematurely white hair, an intensely lined face exacerbated by years of heavy smoking, and the gnomish look of a curmudgeon personified. I think what made our friendship possible was not only the connection of our intellects and sense of the absurd but also the utter ease I felt with him, his tacit permission to just be myself.

That ease was facilitated by his lack of romantic interest in me, his lack of bigotry toward women, and his acceptance of other pilots as flawed humans. On our first trip, he invited me to his room for a drink. (The bars were closed.) When I hesitated, he burst out, "For God's sake, I'm too old to make a pass at you. Right now I'm too tired to even fantasize about making a pass at you. I just don't want to have an after-work drink alone."

I had shown up for our first flight together without my complete uniform because my cleaner had burnt down during my time at home. When I had tried to explain this to him, he waved a hand impatiently and said, "You've confused me with someone who cares about that shit. I don't care what you wear, what sex you are, what color you are; just show up and do a good job. That's all I ask."

Oh, really? I thought, my inner brat becoming activated. Anxious to see his reaction, I reported to work the next day in a red dress and heels. He said nothing. High heels were dangerous on the stairs, so my fun ended quickly.

One of Maxey's character flaws that I shared was impatience with stupidity. As captain, he was able to express his impatience with more panache and more impunity than a junior crewmember could have gotten away with.

For instance, we all found clearing military customs while exiting American military bases in Asia time consuming and pointless. Because we had to file Crew Declarations (decs) to clear U.S. Customs at our point of reentry into the U.S., we generally filled out the form while flying homeward, tallying up our receipts and calculating what taxes we would have to pay on our foreign shopping. For some reason, the U.S. bases we flew out of in Korea wanted to see our U.S. Customs decs *before* we left, though they couldn't tax us or confiscate purchases. They did search for dangerous articles.

One day, the agent examining Maxey's bags found a large bottle of assorted pills.

"Those are my vitamins," Maxey explained. "It's more convenient to carry what I need in one bottle rather than many." The agent rolled several pills onto the counter, touched them with interest, then started to put them back in the bottle. Maxey said, "I'm sure as hell not going to take them after you've fingered them. You can keep them."

Next, the man wanted to confiscate Maxey's pocket-sized Swiss army knife. "This is a weapon. It has to be sealed in a plastic bag and locked in the cockpit en route."

"You want to lock it up with the crew in the cockpit?"

"Yes; the captain needs to be in charge of any weapons."

"So you're going to take it away from me now, then hand it back to me as I enter the cockpit?"

"Yes, sir."

"Let me put it back in my pocket and carry it to the cockpit for you. You'll save yourself a baggie."

I could see Maxey beginning to fume, but he stepped aside in silence while the agent examined my suitcase. I usually added an extra suitcase of purchases when I had access to the Korean street markets. Their goods were varied, plentiful, and inexpensive, rather like the Hong Kong of twenty years before. When the agent had finished searching all of us, he wrote in large red lettering across Maxey's crew dec—suspected drug smuggling. My crew dec had red letters saying, lots of duty to pay. Then the agent signed for our aircraft to depart.

Maxey looked him in the eye, and said, "Are you sure you're done?"

"Yes, sir."

"Really sure? We're free to leave?"

"Yes, sir"

"Good." Maxey grinned. "Do you really think I'm going to turn in that drug-smuggling crew dec on the other side of the Pacific? *Of course*, I'm going to rewrite it en route." He tore apart his red-lettered crew dec and handed the pieces to the agent. "Take care of that *trash* properly," he ordered.

The agent gasped, "You can't do that!"

Maxey said, "I just did," and walked off.

*D*uring one week-long layover in Korea, when the guys were bored to beer daily, I went into a shopping frenzy, doing all my upcoming birthday, anniversary, and Christmas shopping as well as having furniture custom made. Maxey and I went to the Officers Club for dinner; I wore a recently-purchased, low-necked, sleek-fitting aquamarine silk jumpsuit with matching heels and jade jewelry. I curled my hair and slathered on "evening" make-up.

I became uncomfortable with the stares I was drawing at the club. I wondered if I had split a seam in the back of my pants.

"Maxey, have I split a seam? Am I hanging out?"

"Nah, you're all together."

"Why are they staring then?" I grinned. "Could they be wondering whether I'm your mistress, or maybe your daughter?"

Maxey laughed. "Babe, they're just wondering where I found you and how much I *paid* for you."

As we left the hotel at the end of our week in Seoul, Maxey looked with a jaundiced eye at the truck I'd hired to carry my "crew baggage" to the airport. Flying Tigers had recently issued a memorandum saying they were alarmed at the extra weight our shopping was subtracting from the useful load of the aircraft and had decreed that crewmembers were limited to 50 pounds of baggage. This was an uneducated memo because our flight bags alone weighed about 30 pounds. (They carried maps of the world, tools, and manuals.) Together with our ten-day trip suitcase, even with only our uniforms inside, we were already over the 50-pound limit. Maxey pulled his copy of the memo out of his bag and asked if I'd read it.

"Of course, sir; here's mine," I said, as I handed him my carefully altered memo that said the limit was 500 pounds. As soon as he had ascertained the forged difference, he knew he'd been had and remarked that they hadn't sent him a copy of the girl-pilot memo. Upon reaching the airport, where we often helped each other with bags, Maxey watched my crew baggage truck pull up and said, "If you're going to shop like a flight attendant, I'm going to treat you like one. I'm not helping you carry that brass bed!"

Noticing Maxey and me flying together month after month, people began commenting about our pairing. One pilot asked Maxey if he was splitting the legs three ways, because I was qualified to fly the plane as copilot. He replied that when I wanted a leg I could damn well bid it. He wasn't going to give an engineer a leg. This was understandable to me: another airline had recently lost a DC-8 cargo plane with all on board while the engineer had been illegally flying it.

Some captains had allowed engineers to fly at Tigers, but the crash had solemnly underlined the risks involved, and most were reluctant to do it anymore. When Maxey told me I was not going to get a leg from him, I jokingly said, "Ah, you mean I slept with you for nothing?"

This comment was overheard and misconstrued. *Well, of course.*

I hadn't believed anyone would think I was stupid enough to trade sex for flying, let alone announce that behavior in public. But the reactions were so overboard, and Maxey and I got such a hoot from them, that we were inspired to continue our Mutt and Jeff act in different crew rooms, adding variations along the way. When we were bored, we'd treat each other with yelling disrespect, concocting new barbs to sling at each other. The unspoken goal was to slip one past the other guy, one that was so subtle that he either didn't get it at all or was unable to come up with a rejoinder.

When we'd flown together for seven months, Maxey

187

said he'd seen more of me that year than his wife and he was going to bid reserve to break the cycle and ask for a Sydney, Australia, trip. On my first flight of the next month, I was paired with Maxey's good friend, Captain Derrel Gibbins. Just before departing Seattle for Anchorage with Gibby, I saw Maxey getting ready to depart on Qantas for Australia.

Two hours into our flight, Gibby's left eye started swelling shut. By the time we descended into Anchorage, Gibby had relinquished the controls to his copilot and asked operations to call for a cab to take him to an eye doctor. A virus had freakily settled in his eye, and he was grounded. A pilot from the Anchorage hotel was pulled out for emergency duty, and we carried the deadheading Gibby home.

Meanwhile, crew control pulled Maxey off the yet-to-depart Australian flight and replaced Gibby with Maxey for the rest of the week. Maxey was livid about the swap.

"Damn it, O'Neill, you stuck your toenail in Gibby's eye en route. Admit it. You'd do anything to get to fly with me again!" he accused.

"It worked, didn't it?" I sweetly smiled my assent. "Gotcha." It was one of our finer moments. It was also the beginning of our last week together.

I told him I was planning on naming a child for him, in the hope that my child would inherit Maxey's sense of humor. He was aghast. "You can't do that!" he said. "Someone will think it's mine!" I was incredulous that he'd be insulted to have people think I had actually bedded him, but I came to understand that he was only trying to protect me from serious gossip about my child. Nevertheless, my son's middle name is Maxey.

Maxey walked me to my car after that trip. For the first and last time, he touched me. He hugged me good-bye.

*M*axey died on Flying Tiger Flight 73/18 on July 18, 1985. He was in the captain's seat midway across the Pacific Ocean. Deadheading flight attendants gave him CPR for over two hours until they made landfall in Japan. They wouldn't have made that extreme and unpleasant effort for just anyone.

The crew who flew Maxey's body back from Japan listed him in the ship's log as a deadhead. Maxey would have liked that.

I got the news that he had died while I was checking in for a flight in Los Angeles. I burst into tears and sat down. The pilot who had told me kept apologizing. "Norah, I didn't mean to upset you. I thought you hated him."

"I loved him." *I always will.*

24

REAL WOMEN DO PUMP GAS

1984–85

*B*eing accepted as one of the guys didn't change the fact that I was always and ever a woman, though I was no longer harassed except on rare occasions. But our differences were fodder for jokes.

Tigers purchased some used 747s from a company that had ordered their planes from Boeing with a slightly different cockpit setup than in the new Tiger 747s. One difference was a selector switch on the autopilot control panel. The newly-purchased planes had a rotary dial with three positions—heading, navigation, and performance management system (HDG, NAV, and PMS). The PMS selection was new to us and did not go unnoticed.

During my first preflight on one of the new planes, the captain laughed and said, "Norah, look. This plane was custom designed for women pilots. Should I select PMS for you today? You'll have to keep me informed this month."

"Wow. Cool. My very own switch. Of course I have PMS today. I have PMS thirty days a month, twelve months a year. Neato, my very own switch."

"You have female problems? How can you have PMS 365 days a year?"

"Well, of course, it's constant!" I feigned surprise. "PMS

stands for Putting up with Male Shit, doesn't it?"

"O'Neill, it's immensely irritating that you always have a rebuttal ready. Do you lie awake every night thinking this stuff up?"

"No, sir. Tapping into my feminine intuition guarantees that I'll always prevail over male logic."

The publication of the book *Real Men Don't Eat Quiche* was the springboard for running jokes about the things the guys didn't want to do. Real men don't make coffee. Real men don't do paperwork. Real men don't cook. Real men don't make bad landings; they can crash, but they don't make bad landings. Real men don't cry. Also, real men nuked just about everything they did not like—ATC, when it issued clearances for less than optimum routing; Chicago ramp traffic; management, when it asked for work concessions; and ex-wives who wanted cost-of-living alimony raises. Just nuke 'em.

I had fun with the sequel, *Real Women Don't Pump Gas*, though when I finally found the perfect flight situation in which to use its title line, my delivery was met with a scowl.

Captain B.G. O'Hara and I diverted to Fairbanks in 1984, during my first month as a 747 engineer. When a main-tank fueling valve failed shut, I crawled down into the electronics bay to check fuses and circuit breakers. Not finding a remedy there, I studied the manual. I instructed the airport fueler to put fuel in the number one auxiliary tank, where it could slowly be gravity fed to the main tank. B.G. was impatient with the lengthy fueling time and said so.

When we were finally flying to our original destination, I sought to ease the tension in the cockpit. "Sir, I know you have been wondering just what, if anything, they taught me in 747 ground school, but"

"I *never* said that!" he interrupted protesting. "I sure as hell was *thinking* it!"

He watched me closely for the rest of the month, waiting for me to slip up. I tried to be grateful for his scrutiny, knowing I was new and could use practical input. The first officer appreciated the situation. "B.G. was so busy baby-sitting you that I was able to fix my errors before he caught them. Thanks for the pressure-free flying."

A year later, Captain B.G. O'Hara and I flew together again. On the way from Asia to Anchorage, the hourly weather reports showed an unforecast and alarming trend. Both our destination and our alternate, Elmendorf Air Force Base, had ground fog and their visibility was now below minimums for landing. We were still several hours out, so there was time for the weather to change and for us to formulate plans B and C.

B.G. had ordered fuel enough for us to divert to Fairbanks, should we have to go there. We had a laugh about fate wanting us to be in Fairbanks together again, as if it were an exotic and romantic place to be in the winter.

The weather grew steadily worse as we droned closer to Anchorage. Then Fairbanks's weather went down. Never, during all the years I had flown in Alaska, had I seen the coastal and interior weather go bad at the same time. Plan A, Anchorage, was out. Plan B, Fairbanks, was a no go. Plan C, Cold Bay, a windy and inhospitable spot in the Aleutian Islands, became impossible.

I imagined the crews of four other jets, one ahead of us and three behind, all now sitting on the edge of their seats like my crew was. Flying for five hours in trail of each other over the Pacific, we had been up all night. We had taken off from Japan just before curfew shut Tokyo International down for the night, had heard each other calling out position reports, and we had talked together on the Pacific plane-to-plane frequency. We were groggy no longer. Five jumbos were facing an emergency.

Alaskan air charts are pockmarked with airstrips, most of them looking like moose trails in the wilderness and suitable only for small planes. We needed over a mile of asphalt to land safely. *It would be nice also to have a few amenities like a tower and fuel trucks and portable stairs and a telephone. Oh yeah, and a hotel and a restaurant, because we are unlikely to make it out of wherever we land before we run out of duty time.* I radioed Tigers in Anchorage about our not knowing where we would go.

B.G. decided on King Salmon, an airport on the Alaska Peninsula south of Anchorage. It had only 7,262 feet of usable runway, but that was better than the airstrip at our last choice, Kenai Airport. The Tiger 747 ahead of us made the same choice. B.G. briefed us thoroughly on what he planned to do with his landing, which would be nonstandard. He elected to go below glideslope on short final in order to use every foot of runway without dragging our tail in the dirt off the end. We listened keenly to the transmissions of the Tiger ahead of us.

The short runway problem was compounded by the lack of parking spaces for big jets and the lack of a taxiway to get us off the runway. The 747-200 required 152 feet to turn around in and this runway was 150 feet wide. Its only exit points were at midfield, where a general aviation runway crossed. We were going to have to land, make a 180-degree turn at the end of the runway, back taxi to the middle, turn off, and try to find a spot to park in that would keep us from blocking the planes landing behind us.

The plane ahead made its landing, turned at the end of the field, and taxied back to occupy the only area large enough for parking on the northwest side of the field. The rest of us would have to wedge ourselves into the southeast corner around the tower and general aviation ramp. It was critical that we do this speedily, or we would block the landing of the jets behind us that had nowhere else to go.

B.G. O'Hara flew the 747 on approach as if it were a tail-dragging two-seater about to land on a gravel bar in the Yukon River. He ducked under the glideslope and touched down safely well short of our usual 1,000-foot aim point. Max braking, max reverse, and prompt spoiler deployment made it possible for us to exit the narrow runway at its midpoint. We parked with our nose pointing back toward the runway because there would be no tugs to help us push back for our departure. Freed of flight duties, we had the time and seating to view the ensuing airshow.

FLYING TIGRESS

Brand X was the third to land. In the distance we could see the dots of a Japan Airlines 747 and an Air Force jet holding in oval racetracks in the sky, awaiting Brand X's landing and clearing of the runway. Touching down at the 1,000-foot mark, the plane shuddered to a stop with its nose hanging over the end of the runway.

While amusing ourselves by critiquing his landing and his use of thrust reversal, we heard Brand X transmit an astounding message.

"King Salmon Tower, Brand X will be unable to clear the runway. It's too narrow for us to turn around. We're going to park here. We're shutting down now."

"But you have to get off the runway," the tower yelped. "The planes behind you have nowhere else to go!"

"Gee, sorry, but we didn't design this plane."

Silence on the airwaves. What could you say to such stupid and uncaring pilots? They got their spot and didn't give a damn about the 400 people circling on JAL or people on the Air Force plane.

"They've just shut down the only available runway in Alaska. What are the others going to do?" I wondered to my crew. The Air Force plane answered my question.

"Air Force 10 declaring an emergency."

"What are your intentions?" asked the tower. "The runway is closed."

"Not for an emergency it isn't. I'm landing behind Brand X. Hope we get stopped in time."

"Tower, this is Brand X. You can't let him land behind us. He won't be able to stop before he hits us."

"Gee, sorry, Brand X. I didn't design the ATC system," replied the tower. "Air Force 10, you're cleared to land on Runway 11. Be advised that the last 500 feet are unusable due to a parked 747. Good luck."

We had ringside seats for the flying feats that followed. I could imagine how the Brand X pilots must feel, strapped into a plane with its back to the action. If I had been aboard that plane, I would have crawled down into the electronics bay and dropped the mechanic's access ladder and exited over the nose gear tires. I would have run far from the area

194

of potential impact. Why the Brand X pilots didn't do exactly that soon became clear to us.

B.G. radioed Brand X and asked them to switch to ground frequency so they could talk without congesting the tower frequency. The captain of Tiger Flight 78 joined the conversation. He had safely turned his plane around on the runway and thought his having done so was proof that it could be done. Brand X said his plane was at maximum landing weight of 630,000 pounds and therefore could not make the turn.

"What the fuck does your weight have to do with the size of your turning radius?" was the succinct rejoinder.

"Well, uh, duh, our nose is over the dirt. What if our nose wheel isn't clear?"

"So send your engineer out to examine the area."

"But we have no way out of the plane except our emergency exit slides. There aren't any moveable stairs at this airport."

"Didn't you ever hear of the electronics-bay ladder?" Evidently not. I imagined the Brand X pilots rapidly examining the aircraft manual.

"How'd they get type ratings on this plane without knowing how many doors they have?" I asked. I was grateful for the Tiger training center. We had regularly been drilled in topics not necessarily required by the FAA to operate the plane. Flying so many off-route charters required that Tiger pilots be more self-sufficient than other airline pilots.

Meanwhile, Air Force 10 made a fly by to examine the runway. Their incoming roar as they flew low over Brand X was enough to make my heart speed up. I was *really* glad to be safely off the runway.

The Air Force's circling back to approach lit fires under the Brand X pilots. They wanted the tower to send out wingwalkers so they could get off the runway.

"Sorry fellas, I'll send a truck out as soon as it's safe to be on the runway. Probably after everyone out there lands."

Air Force 10 landed and screeched to a halt short of the parked 747. I let out my breath. One down. One to go. Japan Airlines was still circling on the horizon, perhaps getting permission from Tokyo to declare an emergency and waiting to see if they would have a cleared runway.

I crept down the nose-gear ladder, did a postflight inspection, and talked to the driver of a fuel truck that had driven up. I told him we didn't yet know how much fuel we would need.

"No problem, ma'am. I'll come back any time you're ready to put fuel on board. Where's your fueler?"

"My fueler?"

"Yes. Your fueler. He can use my fuel truck. I'm not trained or insured to fuel a 747, but your guy can borrow my truck."

"I'll call you on ground frequency soon," I promised. I scrambled back to the cockpit.

"B.G., they won't fuel the plane here."

"Can't you fuel it?" he asked.

"B.G., I wasn't trained to climb a ladder and fuel the plane." No answer from my captain, just a cool stare. "Real women don't pump gas?" I tried. Big scowl. "I can figure it out. How hard can it be?"

B.G. and the copilot stayed in the cockpit long enough to watch the JAL 747 land and turn around behind Brand X. Then they went searching for a flight-planning telephone, even though we wouldn't be able to take off when the Anchorage weather improved if we couldn't coax the Brand X driver off the runway.

However, we were running out of crew-duty time. If we couldn't take off in the next two hours, we would be grounded for twelve hours. We would probably be sleeping on the plane; there were no hotels in sight. And it was cold outside. Would we have enough fuel to run our APU for twelve hours to provide lights and heat? My head started spinning with numbers. We couldn't wait until the runway cleared to begin our departure preparations; we needed to be ready to go.

Before B.G. and the copilot walked to the tower, the copilot, offered a practical suggestion. "Maybe your being a woman will finally come in handy. Maybe a blow job will get this plane fueled."

Perusing the fueling section of the manual and schematics of the fueling panel in the leading edge of the left wing, I said aloud, "I can do this." The fuel-truck driver loaned me an arctic parka and heavy gloves and gave me general instructions on how to attach the hose to the plane. He settled in the warmth of his cab while I went up a tall ladder, hauling the heavy hose behind me. Buffeted by a freezing wind, I clung to the ladder and started pumping gas.

Two pilots from JAL talked to the fuel-truck driver. He directed them to me. They asked if I would fuel their plane next. I told them I wasn't a fueler, but a pilot. They didn't care. They wanted their plane fueled next. *What the hell* I thought. *They've got 400 people trapped on board with overflowing lavatories and diminishing food and drink.*

"If I run out of duty time with Brand X still blocking the runway, I'll have time to fuel your plane for you," I promised them.

Captain O'Hara returned and gaped in astonishment. "I can't believe you're really doing it."

"Seemed easier to do it myself than to hand out blow jobs to strangers, sir."

The Anchorage weather improved just as Brand X cleared the runway and the two Tiger planes made it to their destination. (Tiger 78 had not needed more fuel.) My copilot remarked that it was unclear why I should be happy to get out of King Salmon.

"Think how much money you could have made, Norah, when those people on JAL found out you were the only fueler in town. You could have passed a hat in the aisles and made a fortune."

The Anchorage evening paper printed a front-page, above-the-fold photo of the 747s stranded in King Salmon. They were still waiting for fuelers and relief crews to be flown in. Only the can-do Tigers had departed, and I was the only 747 pilot who had learned to fuel the plane that day.

Weeks later, I received an "Atta Girl" letter from chief pilot, Doug Happ. I was proud of it because praise from management was rare. We were expected to go the extra mile—that's what we were paid for.

25

LOVE IN HONG KONG

1985

A bar fight, not with fists but with liquor-loosened molten words marked the beginning of my closest friendship on the line. I had no premonition of the depth and trueness of the feelings and bond to come. During the argument, I just loathed Bill Helbig's swaggering smugness and his belief in his rectitude. *Typical ex-Navy carrier pilot—another cocky, self-assured, handsome ace—God's gift to aviation and to women.*

No matter, really, what the argument was about. Twenty years of close and confidential friendship later, we still don't agree who was right that night in 1980, when we argued a point of crewmember ethics in a bar in New York.

Several days after the incident, while flying home to Seattle on United Airlines, I was annoyed to look up and see Bill standing smiling by my aisle seat in coach. Before I could offer him a rude and snarly greeting, he said he had come to apologize. I blinked at that. Perhaps I was going to have to adjust my attitude toward him. But he apologized for the unpleasantness of our argument, not for his viewpoint. I found myself getting heated all over again. He cut it short and sauntered back to his seat in first class. I could acknowledge to myself that he was a better person than I was in that he could apologize for anything at all. I settled into my seat, hoping that I would never have to fly with him.

Two years later on November 1, I flew my first trip with him. While flying from Seattle to Anchorage where we were scheduled to sit on the ground for four hours and then return home, I learned that it was his birthday. Birthdays were special to me, thanks to a mother who always made mine the most memorable day of the year. I didn't understand Bill being so nonchalant about spending his special day working, especially working with someone he didn't like very much.

I decided to spend my four hours in Anchorage acting like a grown-up and putting our differences aside long enough to do something special for him. When he returned to the cockpit for the flight home, he found it festooned with crepe paper and balloons. A card and a gift were ribboned to his control wheel, and there were birthday candles on a small cake. We sang Happy Birthday. "I can't believe you did this," he said several times. In his eyes and in his voice, I could see his opinion of me shifting. I guess he thought I was a big enough girl to have buried the hatchet. He didn't know that I hadn't been adult enough to forgive him. I just couldn't let anyone's birthday pass uncelebrated. But the ice between us had begun to thaw.

A year later, we flew together again. By then, my attitude had progressed to tolerance. I knew he was a good pilot and I decided that I could work with an asshole as long as he didn't scare me. I was proud of that mature bit of professionalism. No segment of our trip went as scheduled, and we spent long nights moving from plan A to plan B to plan C. We were all tapped out.

When he called after a 3 a.m. hotel check-in to invite me to his room for a beer, I was reluctant to go. I thought of telling him up front that I was interested in a beer and nothing else, but I decided to give him the benefit of the doubt. I was glad I hadn't said anything because we shared a couple of beers and relaxed and talked about work with humor and agreement. I learned that he was happily married a long time to his first wife and mother of his two sons. We talked about my recent marriage to the farmer. We had similar thoughts about fidelity in marriage and family priorities. I reluctantly began to admire and respect him. We started to fly together more frequently and found that we had skiing, opinions about child rearing, choice of restaurants, and love of reading in common. I began to look forward to flying with him, knowing that I would enjoy both work in the plane and play on layovers.

Our relationship shifted and grew when I returned to flying after bearing and nursing my daughter, Cameron. Bill loaned me lecture tapes about mothering that his wife, Marilyn, had found helpful. He didn't get bored following me from toy store to toy store in Narita, Japan, while I tested the noise level and educational value of toddlers' toys.

One night in the Narita View Hotel, six of us lounged in the hotel crew room, systematically emptying the vending machine of beer and cheering the players in a backgammon tournament. I always carried my portable board with me and looked forward to finding challenging players.

That night, Jim Bailey, my initial training classmate and a backgammon expert, was present. The championship round was ours. Bored with the small monetary bets we had been making, I challenged Jim to play for his black opal and diamond ring. I had long admired the ring, but Jim had always refused to bet it. Judgment clouded by the flowing beer, Jim agreed to risk it, provided I counter by betting my emerald and diamond wedding ring. That I even thought about betting my wedding ring should have told me I had had one beer too many. Soused or not, I could not quite put my ring on the table. What I did was write a check for the value of Jim's ring. If I won, I got his ring. If he won, he got a big check. He lost. I admired how well that gorgeous stone looked on my hand. As the party ended, Bill suggested that he walk me back to my room. That sent up a red flag for me, but I allowed it. Had the beer changed his attitude toward me? Was I volunteering for a grappling session? He simply walked me to my room and saw me safely inside.

I awakened in the morning when he knocked at my door for breakfast. I blearily cracked my door open the several inches the safety chain permitted and croaked, "Food?

Ugh!" His closed hand shot through the crack. "Take these. You'll feel better," he said as he emptied four aspirin into my palm. I was moved that he would think of nursing me. *Hmm. Smart. Funny. Handsome. Kind. Trustworthy.* My feelings for him were shifting toward dangerous. *Could be trouble, but I'm glad he's my friend.*

Months later, a five-day layover in Hong Kong together forced us to confide about and cope with the new layers our friendship was developing. I was excited when I saw my schedule that month, two weeks of great layover cities with two of my favorite pilots.

Captain Buck Jennings billed himself as a simple country boy who liked to fly. His muttonchop whiskers marked him as not being concerned with current fashion, but his interests and attitudes were quite modern. His love for his wife and family was overt, and he paid more than lip service to the idea of females being equal in intelligence and ability. His attitude in the cockpit was easygoing but thorough. Dicey situations were handled with skill and humor. Better yet, he read the same kinds of books as Bill and I, so I could look forward to book swapping and discussion.

However, when they caught me with a romance novel, Bill said, "How can you read that slop? I expect that from bimbettes, not someone of your intelligence."

"Have you ever read one, Bill?"

"No!"

"Don't you feel a little stupid condemning a whole genre without ever having done any research?"

"I would be embarrassed just to be *seen* with one, let alone read one."

"Why don't I loan you one that I guarantee will not be insulting to your intelligence? After you read it, you can honestly condemn the whole lot if you want to."

Bill agreed to read a book of my choice. I gave him Diana Gabaldon's *Outlander.* I don't know why *Outlander* was filed in bookstores under romance instead of literature, but the odd filing was convenient for my experiment in introducing a macho pilot to the joys of romance. (Later, he said, "I didn't want to like that book, but I really did. Are all romances that good?" No they aren't. But Diana Gabaldon converted another dozen male pilots over the years, and I loved being the agent of the transformation.)

Buck and Bill and I started a month-long backgammon tournament on the first leg of the trip. My board was out in the cockpit, in the crew limo, and in hotel lobbies and bars. I was more skilled. They had to hope for luck. They laughed together at some of my more outrageous suggestions for game stakes. They were good-natured about having to carry my luggage and shopping bags. They served my coffee and meals on the plane and picked up the tabs at restaurants. I had flowers in my room and on my engineer's desk in the plane. They took me dancing, and I never had to sit out a song. They did draw the line at doing my laundry.

Buck contracted a cold just before Hong Kong, so Bill and I did not see him there. Bill and his wife had honeymooned in the Far East and had explored Hong Kong to an extent that I'd never had the time to. Bill became my guide.

I had read about Hong Kong since I was a young child, fiction and nonfiction. I knew the history. James Clavell's *Tai-Pan* and *Noble House* had immersed me in its flavor. I wanted to visit all the places I had seen only in my head as pages had come alive for me. I needed to experience Government House, Victoria Tram, the floating restaurants in Aberdeen, high tea at the Peninsula Hotel, the ships in Repulse Bay, shopping in the street market of the fishing village at Stanley, and the city of floating sampans where some people lived and died without ever setting foot on land.

Bill and I hiked around Victoria Peak, seeing the legendary island spread below us. We rode the red double-decked bus to Stanley. He marveled at my shopping stamina and laughed at my haggling with the Chinese merchants. I had been told it was a terrible loss of face to pay the first asking price, that I must negotiate, even if I thought the first price was reasonable. Bill, more experienced with the Chinese and the normal price ranges, saw that the merchants were taking advantage of me. He also saw that I was having fun and let me go on having it. We sat on the sea wall at

Stanley and lunched and watched the boats on the horizon.

Hong Kong was the most romantic city I had ever been in. I couldn't pinpoint the reason why. I didn't like crowds and dirt and smog and slums and children laboring. I didn't like insane traffic and incessant noise. Hong Kong had all of these. Nevertheless, its ceaseless, churning energy was vitalizing at a gut level. Its blend of history and legend and Asian mystery was intoxicating. As Bill and I explored and learned and played, I found him intoxicating too.

One sunny, hot and muggy afternoon we ran to catch a bus and lurched to our seats in the rear as the driver pulled back into traffic. As we tumbled onto the bench seat, my back pressed across Bill's chest. We were both laughing. We both felt a flash of heat between us. In that moment, a second's connection of flesh, our relationship changed again. Bill had been one of the guys to me, one whom I liked and enjoyed more than most, one whom I had confided in more than anyone at work. But one of the guys. Suddenly he was a man to my woman. And I knew by the way he had fallen silent with me that the same thing had just happened to him.

"We need to talk about this," I said, looking for agreement in his eyes. I had enough experience to know that true friends were forever but lovers came and went. I didn't want to lose Bill over a mating of flesh that could only lead to guilt and remorse and our marriages being blown.

I had not realized until that moment how much I had come to value our relationship and how unwilling I was to jeopardize it. I was more unwilling to lose Bill's friendship than I was unwilling to be unfaithful. My marriage was already in deep trouble, and I was refusing to acknowledge that even to myself.

We did the right things by each other and our spouses. It was very difficult. Because we shared a time in which we struggled to keep our hands off each other and were able to talk about the process, we opened a door to a true intimacy between us that I'd not really had with any other man.

I had a history of falling for the hot and edgy challenge of bad guys. All my men had been bright and funny and charismatic and sexy but emotionally unavailable. I had never been nurtured by a man. I didn't think I even needed that nurturing, but I was mistaken. What was distinctly different about my relationship with Bill was that he *listened* to me and offered support, even if he disagreed with me. He accepted the things he didn't like about me and celebrated the things he thought were wonderful. When I was down, he buoyed me up. When I was up, he laughed with me.

In a perverse way, it was my relationship with Bill that kept me capable of continuing to work on my marriage. My spirit was being eroded at home, and I was beginning an emotional withdrawal and shutdown that would eventually lead to a descending spiral of acute mental disorder. Loving Bill and Bill's loving me was the glue that held my shattering self together.

26

THE
UNDERMANNED 747
1987

"**Y**ay, Barb! We get to fly together for a whole month! I'm so jazzed!" I called Barbara Ganzkow as soon as the schedules were published. "Let's see how our captain takes to being a minority. We're going to have fun!"

"I think I'm going to have to put a leash on you to make sure you behave yourself," she replied.

We had met in 1977, when I was a probationary engineer on my first international flight with passengers and Barbara was a flight attendant. A petite and pretty blonde, she was warm and funny. I liked her immediately.

Barbara had been a flight attendant for Flying Tigers for five years when she sat down next to me in the cockpit and said, "I think I might be in the wrong job." She had earned her commercial pilot's license but hadn't thought that commercial piloting was a viable career option for a woman. She needed to build her flight time, and we talked about what she would have to do to be competitive with other applicants.

Two years later, Barbara became Flying Tigers' seventh woman pilot. When we eventually became good friends, she confided that she had not liked me at first because I had appeared to be full of myself and aloof, but as she got to know me, she learned that my aloofness had been caused by my fear that flight attendants would hate me.

Barbara and I flew with three different captains during our month together. Crew gossips explained that Barb and I kept wearing them out or that our performances were so scary, the captains kept bailing out on us. Actually, it was simply a matter of scheduling around a senior pilot who had vacation that month.

Our first captain was Dick Crawford, a pilot neither of us had flown with. We had met him on layovers but didn't know how he was in the cockpit. It was a good sign that he didn't have a reputation. Captains who were difficult to work with or who had marginal flying ability were widely discussed by copilots.

Barbara and I arrived early at Los Angeles International Airport on the night of our first flight with Dick. We learned that he would be a few minutes late due to ground transportation problems, so we did the paperwork and went to the airplane without him. My intention was to have everything ready except for his signature on the paperwork, hoping that he would be impressed with my efficiency and cut me some slack in areas that I was feeling insecure about.

Even though I had flown the 747 in the copilot's seat before, I was new to it again after my maternity leaves and spending the previous two years in the 747 engineer's seat. Perhaps it was that insecurity or just being around Barb, who always had me laughing, that led me to behave so outrageously when Dick arrived.

We could hear his arrival on the lower cargo deck and the solid clomp of his cowboy boots on the ladder to the cockpit and the upper-deck galley and lounge. Our lounge was filled with fifteen deadheading female flight attendants. As Dick's head came into view, I could see him look around to check who was on board. As he met the laughing and challenging eyes of seventeen women who were waiting for his reaction to an all-female crew, his eyes did not widen. I was impressed with that.

I leaned from my seat, as his body emerged waist high from the opening above the ladder, and said, "Captain

Crawford, the airplane is ready to go. Before you sit down, would you please do coffee? I take mine black and Barbara prefers one cream, one sugar."

Barbara's eyes did widen, and I could sense her unspoken "Bad girl!" But there was no reaction from Dick. *Hmmm,* I thought, and spoke again. "You might want to see if the girls in back need anything."

Dick reached the top of the ladder, set down his flight bag, and poured coffee for everyone on board before he sat in the captain's left seat. The next 20 minutes were businesslike. Dick reviewed the flight plan to San Francisco, checked the weather reports and notices to airmen, read the ship's log, and listened carefully to Barbara's report of her preflight examination of the outside and lower deck of the 747. He checked my loading of our en route navigational data, signed the necessary paperwork, and approved the amount of fuel I had asked for.

Finally, our preparations were up to the reading of the preflight checklist. The pilot who is going to fly the plane, traditionally the captain on the first leg of a trip, normally calls for the checklist.

Dick turned to me and asked, "Whose leg is this?" Captains *never* asked this question. *Yes!* I thought. *I can have some fun here.*

"Well, sir," I replied, working hard to maintain a straight face, "Barb and I have discussed that and we've decided that if you are really nice, if you carry our baggage and buy all our drinks, we might *split legs* with you later."

In my peripheral vision I saw the holy-shit-you've-done-it-now look on Barb's face. I studied Dick's face and saw a decision being made. He called for the checklist and flew us to SFO. The tone was set. Dick Crawford was smart enough to get the jokes. He was man enough to take them. He was playful enough to join in. But there was no doubt about who was in charge.

I flew the second leg from SFO to Anchorage. I felt comfortable enough with Dick by then to tell him I was feeling green at my job. I asked how he personally figured out when it was time to start the descent into our destination.

It was always wise for a copilot to know how a captain did this because there were a number of viable ways to do it, but generally, a captain liked it done his way so he knew exactly what was going on.

Dick and I discussed the options. Then he said, "A crusty old captain once told me that the surefire way to know when to descend is when the captain puts on his shoulder harness." Attaching the shoulder harness to the lap seatbelt was the first item on the descent checklist. *Well, that's cool,* I thought. *I'll just check my calculations against Dick's putting on his shoulder harness. Easy.*

As we neared Anchorage, I figured that we needed to start our descent at 132 miles out, based on our airspeed, groundspeed, weight, and type of engine. ATC had cleared us to descend at our discretion, but 132 miles out had come and gone with Dick not attaching his shoulder harness. I was mentally reworking the descent plan. *What had I not considered?* Then 120 miles out came and went. Still no shoulder harness. When 100 miles out arrived, I was flustered with confusion. *We should have started our descent,* I thought. I could no longer come up with any plan that did not put us too high, too close. But Dick had not touched his shoulder harness.

At 95 miles out, I gave up trying to second-guess Dick and started our descent. Dick turned to me from the magnificent view he had been gazing at through his side window for the last 30 miles and revealed what his averted head had hidden. He was choking with swallowed laughter. He had concealed his glee at my stupidity. *He set me up,* I fumed. I felt zero remorse for his ensuing discomfort in watching me dive bomb at the airport in a nonstandard catch-up descent. When we parked in ANC, I turned to Dick and said, "Captain, sir, you are an asshole."

"Good," Dick replied. "You got the lesson. When you're flying, *you're* flying. Never count on assholes to help out."

Dick was meeting friends in Anchorage so Barbara and I were on our own. We got all dolled up and proceeded to the F Street Bar, a favorite haunt of Flying Tiger crewmembers. It was popular for several reasons. The bartenders and service people were all attractive females. The food and drinks were excellent. And best for me, the place had large windows and airy décor so I could see who was coming and going at the crew hotel next door.

The F Street was where we went to find company for breakfast, lunch, dinner, exercise, or shopping. Barbara and I entered, and all eyes turned our way. I called out, "We need two men for dinner, dancing, and karaoke. Any interested, moneyed hard bodies line up."

The next morning at the airport, while getting ready to fly to Tokyo, Dick scoffed, "You two can get away with anything! If I had pulled that routine at F Street last night, I would have been escorted out."

"Dick," I explained, "there are many disadvantages to being a female in aviation. We have to take advantage of the few pluses just to even out the score."

As I taxied the airplane toward Runway 32 in Anchorage, the tower called Dick to say, "Tiger 72, tell him to keep it rolling. You are cleared for immediate takeoff."

Dick replied, "You mean, tell *her* to keep it rolling. I have a woman copilot."

Tower replied in a bored tone, "Roger."

Dick, intent on enlightening the fellow, said, "*And* I have a woman engineer."

Someone sharp was working the tower because he said immediately, "Now that's what I call an *undermanned* 747!" I was laughing so hard that my centerline positioning was wobbling on the takeoff roll.

"You're not skiing here, Norah; keep it straight," Dick advised. I straightened the plane out, but all three of us continued to laugh.

In Tokyo, Barbara told me, privately, that I had been picking on her. I was aghast to realize that I had several times criticized the way she did her job. We had been trained at different times on the 747, and different techniques had been taught while I was on maternity leave. Unconsciously, in my insecurity, I had been searching for a way to seem competent in some area and thus had been making suggestions about Barbara's job. Barbara did an excellent job without anyone's

FLYING TIGRESS

help. She readily accepted my apology and my promise not to do it again.

I chose to share our conversation and my resolution with Dick and was embarrassed to note that he gave a sigh of relief. He had noticed my bad behavior and was glad that he wasn't going to have to call my attention to it. The captain's job of coordinating his crew to work peacefully together is seldom an easy one.

Our communicating well reminded me of a story another copilot told me of a personality conflict in a cockpit that led to a near-total breakdown of communications. Jack's crew was flying from Honolulu to Fiji to Sydney. This was a killer flight by anyone's standards. They left Honolulu at 3 a.m. local time, having received their wake-up call at midnight. Under the best circumstances, they would have fallen asleep at 5 p.m. and had seven hours of sleep. Unfortunately, at 5 p.m. their hotel was crowded with tourists returning from a day at the beach, planning on having a few cocktails and leaving for an evening of partying. Despite earplugs, it was difficult to sleep in the early evenings at hotels while preparing for a night departure.

Sydney-bound flight crews usually started their flights already fatigued. Then they flew six hours to the Fiji Islands, arriving with the sunrise in their eyes at 9 a.m. Hawaii time. Jack's crew was scheduled for less than an hour on the ground in Fiji. But things slow down in Fiji when the sun and heat come up, and they spent two hours on the ground. Adding to the fatigue level was ongoing tension between Jack and his captain. They had argued in New York at the beginning of their trip. They had argued again in Los Angeles. The engineer might have been able to mediate if he had liked either one of the pilots. But he didn't. He chose to make himself absent from the cockpit as often as possible, saying later that he had only been trying to protect himself from being wounded by the lethal barbs constantly flying through the cockpit.

This dysfunctional crew departed Fiji at 11 a.m. Hawaii time and was scheduled to land in Australia at 3 p.m. Hawaiian time. At 120 miles from Sydney, Jack thought it was time to

210

start their descent. When the captain didn't start down, Jack thought of giving him a reminder but decided not to save the guy from embarrassing himself. At 90 miles out, still at 33,000 feet, Jack thought again of saying something but decided not to. At 50 miles out, still cruising at 33,000, Jack began to feel his years of professionalism win out.

Sure, they weren't breaking any laws. They weren't endangering their airplane. But his captain was making a visible and embarrassing error. The copilot's first job is to keep his captain safe, but making him look good is not required. Finally, at 30 miles out and still at 33,000 feet, Jack overcame his animosity toward the captain and said, "Gee. Have you given any thought to starting a descent here?"

The captain looked at Jack with malice and incredulity. "Hey, Jack, do you remember who made the takeoff in Fiji?" Jack was so tired, he had not remembered that he was supposed to be flying the plane. And his captain chose not to remind him.

I shared this story with Dick and Barbara while we were in Tokyo. It's easy to laugh at behavior when it doesn't end in tragedy but in a lesson learned. None of us wanted to ever take part in a scene like that.

Barbara and I got to swim together in Japan. We were both "water babies." Doing laps together in hotel pools was one of our favorite pastimes. Barbara could imitate the way dolphins swim. I was fascinated with this because I had swum with dolphins in the wild and had a special affinity for their intelligent playfulness. Even though Barb patiently showed me how to wave my body longitudinally and hold my legs together while kicking forward and back, I could never do it as naturally as she did. Watching her undulating around evoked my wondrous memories of dolphins.

My childhood was filled with moves from one coast to another. We grew up on beaches. Sometimes we would see dolphins swimming beyond the breaking waves and even riding the waves into shallower water. It was thrilling to have them catch a wave beside us while we were bodysurfing. But when I tried to touch a dolphin sliding down a wave front beside me, he would move out of reach. I first touched a dolphin when I was twenty-one years old and crewing on a 50-foot sailboat, crossing from Panama to the Galapagos Islands to Hawaii.

Midway across the Pacific Ocean, I was at the helm on the noon-to-three watch when I noticed something odd on the horizon behind us. The sky's milky blue with a few high scudding clouds was meeting the slate blue of the ocean on three horizons in an unbroken line. The horizon to our rear looked as if a white zigzag had been sewn on the line where the sky and ocean met. As I looked with interest at that scalloped line, it began to grow. Facing the stern of the schooner, I saw this line of white foam extend from as far as I could see to the left to as far as I could see to the right. And it continued to grow. I remembered reading sailors' accounts of what tsunamis looked like at sea. They described the horizon looking different, swelling and rising as they watched.

Whatever was happening in the ocean behind us, it was huge and it was growing closer quickly. The line of white had grown from $\frac{1}{4}$ inch to 2 inches. Those inches, from my deck-side view, were actually miles and miles of white water moving toward us. I called all hands on deck. The four crewmembers and the dog, Quincy, watched transfixed as the mysterious phenomenon rolled toward us. An overwhelming sense of inevitability and acceptance surged through me. Whatever was coming, we were going to meet it together and alone. Our radio was no longer operational. We could not send an SOS.

As the white water neared our stern, Quincy's barking coincided with our gasps of surprise because we could finally see what was causing the ocean to boil—dolphins. Thousands and thousands of leaping and torpedoing and playing dolphins were moving in a giant migration that exceeded the speed of our boat. Babies and their mothers, larger males, old and young, all moved together. Soon, the huge expanse of swimming dolphins engulfed the boat and swam on. For some amazing minutes, all distances viewable by the human eye were filled with dolphins. The ocean was frothing from our forward to our rear horizon and from our port to starboard horizons.

I ran to the bowsprit and climbed into the netting below it. On my stomach, nose down to the sea, I trailed my arms and legs in the water. The dolphins nudged my hands and feet. At last I could touch a dolphin. Their skin was moist, velvety-cool suede. They played in the small bow wave beneath me. Some arched into the air above the bowsprit. I wanted to roll in and grab a dorsal fin for propulsion. I wanted to swim with them and undulate along and leap into the air with great splashing joy. The dolphin's sleek body, master dancer in its element, became the symbol of my love of the ocean.

Dolphining around with Barb in the Tokyo swimming pool became a spiritual respite that left both of us calm for the chaos we would face together the next day in the skies over the Philippines.

One-hundred miles north of Manila, we had been told to expect a localizer approach to Runway 12. I was not happy about being given a nonprecision approach because, by their very definition, they are not precise, and flying one meant making many adjustments at the last moment. It was critical, in a nonprecision approach, to get configured and stabilized early. Because I was green, I chose to get set up miles early. Being set up early and totally stabilized was part of what saved our lives.

I had asked for final approach flaps and commanded the gear down at about 10 miles out. The before-landing checklist was complete. As the aircraft flew to 1 mile from the start of the final descent, I reduced the throttle setting to give me the speed I wanted to maintain on the final approach.

Calculating and maintaining the correct approach speed in jets is critical, not only to safely staying in the air but also to being able to stop after landing while still on the runway. The speed is predicated on the weight of the aircraft adjusted for wind and possible turbulence. If the speed gets too slow, the nose of the aircraft gets too high and the wind over the wings begins burbling. Consequently, the lift required to continue flying is lost. This is called a stall. It has nothing to do with an engine stalling like in a car. The wings stall. A sensor on the leading edge of the wing senses

213

airflow and sends a warning to the cockpit if the wing is near stalling. The warning is a riveting attention getter—the control wheel begins shaking and a loud, obnoxious rat-a-tat noise blares. We call it a "stickshaker."

Getting a stickshaker close to the ground indicates an extreme emergency. If the pilot does not take immediate and appropriate corrective action, the plane will crash.

I began the final descent into Manila with the power already set and my speed exact. When we reached our minimum altitude, I adjusted the throttles to maintain the speed in straight and level flight. We entered a low level of scattered clouds, and Dick's attention was out of the front windscreen. We needed visual contact with the runway before we could continue our approach.

Knowing that both Dick and Barb were looking outside, my eyes were steady on the instruments. I saw the airspeed indicator bounce up 10 knots. A sudden and unexplained change in airspeed can be the only indication a pilot will get of an impending windshear, a large change in wind direction that can result in a huge loss of speed. Our plane was not in unstable air, and I had not changed the controls. It looked so like a classic case of simulator-checkride windshear that I doubted what I saw. The correct action was to add power, but if I misinterpreted the situation in this phase of flight, the immediate result would be extra speed that I might not be able to get rid of before landing. Doubtful or not, I pushed the throttles forward. Dick's attention was in the cockpit in a flash.

"What are you doing? We'll have to miss the approach if you add power here," he exclaimed. I was still doubtful; there had been no adverse weather reported, after all, but I was committed.

"I think we're getting a windshear," I said, with not a lot of conviction. Nevertheless, I was pushing the throttles to maximum power, and we were already 20 knots faster than normal in level flight. As both Dick and I opened our mouths to further the discussion, a windshear hit in full thundering fury. We lost 45 knots of airspeed, and the stickshaker beat out its warning.

In that one second of blue and white lightning fire arcing across the windshield, the white-clouded sky gone to charcoal, and the simultaneous bone-crushing, wing-bending turbulence, I was sure we were about to die.

We were 1,200 feet above the ground and our jet had just quit flying. (It flashed through my head that this is how the Delta guys felt in the moments before they hit the ground in Dallas after they had flown into unrecoverable windshear.) *But I didn't do anything wrong!* my mind screamed. Then there was no time for thinking. Just reaction and flying and calling out the checklist that I had memorized and practiced in the simulator.

Max power. Plane nose attitude up to 15 degrees or stickshaker. Maintain heading. Maintain configuration. Hell, the four throttles were already firewalled. They had been shoved full forward as soon as the speed had started to bleed off to that unbelievable 45-knot airspeed loss. I didn't have to do anything about the plane's attitude either, we were in level flight with the full tooth-rattling stickshaker pounding.

My left hand was pinned to the throttles by Dick's right hand mashing mine, as if our hands together could get the throttles to go further than the mechanical stops. My right hand was on the yoke, white knuckled with the effort of holding the plane level. The 747's massive landing gear was down and locked. Raising the gear would reduce drag and allow us to gain airspeed, but it would also, for too many long seconds, open the garage-door-sized gear doors and add to our drag.

That heart-pounding moment in the skies over the Philippines was clearly a case of the if-it-is-still-flying-don't-change-it rule. Dick didn't yell, "I have it!" Later, he would say that it had been his first thought, to take over. His second thought, he said, was, "It's still flying. Don't change it." And so the next seconds in that shaking, howling airplane were spent voiceless in a frozen tableau. There was nothing left to be done but ride it out, to the ground or to recovery. In those hour-long seconds, I thought of my children. In God's hands.

Then the airspeed indicator began to rise; I had time to trim the forward pressure out of the yoke; and the lightning stopped. The yoke quit throbbing with the stickshaker's warning of impending stall, and we broke out of the clouds into a calm summer sky. The airspeed climbed to normal, so I began to ease back on the throttles. We no longer needed 200,000 screaming horses to keep us in the sky.

"Fly the missed-approach procedure," Dick commanded in a normal tone of voice, as he keyed his microphone to inform Manila tower that Tiger Flight 18 was going around for another approach. *This man must have balls of steel*, I thought when I heard his tone of voice.

After Dick reported, "Severe windshear on final at 1,200 feet and loss of 45 knots of airspeed," Manila tower said, "Roger, turn left to 120 degrees and expect vectors for another localizer approach to runway 12."

"I don't think so," Dick replied. "We require a different runway." Dick's maintaining a calm professional tone of voice while reporting the massive windshear had not conveyed to Manila that we had *just cheated death of three pilots.*

While Dick talked to Manila tower, I noticed that the plane was not accelerating to the speed I had set the throttles for, and, indeed, there was a rumbling vibration that was not normal for this phase of flight.

I searched the cockpit's forward instrument panel for some sign of abnormality and found none. There were no yellow warning lights illuminated. There were no red do-something-now lights illuminated. Our front panel was all white and black and green, just the way it should be. I voiced my concerns about the airspeed and vibration to Dick and Barbara.

Dick was the one who discovered the problem. He had the grace not to laugh as he pointed to our front instrument panel and its three green lights that indicated our landing gear was down and locked. Normally, on a missed approach, the flying pilot's first callout would be, "Going around. Max power. Positive rate. Gear up." In the flurry of activity required by the emergency, and in the moments that I realized we were not going to crash and tried to return my racing heart and mind to normal, I had completely missed the go around procedure.

No wonder the airplane wasn't accelerating. We had eighteen huge tires hanging out in the slipstream. And no wonder the aircraft was still vibrating. It was not designed to fly around at high speeds with the wheels dragging underneath the fuselage.

After an uneventful second approach and landing, we parked at the cargo terminal in Manila. I exited the airplane to exercise off some of the adrenaline pounding in my bloodstream. Barbara was close behind me.

We talked about what had just happened and how we were going to con our nervous systems into thinking that it was perfectly okay to get back on that plane and fly it on to Hong Kong. We also worked out a plan about how we could be nonchalantly "macha" about the whole experience and *still* get Dick to pick up the tab for the bottle of Dom Perignon we deemed necessary to celebrate surviving our near-death experience.

In Hong Kong, over dinner and drinks, Dick and Barb and I reviewed the incident. We agreed that my having gone through a checkride in Los Angeles right before leaving on this trip had been a factor in the Manila approach turning out so successful.

In real life, the first subtle signs of windshear are hard to diagnose correctly, mainly because every approach to land in a jumbo jet is filled with constant small adjustments to all parameters. But I had been spring-loaded by recent training to call an airspeed fluctuation an emergency.

That night in Hong Kong, Dick and Barb and I raised our glasses. "Here's to cheating death again." *Being macha about emergencies is so much more fun on the ground.*

After ten days of thoroughly enjoying flying with Dick, Barbara and I decided to show our appreciation of his humor and camaraderie by making him officially "one of the girls." Barb and I had bought matching navy blue roses sewn on ribbons to wear as our "uniform" ties during our month together. Tiger women pilots were rarely seen together so their uniforms could be compared, which left us free to be

217

creative with what we wore. Essentially, anything we had on was the "official" uniform.

While waiting in a hotel lobby for our transportation to the airport, we presented Dick with the lady pilot's blue-rose tie and helped him replace his boy's tie with it.

"Looks good on him, doesn't it, Barb?" I said while adjusting the rose to center. "It sure brings out the blue in his eyes. I bet the guys will be jealous."

Dick wore his fluffy rose with dignity. If anyone dared to say, "Captain Crawford, nice tie," Dick would respond by fluffing it and grinning. He wore it for the rest of the trip.

Yellow magic markers are a part of every pilot's flight kit. We use them to highlight pertinent weather on our ten-page international weather "briefings" and to mark our route of flight on densely printed aviation charts. I noticed that Dick carried six colors other than the standard yellow, each color assigned a specific duty. Red was for east-west routes; green was for west-east routes; violet was for north-south routes, and so forth. This seemed like a dandy idea, so I frequently borrowed Dick's markers to augment my yellow. This borrowing was so regular that Dick started each flight by placing his markers on the center console where I could reach them without having to disturb him.

Two weeks after our flight together, I received an unmarked brown paper parcel at my home address. There was no note. The package contained six different shades of pink magic markers—rose-petal pink, petunia pink, sunset pink, shocking pink, iridescent pink, and pastel pink. *Ah Dick*, I thought, *of course a lady pilot should have lady-pilot-pink markers. How clever.* What was puzzling to me, though, was the inclusion in the package of a large dark green marker. It took me a long time to finally get it. Across the side of this wide marker was printed, BROAD marker.

Our second captain that month was Garrett Wight. Barb and I had flown with Garrett before and knew him to be bright and funny. My first mistake on that flight was to think that the bawdy, irreverent humor so enjoyed with Dick would be equally acceptable to the more cerebral, born-in-Maine conservative Garrett.

We left LAX at midnight for a stop in SFO before going to Anchorage. At 4 a.m., we were abeam Seattle, with hours still to fly. Garrett slid his seat back as far as it would go. "I'm sorry, ladies. I'm enjoying your company, but I think I'm going to have to shut my eyes for a while. I'm getting too old for this all-night stuff. Are you okay with that, Norah?"

"Don't worry about *staying up* Garrett. I' m really, really good at getting men to *stay up* all night. Lots of practice. You won't be sleeping *on me*." I gave him a bold wink and laughed. The look on Garret's face told me I had gone too far just as accurately as Barbara silently mouthing, "Down girl!" at the edge of my peripheral vision.

He replied, "Do you always open your mouth before your tongue has a chance to connect to your brain?" *Oh no. I've made an error in judgment here.* My vivacious, anything-goes attitude squashed, I turned a somber face to Garrett.

"I am so sorry. I didn't mean to offend you, and I can see I have. I promise you I will control myself in the future and behave in an appropriate manner. While you're sleeping, I'll ask Barb what appropriate looks like." He did laugh at that and rolled into his nap.

We flew with Garrett to Tokyo, where he ran out of flight time for the month and flew home on JAL. I had restored myself in his good favor with professional *and* ladylike behavior. He had ramp personnel take photos of us three. Like Dick Crawford, he had never flown with two women pilots before.

While waiting for Garrett's replacement, Barbara and I had time to walk to the ancient temple in the heart of the village of Narita, a serene spot we had visited together before. Tiny things like the turn of a word and the subtleties of creating a working atmosphere in the cockpit and the differences between how men and women communicate became inconsequential amongst the centuries-old stones and gardens and fishponds.

Captain Bob Poindexter was our third and last man of the month. I had worked with Bob many times before and didn't think my humor would surprise him, but I was careful not to frivolously blurt out everything that came to mind.

He, too, was flying with two women on his crew for the first time. He said he was delighted at the prospect.

I took advantage of his having taught in the simulator and on the line for many years and appealed to his teacher persona. I knew he liked to share his vast knowledge of aviation. He had a special way of proffering information without inferring that the student was stupid. He had mastered the art of constructive criticism. Bob and Barb and I flew uneventfully from Tokyo to Seoul to Osaka to Tokyo and Anchorage. We parted there.

True to how it seems to go in airline flying, whenever I particularly enjoyed working with a special crew, we never flew together again.

27

WINDSHEAR OVER THE VOLCANO
1987

*O*ur years as pilots were filled with moments that could have gone terribly wrong if we had made different decisions. Our good judgment and the experiences that contributed to that judgment were what we got paid for. I had one of those definitive moments while flying with Captain Ron "Santa Claus" Hall in 1987.

We were flying through storm-filled winter skies with a load of horses destined for Kagoshima, Japan. This particular runway, though wide and long and serviced by a trusty instrument landing system, was nevertheless a red-flagged landing spot. Not only was the approach end over the ocean but also a tall, sheer cliff marked the meeting of sea and land. A rapid change of ground temperature usually produced turbulence or windshear. Complicating that natural phenomenon was the presence of an active volcano on an island not far offshore. I had rarely seen it without some type of emission coming from it. When we approached this airport in bad weather, we didn't know if the clouds might contain rain, hail, turbulence, volcanic ash, or live embers.

That day we were tossed around the cloud interiors with seatbelt-tightening regularity. We always used engine anti-ice on descent in the 747, but seldom needed wing anti-ice. We needed its blasting heat that day. The reported ground visibility would not allow visual contact with the airport environment until we were 300 feet from the ground on final approach. Because of ATC instructions for our descent, it was not practical to have the autopilot do the flying.

I was flying and had the guys configure the plane and run the checklists as soon as they could. We were carrying a maximum additive of 20 knots on our approach speed because of the wind velocity and gusting. Though we always do approaches with the engines spooled up so we have the least lag time if we need extra power, the fact is, in jets there *is* some lag between pushing the throttles forward and producing useable thrust. (One reason propeller-driven planes recover from windshear better than jets is that their power increase is almost instantaneous.)

Ron, with many years of being a pilot instructor, frequently had interesting tidbits of fine-tuning instructions to relate. On our layover fast walk of the day before, I had asked him what single thing he had seen most frequently screwed up in the cockpit. His response was that when pilots needed to add power on an approach, they seldom added enough. It was an understandable error because landing a jet with too much speed is arguably as dangerous as landing one with too little; the great mass of the 747 does not slow down quickly if too much power has been added.

Bumping along through the ice-driven sky toward touchdown at Kagoshima, I did not have time to reflect on yesterday's conversation. Ron called out runway in sight at 300 feet, and I looked out the window. The runway centerline was lined up straight ahead. We were on speed and on glideslope. I was still using large aileron input to keep the wings level but feeling comfortable with our position. We were in the slot. Descending out of 150 feet at a sink rate of 800 feet per minute, we suddenly heard "Glide Slope. Glide Slope. Sink Rate." It was our mechanical-voice warning of an out-of-parameters situation.

At 100 feet there wasn't time to fix it. I jammed the throttles full forward and raised the nose. "Going around,"

I gritted out. How I hated to get that far and then have to abandon the touchdown. My eyes were still directed outside the plane as I waited for Ron to call "positive rate," indicating that we were climbing and could raise the gear.

To my horror I could see that we weren't going anywhere upward. Max power had not been enough. Then the main tires slid on the ground and our ground spoilers extended, breaking the airflow over the wings. I yanked the power levers to their rear stops and pulled the four thrust reversers back to maximum reversing. Now my problem was getting the plane to stop before all the horses were knocked to their knees with the deceleration forces of brakes and reversers. Water on the runway didn't help. *Too late to worry about hydroplaning.* We slid down to the end of the runway, and finally stopped. Only then did I notice people with TV lights and cameras at the end of the runway. They were filming us, unaware of their precarious position.

As I steered the 747 through a 90-degree turn at the end of the runway, Ron made eye contact and queried, "How're you doing Norah?"

I assessed exactly how I *was* doing.

"Hair's standing up a little with the adrenaline rush, but that won't interfere with my parking this bird." I looked at Ron again. "Babe, you're looking a little peaked yourself. You want to park her and save yourself any more O'Neill-generated excitement today?"

"Nah, chicken, you got her. I'm really glad you didn't hesitate with the power."

"Yeah, well Santa wasn't a half bad instructor."

Turned out we had the Japanese version of Mr. Ed on board. That's why our arrival was being filmed. Luckily, all the horses were still standing uninjured when we parked.

Perhaps because I had children I wanted to be around to raise, or perhaps because I was getting older, the we-cheated-death-again experiences were beginning to be less thrilling and more wearing on my psyche. I loved flying and liked my job, but I sometimes wondered about a profession where I spent the bulk of my time sitting on the edge of an uncomfortable seat in a noisy, dirty place just waiting to respond quickly to the next life-threatening emergency.

*L*aughter lightened our stress and fears, and we laughed often. On a muggy but brilliant morning in Fiji, I walked with my crew along a lanai in the restricted area of the Nandi International airport. All transiting jumbo jets nosed up to this raised deck and loaded and unloaded passengers from it.

As we approached our silver 747, we could see the previous crew still in the cockpit, getting ready to leave it for us to fly on to Sydney. When they noticed our approach, all heads swiveled in our direction. Then there was an unusual flurry of activity around the copilot's seat that I was to occupy. We could see one grin-stretched face.

When they climbed down the stairs to where we were waiting, I knew in my gut that another "box-office" moment was coming. Bob Stickler was the deplaning copilot. He and I went way back, and the memories were good. His no-bullshit manner and bawdy sense of humor had earned him the nickname "Max Gross" among the pilot group. He deserved that name. What I appreciated about him was not only his treating me with professional respect and his entertainment value, but also his strong insistence in the cockpit that pilots not get creative about flying on his shift.

Our first flight together had been with Captain High and Hot, a copilot's nightmare. This man consistently approached airports by diving from too high an altitude with too much airspeed and the throttles full back at idle. I thought this formula was a recipe for disaster. That H and H had not had a disaster in his career was a miracle, but he saw it as proof that his way worked.

I was an engineer when I first flew with H and H and had told him repeatedly that I was uncomfortable with the way he approached airports. When my concerns were not echoed by the copilot, H and H ignored me until I just shut up and held on. When Stickler, who had replaced that co-pilot, saw the captain's first approach into Rio de Janeiro, he explained to him why his approach was unsafe and asked him to do it differently. H and H ignored him. Stick then said, "In which direction do you want me to tell ATC you are going to do your 360-degree turn?" H and H was confused by this question.

"Why would I want to make a 360-degree turn?"

"In order to lose this extra altitude safely," Stick replied. H and H mused that answer while he continued to plummet toward the airport. When it was clear the captain was not going to change anything, Stick keyed his microphone and requested a left 360-degree turn from ATC.

Addressing the captain, he said, "Either you start the turn now, or I'm going to take the control of this fucking airplane away from you and do it myself." H and H made the turn. *Thank you, Bob!*

We paused for Bob Stickler's inbound crew on the lanai in Fiji that day and exchanged information on the airplane. As I climbed into the cockpit, I could see through the front window that Bob's crew was lingering on the lanai, watching for my reaction to whatever their joke was.

The joke was easy to see. Strapped to the center of the copilot's control wheel was a large yellow banana. Printed on the banana's skin in ballpoint pen were detailed instructions as to what I could use this banana for. The instructions were of a sexual nature—batteries not included.

My captain, a conservative man, was astonished that someone would make this kind of joke with me. He watched my next actions with relief that I was going to handle the situation myself and he would not have to get involved. I yanked the banana from the steering column, climbed with it onto a seat in the cockpit that allowed me to extend my upper body through the overhead escape hatch, and tossed that yellow fruit at Bob's feet.

"Hey, Bob," I yelled, "You're going to need this a lot more than I am on our layovers! But thanks for thinking of me. I appreciate it!"

225

Everyone laughed. En route, my captain asked how I could put up with such shit and still smile. In forming my reply, I realized what a long way I had come from being prickly and having chips on my shoulders. I was confident in having learned how to let things roll off my back. I also accepted that I had established a certain reputation with the men about just being one of the guys, which allowed them to say things to me that they would not say around other women. For instance, a man had recently told me a particularly crude joke in the cockpit, and I had responded with, "Oh, ugh! That's too nasty to be funny." Because I knew he had recently flown with Pauline Goslovich, another Tiger pilot, I asked curiously, "What did Pauline say when you told her that one?" He replied, with a surprised look, "I would never tell that to Pauline! She's a *lady!*"

So I guessed that no one was going to confuse me with a lady. I could live with that. What was harder to accept about myself was that I had developed a double standard. I, who had fought so hard against double standards, had created one myself: For men who were never going to think it was all right for women to do men's jobs, it was *not* okay to tell jokes that denigrated women or to make sexual comments to me. Because, from them, it *was* harassment. For those men who treated women with professional respect, it was okay to say whatever they wanted to me because it was innocent of bigotry. It was a fine distinction to draw, but I had learned to do it.

28

YOU CHANGED MY LIFE

1988

I met two women in 1988 at the tenth annual meeting of the International Society of Women Airline Pilots who told me that the public relations I had been coerced into doing for my employers had paid off in ways I had never imagined.

Binka Bone, a petite, brunette Eastern Airlines pilot, introduced herself to me saying, "I have been wanting to meet you for years. I was so excited to hear that you would be at the convention. You changed my life. When I was in junior high school, I heard you interviewed on the radio. I knew right then that I wanted to grow up to be an airline pilot. Thank-you, thank-you for paving the way for me. It was you who got me here."

A TWA pilot, Linda Sartnurak, introduced herself during that convention and also thanked me for my help. It was clear that I did not recognize her name, so she jogged my memory. She had been an airline ticket agent when she read an article about me in *The Seattle Times.* She got my phone number from directory assistance and called me for advice on how to become an airline pilot.

At the time of her call, I was heavily pregnant and three weeks overdue with my first child and, at the same time, was additionally hobbled with a hip-to-ankle cast on my right leg from knee surgery. I welcomed diverting phone chats. Because my short-term memory was frequently hazy during those raging-hormone days, I enjoyed talking with Linda for an hour then promptly forgot that I had. Four years later, she credited me with convincing her that she could be an airline pilot if she really wanted to. She had wanted it enough to do huge amounts of work in those intervening four years. She stood before me, arms outstretched, showing me the stripes of her pilot's uniform with great pride.

Binka and Linda changed my life that day just as I had changed theirs in the past. I had given many career-day talks at schools and colleges and had received thank-you notes from some young people who said that I had inspired them to want to fly. But I had never met someone who had gotten inspired and then done something about it.

"You changed my life." How amazingly awesome to know that. My eyes filled with tears.

Shortly after the convention, vertigo visited me again, suddenly and startlingly. I was flying a 747 with Captain Jim Theobald through a torrential downpour to Tokyo's Narita Airport. As ATC vectored us into a long downwind leg, we bumped through low clouds and the staccato pounding of heavy rain.

My plan as the flying pilot was to not look out the window until we were established on final approach. Transitioning from relying on instruments to relying principally on visual cues is a tricky time in flying.

It was important not to attempt the transition too early in the approach. When flying out of a black hole of an unlit area toward distant lights, the tendency is to descend too soon. It was equally important not to go visual too late because there might not be enough time to adjust to what can be seen from the window, such as being slightly off the centerline or having to correct for the drift of a crosswind. We generally try to alternate from instruments to visual in the last 1,000 feet of descent.

That night outside Tokyo, the measured ceiling of clouds would prevent me from seeing outside before 500 feet above the ground. Jim was briefed to call out any signs of the ground as soon as he saw them and to describe them to me. As my engineer called out his reading of the radio altimeter, "500 feet," I raised my head to look at the runway for the first time. It should have been lined up directly in front of us, stretching into the distance.

What I saw instead was Narita's Runway 16 sitting sideways across the windshield and undulating up and down while its lights blinked on and off. I went from calmly concentrated to shocked. *That can't be right.* I reverted to my instruments that plainly said I was on course.

"Windshield wipers!" I ordered Jim.

"Book says not until 300 feet," he replied.

"Windshield wipers, now!"

"You got them," he said.

When I heard the wipers' loud sweep, I dared to look out the window again. Without rivers of rain on the glass, Runway 16 was now sitting where it should be—lengthwise in front of us.

After we shut down for the night, Jim asked what had happened on final. He had flown with me often enough to know that raising my voice in the cockpit was unusual. I told him of that surreal split second when the world had tilted sideways on its axis and started to spin and blink. Only my instruments had kept us shiny side up.

"The lessons out here never end," I said to Jim. "Have you ever had a flight in which you weren't surprised at least once?" He thought for a moment and replied, "Nope. Not yet. The day I quit learning will be the day I die."

29

THE BEST LINES I EVER HEARD
1988

*O*n September 26, 1988, I started a three-week flight with Captain George Gewehr and Second Officer Jim Brendel that flew into my record book as one of life's grander times and perhaps the best trip I ever worked. What made it so magical was the electric chemistry among the three of us.

I have a weakness for smart, funny, and charismatic people; George and Jim had those characteristics. They were also warm and compassionate when I needed warmth and compassion in those days when my marriage was becoming deeply troubled. We worked together around the South Pacific and exotic Oriental ports of call; we played together; we became vulnerable together; and we fell a little bit in love. We ended up life-long friends. Maybe it doesn't get better than that.

We started with a night flight from Los Angeles to Honolulu. Amidst the minutiae of our normal technical routine, I noticed that I was laughing often. Brendel was on a roll with nonstop one-liners. We had deadheads going to Honolulu with us, and when we had been cleared for takeoff in Los Angeles, Jim made the required PA announcement. "Buckle up! Hang on! Here we go!" was hardly standard phraseology, but what Jim followed that with was even more creative. He held a long wooden whistle to his mouth and played a whoooo-wooo sound of an accelerating train into the open microphone. Laughter from the cabin accompanied the engines roaring on our takeoff roll. When George leveled off the plane at our cruising altitude and called for cruise power, Jim pressed a button on a tiny electronic box that belched in a surly tone, "No way! Fuck you for asking." He then set the throttles to the required power setting.

He said his electronic toy voiced a number of other choice things, not always appropriately selectable. One time, the box, which he carried in his flight bag, was jostled as he was clearing U.S. Customs and started singing out crude suggestions. The insulted customs' agent spent time looking for the disrespectful speaker. He didn't think of looking inside Jim's bag.

Captain George shot the approach and landing into Honolulu that night. The weather was unusually challenging; limited visibility in rain and gusting crosswinds were complicated by low level windshear. We bounced down final to an unexpectedly soft touchdown.

"Whew, nice job," I commented. Jim said nothing.

Days later, when Jim knew me better, he gave me this advice, "Norah, men don't compliment each other on their flying. We don't acknowledge good landings. We don't acknowledge bad landings. If you want to fit in with the guys, you just keep quiet."

I thought about that. I asked if there were any exceptions to that rule, like when someone had just saved your life by doing some astounding stick work. Could you mention that you had noticed that?

"No," said Jim firmly. "No exceptions."

"No wonder God doesn't allow men to be mothers," I bit out in reply. "By nature you're incapable of nurturing." But for some time I didn't say, "Nice landing" to anyone. Eventually, I decided that the no-nurturing boy's rule was not for me.

*T*he next morning in Honolulu, I awakened before my body was ready to get up. I knew that something other than my own inner clock had awakened me and I lay in bed alert for another noise. Then it came again. There was the tap, tinkle, thud, roll of a pebble hitting my window, bouncing down the glass and hitting the floor of my lanai in the bright sunshine. I was on the fourteenth floor. *What the hell?*

I pulled my billowing nightgown against my body and tiptoed out onto my balcony, ready to duck any incoming missiles. Jim was leaning precariously over the balcony nearest mine, tossing stones against my sliding door.

"Good afternoon," he called, "I brought you some coffee." He leaned into space proffering a lidded cup as if he might reasonably expect me to extend my body over the abyss just for a cup of coffee!

"You woke me up," I said ungratefully while holding my position safely back from the edge of the deck.

"You should be up," he insisted. "You need to get your sleep schedule adjusted for tomorrow's flight."

"Well, thanks for nursemaiding me," I grudgingly acknowledged. I did need to be up. I inched forward to see if I could reach the cup of coffee without revealing my fear of heights. I sensed that Jim would be unmerciful in his exploration of that avenue for teasing, and I was unwilling to give him any ammunition.

I sipped the coffee while leaning against my terrace wall and studying Jim's face and lean, tanned body, while he regaled me with stories of his morning adventures.

"You got up at *what* time?" I asked him. "You must need a lot less sleep than I do." After all, we had flown until 2 a.m. that morning and it was now barely noon.

"Well, I'm younger than you are," he said.

And he looked younger, I thought. His gracefully formed body and long, sleekly-muscled legs looked younger than his thirty-five years, but my body, despite having born two children, looked younger than its years also. The difference between us was around the eyes, and I wasn't counting crow's feet. Jim's wide-set, round, sky-blue eyes looked like they belonged in the face of a ten-year-old rapscallion. They twinkled with mischief in the making. As I got to know him better, I realized that part of Jim would always be ten years old and cooking up trouble. I found that to be the most endearing aspect of his personality. My eyes, I was afraid, were beginning to show the haunting sorrow of a marriage gone awry and the pain of it that I was unable to speak of yet. Part of me hoped that if I didn't say anything, the problem would go away; and part of me knew that if I gave words to it, the pain would give way to tears, and I feared that once loosed, the tears would never stop. Crying vulnerability was forbidden in the boys-only club that I had worked so hard to be accepted into.

I shoved those thoughts away with my empty coffee cup and made plans with Jim to join him at the beach. We ambled along Waikiki, chatting idly and enjoying the views of scantily clad, firm bodies. At one point, Jim strode ahead of me and talked briefly to a woman who was lying on the beach. I walked on. He caught up to me soon and did not offer an explanation, so I asked, "What was that tactless detour all about?"

"Oh, I was trying out a line I just thought of. It's always fun to see the reaction," he blithely replied.

"A line?" I puzzled.

"Yeah, you know, astonish them, then leave them wondering."

"No, I don't know. Fill me in," I replied, intrigued.

"Well, I just asked her what she was reading. Told her that whatever it was could not be half as exciting as getting a chance to talk to me. Her lucky day, you know."

"How does this honing of lines fit in with your being married?" I asked.

"Has nothing to do with it," he said. "It's not like I'm trying to pick women up. I'm just having some fun, and so are they."

"Fascinating," I mused. That was the seed for Jim and George and me spending weeks swapping stories of the best lines we had ever heard.

233

We left Hawaii for Fiji at 1 a.m. and flew on from Fiji to Sydney, putting in a maximum duty time of fifteen hours. I was walking wounded when we hit the tarmac in Australia. Jim looked fresher, mainly because he had been able to nap en route. I always had trouble sleeping in an airplane seat.

Nonpilots thought it was good that I could not sleep in the cockpit. Pilots knew that not being able to nap was detrimental to safety for everyone flying oceanic routes. Conscientious pilots assessed their alertness after the first departure and decided who was going to take the first nap. They allotted oversight duties, and someone was always in charge. They arrived at their destination with all pilots awake. Stories abound about crews who held strictly to the FAA rules about never sleeping in the cockpit. They hung on to wakefulness and their shoulder straps to keep erect in their seats. What they got for those fruitless efforts were three guys sleeping at once. Tigers had one crew that overflew their coastline destination. An alert flight attendant saw the coast come and go, figured out that something was wrong, and went to the cockpit to investigate. She woke up the crew before they had to write an incident report about why they had not responded to their radios and ATC instructions. They turned the plane around and landed.

Scheduling of international pilots has long been an open debate, with economic factors winning the day. We are sanctioned if we sleep, so there is a conspiracy of silence as we, quite practically, take matters into our own hands. Every generation or so there comes along a brave Ralph Nader of airline pilots who tells the truth to the media and is usually out of a career later. I say this now as an explanation of why Jim got uptight with me when he heard me laughingly comment, "Oh, Jim is a ball on layovers. He's always prepared—sleeps from gear up to gear down."

"How could you?" he asked me. "People are going to think I don't do a good job."

He was right in that I had been indiscreet. Saying it to a nonpilot was to court misunderstanding. And Jim was one of the best men I had ever flown with, bright and thorough *and* very astute about when a nap was safe and productive.

I had plans for dinner that night with an Australian barrister whom my husband and I had met skiing in Idaho. I fantasized about more than dinner with him. It said a lot about the state of my marriage that I was so attracted to the barrister and still willing to risk seeing him. He—smart, funny, and experienced—certainly was not interested in having an affair with a married woman. I had thought I would spend our five-day layover in Sydney with him, but he was unable to see me after the first evening.

I saw Jim at breakfast the next morning. George had already left for Melbourne to visit with his wife's relatives, and Jim had thought he would not see either of us for this stay. When he said he was surprised to see me, I started crying. I hated that! I didn't know Jim well enough to trust him with my feelings or my secrets, and here I was exposing myself like a ninny. He chose to put a lid on his brat persona and momentarily allowed me to see the compassionate man he could be. He trusted me, as I cried, with a recent painful incident in his own life. Taking the risk of being vulnerable opened an intimacy between us. I was grateful for his sensitivity and his willingness to share it.

We had landed in Sydney just as they opened their bicentennial celebrations. Jim and I spent the next days exploring and joining the parties from sunup to sundown and beyond. The fireworks every night were so spectacular, they eclipsed all my previous Fourth of Julys rolled together. We watched the night sky exploding from the Circular Quay with the Sydney Harbor Bridge and the Opera House as a backdrop. We would gravitate, pushed along by the milling crowds, toward the Rocks area. British convict ships had first landed at the Rocks, and it was the oldest historical section in Sydney, replete with well preserved low-ceilinged stone buildings, narrow cobblestone streets reeking of old tales, and wall-to-wall taverns and cozy restaurants.

Often, we'd find ourselves unable to get closer to a bar than midstreet, but the ever-adaptable Aussies, intent on their daily beer allotment, figured a way around that. All we had to do was pass our beer order to the mate nearest us, and somehow the order got passed inside, and ten minutes later out would float two beers over the heads of those in front of us. Our money would make the same transit.

There was dancing in the streets, and I joined in, though Jim would not. He refused to even pretend to be dancing with me. The crowds were so dense, it was impossible to tell that I was partnerless. What a heady, laughter-filled time it was—a time for Australians, no matter their differences in politics, creed, race, age, or intentions, to join one another in just being glad that they were alive in so beautiful and so free a country.

Jim and I took the hydrofoil to Manley Beach and walked for hours in the spring sunshine along the coastal trail. I learned that his marriage, also, was at a troubled point. We talked about marriage counseling. Scott and I had been going for almost our entire five-year marriage; I was getting worn out with the effort and was fighting despair that it would not work anyway. Sometimes, I told Jim, I think that the very act of going, the hopefulness of that effort, was the only good we were getting out of it. Still, I was nowhere near ready to give up.

On our last night in Sydney, Jim and I joined a large group of other Tigers in the Henry VIII bar. I was the only woman. When the band started playing, I jumped up and said, "All right. Who gets the first dance?" There was a long silence until finally, Lenny Sulewski, a Tiger mechanic, stood and said, "I guess I get the honor." I could have kissed him for the reprieve. On the way to the dance floor he confided that he didn't know how to dance well, but he couldn't just sit there and watch me be embarrassed.

"God bless you, Lenny," I whispered. "I'll lead. You needn't worry."

I hugged Lenny goodnight as Jim and I left the bar. It was our one and only hug. I never saw Lenny again.

A day later, on the evening of our flight leaving Australia, Jim and I had dinner with Deborah Lawrie and her fiancé. Deborah, another 5' 10" redhead whose legal battle to be allowed to fly had changed state and federal law in Australia, was that country's first woman airline pilot. She was also my daughter's godmother.

After dinner, we four waited in my room for the phone call from the station that would alert me to the scheduled arrival of the crew transport. When the phone rang, Jim, to my consternation, grabbed it and answered.

"Yes, this is First Officer O'Neill's room. She's too, ummm, busy to talk to you right now. I'll take her alert for her. This is Second Officer Brendel, and as you can tell, I'm not in *my* room right now, so I'll just take my alert here." A pause while Jim listened to the station agent, then, laughter, "Yeah, well, I'm pretty sure we'll be ready on time for pickup. I'll hurry her along." More laughter and good-old-boy chuckles. I could have wrung his neck then and, again, when we arrived at the station and the agent gave me knowing looks and Jim a congratulatory handshake.

"You incredible asshole!" I fumed at Jim as we walked to our plane. "What is everyone going to think?"

George, whom we had not seen for days, offered, "I'm thinking that you two had a *really* good time in Australia. Want to tell me about it?"

What we did relate to George en route was our continuing compendium of best lines heard or delivered. Amidst our revelry in the boys delivering lines in their best Bruce Willis voices, I told them that my favorite pass had not involved a line at all but a strategic maneuver. I had been interested in a man I saw frequently in the crew hotel in New York. I was practically living there because I was a commuter pilot on reserve. I had had several conversations with him, immediately struck by his wit. This sunny-faced man seemed to enjoy the conversations but he didn't indicate any romantic interest. I thought I had given him clear signals about my willingness to pursue a relationship but I saw no warming in return. After more talk, some walks, and two lunches, I attended a party in the hotel where he was present. I told myself that if he didn't try to kiss me that night I would shelve my desire as unrequited.

Hours later, I was disappointed to see him prepare to leave the party without having made any plans with me. He stopped by each grouping of people at the party to say his goodnights. After he said goodbye to my crowd, he discreetly

237

whispered in passing, "Use it if you want to." Unbeknownst to me or to anyone watching, he had slipped his room key into my purse. I found it an hour later when I returned to my room and could not get his key to work in my door. I always admired him for his discretion.

As I shared the story of the key drop with George and Jim, Jim wanted to know, "Did you use it?"

"Oh Jim, I don't kiss and tell."

George told of a midnight visit during his single years from a Tiger flight attendant.

"George, someone keeps knocking on my door. I don't know who it is and I'm afraid. Could I just sleep in your room?" she said. "I'll feel safe with you."

"So just how safe was she with you?" I asked. "Did she sleep in your spare bed?"

"Norah, I don't kiss and tell, but of course she was safe with me. It's a captain's job to take care of his crew," George piously replied. Jim and I snorted at that one. Bratty ideas were already hatching in my mind about testing George's limits in taking care of *this* crewmember.

Tall stories, laughter, companionable silences, and the New York Times Sunday crossword puzzle filled our seven-hour flight from Melbourne to Guam, a tiny speck of a Pacific island that appeared after hours of open ocean. I was grateful for three inertial navigation systems that gave us a constant readout of our latitude and longitude. I had zero envy for Amelia Earhart trying to find Howland Island with her devilishly dinosauric radio equipment. The lights of Guam shone visibly through rainstorms exactly when and where I expected them to.

The next day was George's fifty-third birthday. Quite dutifully, Jim and I worked to make sure that George had a good time, complete with champagne, a live band, and dancing girls. God threw in stars and moonlight on a terrace overlooking an azure lagoon. George even coerced Jim into dancing with me when he needed to sit one out. We all sang oldies and watched the sun come up together.

The next day, we flew as passengers to Manila and then embarked on a four-hour "limo" ride to Cubi Point, Subic

Bay. The rattletrap jeep that was our crew transportation bucked and belched smoke as our driver navigated through heavy traffic in the city and then around animals and children and buses in the potholed countryside lanes. Two hours into that white-knuckled ordeal, Captain George had the driver pull over to a roadside stand for crew fortification. Lumpia (Philippine version of wonton) and a few beers dimmed the fright and discomfort of the rest of the ride.

We were ready to rock and roll away from the road by the time we reached the White Rock Honeymoon Resort. We were supposed to stay at four- and five-star hotels on layovers, according to our contract, but in some parts of the world, five-star, comparatively speaking, was somewhat like a Motel Six. The white rock of this resort, as far as we could tell, was a guano covered lump on the sand out in front of the sprawling, clapboard, roach-infested place. One look at the rooms, and we knew they would be for sleeping only.

Out to the pool we ran, discussing briefly which looked less polluted, the pool or the ocean. Well, they're probably not dumping sewage into the pool, we surmised. The pool was a curving lagoon of light green water set among lush tropical foliage and palm trees. The deep end rose up into a natural rock cliff where a trail of tiny footholds led up between the white-dripped outcroppings to narrow ledges of varying heights.

"Look! Olympic-height diving boards!" Jim whooped. "You have to be the judge, Norah," he called while starting to scale the wall.

It made me dizzy just to watch the guys climb up that wall. No fear of heights there. I treaded water in the center of the pool, working hard not to notice that the green water was not clear enough for me to see my lower body. My legs disappeared into the murk as I fluttered my feet and raised my hands to flash the boys their diving scores. The competition continued while the guys discussed what prize I ought to reward the winner. We stayed out of our hotel rooms as long as we could, then trooped back when we had just enough time to get a good night's sleep before our early morning departure.

I was exhausted when I stepped into my tiled bathroom shower. As the sluicing water began rinsing the sand and moss from my hair, I reached to adjust the showerhead, and the whole head and its attached pipe came off in my hand. I looked dumbly as water squirted from a hole six feet up the wall in an arc, hitting six feet up the other side of the shower stall. There was no tub. The sink was only a few inches deep. Hell. There was no place in my room to wash my hair. The rest of my body I might have managed, but not my hair.

The thought of toweling the sand from my body, finding clothes to put on, packing my suitcases, going out to the desk to tell them I needed a new room, getting my suitcases to a the new room, unpacking, getting back in the shower, and then calling the guys to tell them my new room number was just *too* much. I decided to simplify the procedure. I wrapped my dripping body in a towel, threw shampoo and crème rinse and room key in a bag and walked two doors down the hallway to George's room. I knocked.

George opened his door and allowed his eyes to widen only slightly at my towel-wrapped torso.

"George, could I borrow your shower. I promise I won't take long."

"Uh, yeah, sure," he stepped back, his eyebrows rising in query.

"Thanks." I strode into the bathroom and closed the door. Ten minutes later I stepped out still clad in my wet towel and said, "Good night" as I left.

George stood holding his door, as he waited for the punchline that never came. A good captain always takes care of his crew.

We departed the Philippines the next morning in a torrential tropical downpour. Jim did his preflight inspection wading through ankle-high pools of water, thoroughly soaking his white Reebok "uniform" shoes. He had left his black uniform shoes in his Sydney hotel room days before. Though I had heard him call the Sydney Hilton from an airport phone asking that his shoes be shipped home for him, the explanation he gave his captain for being out of uniform was, "You know how it is, George. Some women have to collect souvenirs. I didn't realize she had taken them until it was too late to do anything about it." Much laughter. Boy stuff.

We flew north to Japan. As we began our descent preparation and I was studying the approach plate to Iwakuni, Jim leaned forward and whispered in my ear, "After 12 years in the minor leagues, I don't try out. I don't believe in quantum physics when it comes to matters of the heart. I believe in the soul, the small of a woman's back, the hanging curve ball, the sweet spot, opening your presents Christmas morning rather than Christmas Eve. I believe in long, slow, deep, soft, wet kisses that last three days."

"Norah. Norah. Are you with me?" George had been speaking to me about the approach. I was hearing only Jim.

Eyes fogged, breath heavy, I turned astonished eyes to Jim. "You memorized Kevin Costner's speech from *Bull Durham*? My God!"

"Just thought I'd help you focus on the job at hand," Jim smirked. "Great line, huh?"

We should have flown on to Hong Kong that day after a brief stop at Iwakuni Air Force Base. A broken cargo loader and a problem with the fuel truck delayed us until we ran out of duty time. We left our frustrated charter representative, Brian Gorrell, to sort out the problems.

We spent our unscheduled night in Iwakuni at the "best" hotel around. George had done the unexpected and said I could fly the IGS approach into Hong Kong the next day. Many captains would not let their copilots, no matter what their experience, fly that "checkerboard" approach. It was arguably the most challenging approach on earth for jumbo jets. I had never been allowed to fly it before. I was honored and terrifically excited about having the opportunity.

I spent that evening studying and memorizing the Hong Kong maps. I arranged my room furniture to resemble the islands I would fly over while descending into Hong Kong. I flew an imaginary airplane from one island to the next, rehearsing what I would do over each one. "Okay, flaps 10 degrees, engines at 55 percent EPR, speed 180, heading 270 degrees departing Cheung Chau Island, descending to 6,000 feet. Anticipate and lead the turn while nearing the 360-degree bearing to Sha Lo Wan. A 45-degree heading out of Sha Lo Wan and down to 4,500 feet to intercept the 88-degree inbound on the instrument guidance system. Flaps to 20 degrees and slow to final approach speed, checklist out of the way before intercepting the glide slope.

I repeated the call outs and commands and actions over and over until I could do them without thinking. Then I imagined the checkerboard painted black and white on the hillside dead ahead and started the final turn to runway heading. I reminded myself not to choke up and slow the descent; not to let speed bleed off; and to hold crosswind correction in. I ignored the laundry flapping from the balconies now higher than the right wing, which was pointing toward the nearby building-covered ground on my final turn. Remember to flare. Full reverse on all four. Yes.

I crawled into my slender bed tired from my imaginary flying and ready to sleep. My eyes popped open at 2 a.m. Was there an earthquake? Once before, my bed gently rocking with the earth's tremors had awakened me in Japan, land of daily little quakes. No, my bed was not shaking, the curtains were not swaying, but there was movement; movement on my hand. I raised my hand in the darkness and shook it. *Holy shit!* I plunged for my bedside light switch and turned the light on. My bed was covered with cockroaches! They were scurrying from the light back into the darkness, leaping from my bed and running for the corners. I was horrified. I had been covered with them! *What am I going to do?*

I thought of my options. Not many. Changing rooms would not help. They're everywhere. I'm flying to Hong Kong tomorrow; I have to be well rested. So I did what I could do—shook out my bedding and remade the bed with everything tucked under the top mattress. I lowered my bed's feet into glasses of water, so the bugs would drown before they could get on the bed that way. I moved all furniture away from the bed so the roaches could not leap across the small gaps.

My first experience with six-inch-long cockroaches had been on my first trip to the Philippines with a DC-8 load of military personnel headed for Clark Air Force Base. The Tiger flight attendants had tried to prepare me.

"The hotel is not up to our usual standards," one said. "Always keep your room lights on," another advised. "They will usually stay at the edge of the light." *They?* I wondered. Always keep your suitcase closed. Take your shoes to bed with you, in case you have to get up in the middle of the night. Never walk anywhere barefoot.

This place can't be that bad, I thought. I was wrong.

I awakened there, in the hour after dawn, to the ringing of the phone. I reached for it, knowing that it was my final alert, before I realized that the phone was ringing in the room next to mine. The walls were so thin, I could hear my copilot, Chuck, rolling over, groaning, clearing his throat and barking, "Hello," as distinctly as if he were lying beside me. I heard him hang up his phone, creak out of bed, and pad across his room just before my own phone began to ring. As I replaced my receiver in its cradle and sat up, I could hear Chuck run water in his sink, then lift his toilet lid and begin to pee. *Oh brother, we might as well be sharing a room*, I thought, as I started to tune his sounds out. What I heard next was impossible to ignore.

I heard a blistering yelp and then a crashing and a whomp-whomp-whomp pounding noise. Then another yell, a bellowing "No!" and the sound of a door crashing open against the wall of the corridor. Whomp! Whomp! No! Whomp! Next, there was the sound of feet tromping on the hallway linoleum.

I ran to my door (shoes on) and stuck my head into the corridor. There was Chuck, stark naked, swinging a bath towel over his head and down in a powerful arc to slap against the floor and walls, always narrowly missing the largest cockroach I had ever seen. Soon, Chuck began to focus on his situation. He stood, towel drooping at his side, and eyed the faces looking into the hallway.

All of the flight attendants and I were looking at the scene. Chuck, truly a man's man macho kind of guy, built

243

solid as a tank and blessed with granite-chiseled cheeks and chin, looked at us giggling females and began to blush. He lunged for his door and found it locked. I took pity on him and offered a solution to his dilemma.

"You can use my phone to call the desk to bring another key. Or you can *hang* out there and I can call them for you." Another burst of giggles from the girls when I emphasized the word "hang." He decided to make the call himself and get out of the hallway.

Later, I let Chuck, who was a nice man, tell his own, perhaps less embarrassing version of the story to our captain. It seemed that the giant cockroach, which was crawling across the ceiling when Chuck started to pee, had fallen directly on top of Chuck's extended member. Small wonder that banishment from the room had not seemed fitting enough for that bug. Chuck had total annihilation on his mind.

Thinking about Chuck and the cockroaches put a smile on my face, and helped me to accept the inevitable in Iwakuni that night. *Just deal with it, O'Neill. Go to sleep.*

George and Jim and I were all light hearted as we boarded our finally-fueled airplane in Iwakuni on a calm and sunny day. My heart was singing with the joy of getting to fly to Hong Kong. My exuberance led me to pull back the yoke an inch farther than normal as we climbed our nearly empty 747 into the blue. All 208,000 horses really perform well when they don't have much to lift. The tower at Iwakuni had never seen a 747 departure like ours before.

"Thanks for the airshow, Tigress. You're cleared to contact ATC. Bye. Come back soon."

As fate would have it, Hong Kong ATC did not have any surprises for me that day. The wind was calm. The air traffic was light, and our visibility was unlimited. My IGS approach to Hong Kong went exactly as rehearsed and our touchdown was right on target, the speed exact and the wheel contact smooth. I taxied off the runway knowing, really knowing, that I couldn't have done it better. What an incredible adrenaline rush. The boys, of course, said nothing.

Brian Gorrell said, "Thanks for not pounding me against the ceiling, Norah. Nice landing." It was okay for Brian to critique pilots. Charter reps were all eccentric characters. If someone wrote a macho rulebook for them, they would ignore it.

Jim did his postflight aircraft inspection and waited until everyone had exited the airplane to walk up to me.

"O'Neill, I don't *ever* do this, but...**Hot shit, O'Neill! Hot shit!** Great job!"

Coming from him, it meant more to me than he could possibly have imagined.

Still elated from my arrival into Hong Kong, I was only mildly annoyed when I reached my hotel room and discovered that my room key did not fit my door. Muttering with the frustration of slogging my suitcases back to the lobby, I was waiting for an elevator when Jim emerged from the fire stairs.

"Got tired of waiting in my room for you," he said. "I'm hurt you decided not to use *my* key. Maybe it's just as well. I wouldn't want to ruin all other men for you." He extracted the key to my room from his pocket, threw it to me, grabbed his key from my hand, winked, and departed.

I replaced my old suitcase on that Hong Kong layover. Of course we were having too much fun together for me to read the instruction manual about how to reset the combination lock from the manufacturer's 0000 setting. Time enough for that when I get home, I thought. I was soon to regret that mistake in judgment.

Next stop, Taipei. We agreed to meet in the Galleon Bar for an after-work drink. I was quick in shedding my hot and dirty uniform, so I beat the boys there. I was surprised to hear a page for Captain Gewehr. We had not been in the hotel for more than a half-hour. *Who could be calling?* I asked the bartender for the phone. He looked both surprised and reluctant to hand it over.

"This is First Officer O'Neill. I'm expecting Captain Gewehr soon. May I take a message?"

"Oh. So sorry. Did not know the captain already had

company," said an Asian woman before she hung up.

Hmm, I puzzled, as I walked back toward my seat. *I wish I had gotten her name.*

"Phone call for Officer Brendel," came the next page. I swiveled back toward the bar and grabbed the phone.

"He's not here yet," I said.

"You with him too?" an outraged and familiar voice said. "When you start working?"

Click went the phone. Click went my brain. Sometimes I can be slow. The men walked into the room then and the pieces quickly came together. A desk clerk regularly sold the names and room numbers of inbound crewmembers (maybe any inbound men) to a call girl service. That night, the clerk had even told them that the men were on their way to the bar. Nobody ever paged O'Neill. I felt left out.

"Of all the sexist bias," I huffed. "Can't women get serviced in Taipei?" I asked indignantly.

Stunned silence. "Ah, come on guys. You can't say I didn't feed you a good opening. Where's your best stuff?"

*J*im boarded the plane to preflight while George and I sat in the car doing paperwork as we prepared to leave Taipei. Noticing that we had female deadheads going with us to Tokyo, my bratty brain hatched a plan as we climbed the boarding stairs. A quick peek into the passenger compartment affirmed that we had a few young beauties with us. Jim always did a particularly charming version of the emergency equipment briefing for good-looking women.

"Watch this," I instructed George as I stopped by a mirror to apply a few more layers of lipstick over my usual one coating. "How's it going, babe?" I sang out to Jim as I leaned over his shoulder and pressed my lips firmly to his cheek. "What a great morning," I enthused, stepping back quickly to dodge his swatting arm.

"What the hell, O'Neill," he groused. "Yuck!"

George and I climbed into our seats, stifling smirks. Business as usual for a while; then Jim went back to brief the ladies. He sighed at the heaviness of the chore, as if he didn't enjoy every second of being the center of their attention. I crept silently back to watch the women's faces. Jim didn't have a clue as to why they were smiling so freely.

At the top of our climb to altitude, when our workloads lessened, I turned in my seat to look at Jim. George turned also in silent perusal.

"What are you staring at?" Jim grumped.

"Nice color," George said.

Jim looked back at me, light dawning. He raised his hand to his cheek.

"It'd better not be what I think it is," he warned. He rose and went to a mirror. "No!" He started rubbing at his face and the large, bright, peach smiling lip print began to smear and then to disappear. "Did you do this before the briefing?" he demanded.

"Whenever else?" I yawned. "You should have seen their faces! You were sooo cute."

"I will pay you back for this, O'Neill. You *will* be paid back," he promised.

"We'd better set out flares, George. He's gonna frump for a while."

Later, when Jim had changed into his en route jammies (navy gym shorts that day) I swished my long ponytail over my shoulder into his face and asked for coffee.

"Get your own," he snarled, "and keep your engineer's whip out of my face."

I languished into my seat and pouted while feigning a lengthy examination of the inside of my eyelids. Okay, I did nod off. Jim should have brought me that coffee.

I awakened to find my head immobilized against the seat. Jim had speedtaped my hair to the back of my seat.

They laughed at me while I struggled to free myself. I let loose with a few sharpened barbs. Jim returned them.

"Children behave!" George admonished. "What will our passengers think?"

George greased the landing on the runway in Tokyo. I didn't say, " Good job." Instead, I made a lascivious stroke down his arm followed by a hand warmly on his and lingering eye contact beneath half-closed lids, a delicious sigh, and,

247

"Oh, babe. Was that as good for you as it was for me?"

We dropped all our passengers in Tokyo and took off again to fly away the rest of the night eastbound to Anchorage. I told Jim I didn't appreciate his flaunting his legs in gym shorts and asked, when he rose to change, that he wear something decent. His response to that request was to come back minutes later wearing skin-tight red satin short shorts. He moved forward with a bump and a grind, wagging himself in my face.

I groaned, "It wouldn't be so bad if you didn't have such great legs. Have mercy on a woman who's been away from her husband for too long."

As Jim reclined in his seat later, George saw my face break into a grin that was not in keeping with the low-key conversation we were having.

"You've thought of something haven't you? A suitable revenge?" he queried.

"Oh George, it's the perfect cure for his hot pants! You're going to love it. I need your permission to go in back for about ten minutes. Are you wide awake here?"

We spent minutes confirming waypoints loaded, heading and altitude checked. My work in order, I tiptoed past Jim into the seating area. There were Jim's pants where he always left them, neatly folded over a seat back. I carefully sealed off the bottom hems with rubber bands and then stuffed the pantlegs full of ice cubes and dry ice pilfered from our catering chest. That done, I tiptoed back to my seat. We had only about an hour left until the top of our descent, time enough to freeze his pants solid if only he didn't discover them before then. No worries there. Five minutes before descent, I carefully skirted Jim's outstretched legs and proceeded in back. I emptied the ice out of Jim's pants and smoothed them back into their previous well-pressed position. That took some work because they were hard and crackley. With luck, in the dim light, Jim wouldn't notice anything until he slipped his first bare leg into them.

I returned to my seat just as Jim yawned and stretched and rose to go change back into his uniform. George and I leaned toward the middle of the center console in hopes of being able to see Jim in back. No luck there, but we could hear every sound. We burst into hooting laughter as we heard Jim's first bellow.

"O'Neill! I'm going to kill you!"

"Gee, George, how do you think he knew I did it? I mean, it could have been you, couldn't it?" I asked.

"I don't believe you did this!" Jim screamed as he struggled into the cockpit, waddling with stiffened legs. "If you put a stick up my butt I'd be a popsicle!"

"That'll teach you. Cooled your hot pants right down, didn't I?"

Jim stood aghast, disbelief on his face, but belief written in his posture. I couldn't stop laughing. I was afraid I was going to wet my pants if I didn't get myself under control.

George called my attention back to the job at hand, flying the plane. It had to have been a bitch, being the only grown-up on board. Not that he wasn't laughing as hard as I was. He was somehow managing to function at the same time. I pulled myself together and started to work while Jim stomped down the ladder to the lower-deck baggage area to find something dry in his suitcase. He was gone a long time. I didn't have time to worry about his absence at the moment because I was busy. He eventually returned wearing jeans, a tee shirt, and white Reeboks.

"Look what you've reduced my uniform to, O'Neill. Lipstick on my shirt, my pants frozen into position. The shoes are your fault too."

"How do you figure that, Jim?"

"Male logic."

We had to clear U.S. Customs in Anchorage. I had my declaration filled out with details of the shopping I had done in Asia. I owed some duty. The agent wanted to see my purchases, so I lifted my new suitcase onto the examination counter and confidently dialed 0000 to open the combination lock. It wouldn't open. I dialed and pressed and pounded. Nothing worked.

The agent began to take even greater interest in that locked suitcase. I explained about its being new and not having set the lock yet.

"Maybe we can borrow a saw," he suggested.

"Oh, my brand new suitcase sawed open," I lamented.

Jim moved close to me then, put his arm around me, and whispered, "I'll trade you a blow job for the combination."

"What?" I sputtered. "Give me a damned saw!" I realized then what had taken Jim so long downstairs on the plane. He'd opened my suitcase, read the instructions, and reset the lock. He had even left a note inside for me to find. I had to admire his inventiveness.

George and Jim and I were having our last evening together. I was already sad that our time together was ending but determined that the maudlin would not interfere with the night. The F Street Bar was crowded and boisterous when we arrived. We squeezed in and began mingling. A couple of glasses of wine later, we were standing together when a man told me I had the most beautiful hair he had ever seen. I thanked him. Jim asked if I ever got bored hearing that; I must hear it so often.

"No, Jim. My hair has been one sure source of compliments in my life. I welcome comments on it," I said. "Don't you have something you always get compliments on?"

George and Jim gave that some thought. George responded first.

"Women have always complimented me on my kissing," he mused, then he blushed.

Jim laughed, then said, "Yeah. Women have always liked my kisses too."

I was intrigued. Had I been traveling in the company of two of the world's greatest kissers? I wanted to know but couldn't figure out a discreet way to find out. It seemed an odd subject to phone their wives about.

Jim came up with a solution—a kissing contest with Norah as the judge. Uh-oh. I felt some serious bad-girl behavior coming on. It was disreputable enough that I was passionately kissing two crewmembers in a crowded bar, but my real dilemma did not penetrate until about midway through the second kiss. These two men, whom I liked and respected, were going to be waiting for an answer from Norah. How could I tell one man that he kissed better than the other without hurting someone's feelings or damaging an ego? Hell!

The solution came to me as the raucous people around us asked for my judgment. Well, it certainly wasn't any of their business. That was it. I would not announce my answer to the public, but instead whisper it to each man. And this is what I said.

"George, it was really you, but I am going to tell Jim it was him so his feelings won't be hurt."

"Jim, it was really you, but I am going to tell George it was him so his feelings won't be hurt."

Whew! Close one.

The next day we flew together for the last time from Anchorage to San Francisco to Los Angeles. We handed in our trip-closing paperwork and turned to each other to say good-bye. There was a hesitation. The traditional shaking of hands and saying "Thanks for a nice trip" felt inadequate to me, but I didn't know what to do. We three moved toward each other with hands extended, and I looked into their eyes. I saw a flash there of their humor and incisive intellect and their sensitivity and I just couldn't do the normal handshake.

My one outstretched hand turned into two and I stepped forward and drew them into my arms for a totally unprofessional three-way hug. And *then* my eyes filled with tears. "It's never going to be this good again," I sighed. I was right about that. We three never flew together again.

By the time we saw each other again, Flying Tigers was history. Our carefree ease was forever gone.

30

N2 AND C1

1989

*I*n 1989 I had the opportunity to make a difference in someone's life and was elated at the chance. I was taught, as a child, that everything I did had an impact somewhere. That was usually too daunting a responsibility to keep in the forefront of my consciousness. But the time I flew copilot for Frank Campbell, I could see the ripples my actions might form and was determined to have those effects be positive. Frank was newly checked out as the world's only black 747 captain. (Flying Tiger pilot George Rainer had been the world's first black 747 captain, but he was medically retired.)

Unaffectionately known as N-2, Frank had a mixed reputation on the flight line. I had flown with him when he was 747 copilot and I was 747 engineer, and his performance in the plane had enlightened me about some of the nasty and subtle side effects of prejudice. Knowing him had taught me things about my own reactions and myself.

Frank had had problems in the dark ages of his early career checking out on a new plane. Tigers had bought him extra time, in a light twin-engine aircraft, to hone his skills and reach his own comfort level. This was not unheard of at Tigers. In fact, when Flying Tigers decided not to have professional engineers any longer, they gave the eighty-four mechanics/engineers on the flight list time off and money to learn how to fly. Some of those men took years to get ready to fly. I first heard of the "dirty eighty-four" at the end of my probationary year and was told to watch out for them because they were all terrible pilots and required massive efforts from their crews just to keep them alive. When I checked my seniority list for the dirty eighty-four section, I was surprised to see that most of the captains I had flown with that first year were ex-engineers. It was obvious that they had learned to fly quite well, yet the rumors about them didn't stop until they retired.

The rumors about Frank hadn't stopped either. When I flew with him while he was still a copilot, he had done a scrupulously good job. He was professional and thorough. But, and this is a really big *but*, I noticed that whenever a captain asked Frank to do things that were not directly in the line of proscribed duty, Frank got bristly with attitude. He would do as requested, but only after making sure that everyone was aware that he was doing something extra. I realized that he wanted to make sure everyone knew he had not forgotten to do part of his job. My first reaction to this behavior was to think, *Oh, just relax! This isn't a bloody checkride! You're making a big deal out of nothing.*

The more I observed Frank, the more I realized that he had big chips on his shoulders, and those chips were interfering with his doing the best job possible. He did a good job, nonetheless, but those chips regularly interfered with an open and easy flow of communication in the cockpit. (My shoulder chips looked just like his.)

During one of my trips with Frank as copilot and me as engineer, I heard a group of pilots joking about us in a crewroom. They made some quips about how hard our captain must be working in order to get a three-man jumbo jet from point A to B without any other pilots onboard. As if Frank and I together, N2 plus C1, did not add up to one pilot, let alone the two pilots required to work with the captain. I thought I had grown immune to such jokes. I had not. They still hurt.

Frank had also heard the jokes about himself for many years. Flying with Frank and seeing the results of the jokes made me angry for both of us. How could we get rid of our chips? How could I keep them from interfering with my own performance?

This was my background with Frank when I received the assignment to fly as his copilot for his first trip as 747 captain. I promised myself that I would make his first trip as trouble free and as positive as was humanly possible. I pulled our engineer aside before the first leg and asked for his cooperation in making this a memorable trip. The ex-Navy pilot, noting my intensity, didn't appear insulted that I thought I had to ask for his best work and best attitude.

As it turned out, Frank didn't need either of us working at 150 percent to make the flight smooth. The miracle of Frank's changed demeanor was apparent soon after we climbed the ladder to the cockpit in Los Angeles. I was waiting to see his feathers get ruffled, but what I saw was Frank's shoulder chips floating away. Getting into the left seat, where he was running the show and setting the attitude and atmosphere, had accomplished what years of politically correct therapy could not have. This was truly a prejudice-free cockpit where everyone could do the best job with no preconceptions in the way.

We had four uneventful days of working together and meshing our communications before we experienced a problem with flight planning. Tigers had lost a 747 and everyone onboard in Kuala Lumpur in February 1989. Flight 66 had flown into the ground while navigating a nonprecision approach. Three pilot friends and my dancing partner from Sydney, mechanic Lenny Sulewski, died on impact. (For a while after the accident, 66 had not been used as a flight number.) Frank and I were scheduled to fly Flight 66 from Singapore to Bangkok in the dark hour past midnight in July of 1989.

I had a bad feeling about flying a Flight 66. I am not a superstitious person nor am I given to powerful strokes of intuition, so I had no viable reason for my "bad" feeling other than I had had friends die with that number, late at night, in this small corner of Asia. I shared my bad feeling with my crew after I had perused the weather and NOTAMs for our flight and discovered that all the precision navigational aids for Bangkok International Airport were out of service and the weather was marginal. We were going to have to fly a nonprecision, ADF approach to Bangkok. I didn't like the situation and said so.

In saying so, I saw an imaginary chip materialize and plant itself on Frank's shoulder. He turned to me and said, quietly but with force and a dark underside to his melodious voice, "Norah, I'll have you know that I am fully qualified to fly an ADF approach safely in this airplane."

"Oh fuck, Frank! This isn't about *you*. Of course you can fly this type of approach. You just practiced it for weeks in the simulator (normally the only place jumbo jet pilots had to fly nonprecision approaches). This is about *me*. I'm scared! We shouldn't have to fly a chickenshit, 25-cent approach with a 100-million-dollar airplane! And with the flight number 66! And with lousy weather! I don't *care* if you are Frank Campbell or Frank Christian! (Frank Christian was a Tiger pilot other crewmembers cited as an example of everything a pilot should be.) I just don't want to go!"

Frank stared at me for a moment. He had counted on me to be helpful, not to present him with problems. A pilot admitting to being scared was just not done—the Crew Resource Management textbook didn't cover that problem.

There were a number of ways that Frank could have responded. He could have said, "If you're scared, maybe you're in the wrong job." He could have said, "Oh, get your act together." Or he could have said, "How dare you cuss at me and impugn my skill level?" But he said the only thing that could make it all right for me. "Norah, we are going to fly this plane together to Bangkok. Let's work out a way to make it okay for you. What's it going to take to get you comfortable with this?"

The three of us together worked out a plan. We were faced with not only bad weather and a nonprecision approach to Bangkok but also those same conditions at our alternate airport. We changed our alternate to a larger airport with better weather, approaches, and runways. We added the fuel required by the change. We thoroughly briefed the ADF approach to Bangkok while still on the ground in Singapore. Then off we flew.

As so often happens when one is fully prepared for a dire situation, nothing out of the ordinary occurred. While we were descending into Bangkok, prior to reaching our initial approach altitude, we broke out of the clouds earlier than expected. When it was evident that the final sections of our approach would be flown with unlimited nighttime visibility, I was so relieved, I was able to joke with Frank. I positioned a large sectional chart on top of his instrument panel, effectively blocking his view out of his windscreen, and said, "Go ahead, Frank. Show me a perfect ADF approach down to minimums. When I see perfect, I'll remove the artificial cloud." Instead of grabbing the map out of his way, as I might have done, and saying, "Be glad you don't have to watch one," Frank rose to the challenge and executed a textbook-perfect nonprecision approach. I was impressed.

As our trip proceeded, I could see Frank visibly relaxing, and we swapped jokes. I ran a few of my best male-bashing jokes by the guys, and they told me the latest girl-bashing jokes. We ran through our repertoire of blonde jokes and Polish-pilot jokes and we laughed a lot. Perhaps I became a little too relaxed.

One night, at the Taipei International Airport, after our limo dropped us off, I looked around for a baggage cart. It was a long walk from the drop-off point through the ticketing area and on through customs to the departure gate, and we had heavy international-trip suitcases and flight bags. The ordinary procedure was for the engineer to push the baggage cart carrying everyone's luggage while the copilot collected flight paperwork and the captain consulted with the agent and signed the departure papers. That night, Frank exited the car nearest to the baggage cart, and I breezily walked to the terminal door, clicked my fingers over my shoulder, and called, in an imperious tone, "Boy, bring the bags, will you?" I don't know how that slipped out; I would never have addressed a baggage handler in that insulting manner. But I couldn't take the words back, and I stood, foot firmly planted in my mouth, awaiting flying shoulder chips and Frank's response.

Frank paused, then burst into laughter. "Only for you, O'Neill," he said. Then he loaded all our baggage onto the cart and pushed it to the gate.

Our last layover together before we flew home was in Anchorage, Alaska. I ran upstairs to turn in our flight paperwork while the guys waited for me in the crew transport. I saw three pilots facing the window that overlooked the ramp. They had just watched us land, park, and walk into the building. They didn't notice me enter the room.

"I'm sure glad I'm not on that plane. Want to bet on whether they make it through their trip alive?"

"The odds aren't good enough for a bet. It's a miracle they've made it this far without killing an airplane."

"The real miracle is that they were scheduled with an ex-Navy pilot for an engineer. I wonder if they're paying him extra for baby-sitting N2 and C1."

I dropped my paperwork noisily on the agent's desk and announced that "Miracle Flight 72 blocked in at 1400." I looked into the faces of the three men as I stomped out. Two of the offending pilots had the grace to look embarrassed.

That night, during happy hour at F Street, I was approached by two crewmembers who wanted to know how my week with Frank had gone. I was pleased to tell them how well it had gone and how much easier Frank was to work with as a captain than as a copilot. One man looked at me with puzzlement, and said, "No one else is listening. Frank isn't here. You can tell us the truth."

"I did tell you the truth. Have you ever known me to lie?" I said with heat.

The man looked puzzled again. He said, " I guess I should have known that you would stick up for the underdog. That's like you."

"There's nothing to stick up for! He did a good job!"

"Yeah, if you say so."

I gave up trying to convince them. It was one more lesson in accepting the things I could not change.

31

B.I.T.C.H.

1989–90

Federal Express purchased the Flying Tiger Line in 1989. The merger of the two airlines was not a happy one. Someone said that the definitive test of fairness in a merger is that both sides are equally pissed off. So perhaps it was a fair merger.

I struggled to manage my anger and stress and worry by trying to focus on what I still had, a job flying airplanes for an extremely successful company.

The Flying Tiger 747 pilots were fortunate during the early days of the changeover to be buffered from some of the crazier events. Tiger 727 and DC-8 pilots were merged into the FedEx domestic routing system almost at once. Feelings ran high. Domestic silver pilots (Tigers had silver planes) had to share intimate cockpit space with purple (FedEx) pilots, and only the coolest tempered managed any type of congeniality. Added to this volatile mix was the fact that domestic all-night flying was physically brutal and thus exacerbated frayed tempers. The 747 pilots flew the international routes, had layovers in foreign cities oceans away from purple pilots, and flew with their Tiger buddies.

Beleaguered silver domestic pilots accused the 747 drivers of having an exclusive country club that had yet to truly awaken to the less palatable effects of the merger. The running joke was "Hey, have you heard the news? While you were lying on the beach in Fiji, a merger happened in the states."

We were dealing daily with a new set of rules. The Flight Crewmembers Handbook (FCH) was the FedEx nonunion version of a pilot's contract. The FCH spelled out how much pilots were paid and for what, how many hours they could remain on duty, when they got time off, when they got assigned schedules, and when they took vacation. This was vitally important stuff, and we memorized sections. An irritating aspect of the FCH was that it came in a small, loose-leafed binder and its pages were subject to revision, much like our Jeppesen portfolio of world maps that got updated weekly. We discovered that sometimes, when we relied on the FCH for an overseas decision while out on a two-week international trip, the pertinent page had been revised after our departure.

Tiger pilots had been staunch ALPA members ever since Tiger's founder, Bob Prescott, had encouraged them to join a union. Prescott said that the airline had grown too large for individual problems to be solved any longer on a one-on-one basis. The management-union interface had been friendly and mutually beneficial until after Prescott's death in 1978. Tiger pilots had no experience with a "contract" that could be unilaterally changed. Knowing that we had no input or control over our work rules increased our sense of powerlessness and paranoia.

The silver 747 pilots were in the front seat for FedEx going international. There were expensive mistakes made while FedEx management teams were on their learning curve. In fairness, I had never seen management teams so willing to admit to their mistakes and change their ways. Of course, when you start parking jumbo jets around the earth at a grounded cost of at least half-a-million dollars a day, it is hard to pretend that you didn't screw up. But for us, who had watched bad management decisions nearly destroy Tigers, viewing the costly mistakes was painful and scary. I had no desire to bite the hand that fed me my paycheck and

I hoped to be part of the team that helped FedEx through their growing pains.

Being helpful was not always allowed. Once, Captain Karl Krout, Second Officer Blackie Jorgenson, and I had a Sydney, Australia, layover that was scheduled for 36 hours on the ground. We slept after flying in and met for dinner later. At 11 p.m., I left the crew listening to music in a nightclub and crawled into my nightgown. I then received a phone call from a distraught Sydney Airport agent.

Nick said he was giving me a final alert to operate a flight from Sydney to Hong Kong, departing in three hours at 2:30 a.m. A final alert was an official go-to-work call that put pilots on the clock and started their duty time running. The maximum time a three-man crew could work was 16 hours. The Sydney International Airport was closed from midnight to 6 a.m. daily to all except emergency operations. We could not possibly depart until 6 a.m. So accepting a final alert and leaving the hotel for the airport at half past midnight would mean that we would be out of duty time before reaching Hong Kong and would not be able to legally depart at all. I knew that Nick knew all these timing parameters. He had long experience in getting jets and crews ready for lengthy flights leaving Australia.

I said, "Nick, this is nuts. I would be grounding an airplane to accept this alert. And why are you calling me anyway? Call Karl, like you're supposed to." The captain was always alerted first, precisely to avoid the kind of problem I was now dealing with. It was the captain's decision to not accept an alert, not the first officer's.

"I couldn't *find* Karl," he yelled into the phone. "The fine print in the FCH says that I can alert *any* crewmember and they are responsible for the rest."

Oh brother, I thought, another wonderful change in the work rules. If I spent an hour looking for the other crewmembers, I would have no time to shower, dress, pack, check out of the hotel, and be on the curb for the crew transportation that always arrived one hour after the final alert. It didn't help the situation that the other crewmembers were not in the hotel but a cab ride away at a nightclub.

"It doesn't make sense for you to give me this alert," I repeated.

"They said they would fire me if I continued to refuse to alert you!"

"I'll take care of this Nick."

I called Memphis and explained the situation. I offered to pretend that I had not gotten an alert so they could call me out when the airport opened.

"First Officer O'Neill, if you don't accept this alert, you're fired."

"Fired? I'm trying to do you a favor and you're firing me?" I was stunned. "I'll take your damned alert and *you* get to explain why you parked a 747 in Sydney."

I threw a raincoat over my nightie and went to get Karl and Blackie. We went to the airport and officially checked in. Karl called Memphis and essentially said the same things that Nick and I had already said. Some sane person in Memphis allowed as how a mistake had been made and asked if we would pretend that we hadn't been at the airport so they could call us five hours hence and move the plane at daybreak.

"You offered to *fire* Norah when she made the same suggestion. I'm not going to make the same deal. We won't be legal to accept an alert for 12 hours, starting when we reach our hotel. And just for your information, if we leave *then*, Hong Kong will be closed when we arrive. Good luck figuring it all out and explaining it to your boss."

The incident in Sydney and another in Hong Kong, where they again threatened to fire me when I tried to save them from a costly mistake, dampened my enthusiasm for being an active part of the team that spearheaded FedEx's international foray. As purple pilots began to fly the 747, I was wary of working with them.

When scheduled to fly with my first purple captain, Jim Shreve, I had a chat with myself about professionalism and attitude that I hoped would get me mentally prepared for whatever problems arose. None did until the day he called me B.I.T.C.H.

Lanky Jim was a cross between a Hell's Angels biker and a cowboy. Indeed he owned both motorcycles and horses.

His personality was an easy combination of laid back and off the wall, but in the cockpit he was all pro. Meshing as a cockpit team was simple. Jim was new on the 747; I had many years on it so I was able to make suggestions about autopilot use that were helpful. Jim seemed to welcome that input. Otherwise, it was piloting business as usual until the day we landed in Okinawa.

We were running late, and it was critical that we perform our tasks with dispatch so we could reach our destination before it closed. Our flight plan looked ballpark; weather was not a factor anywhere. But the flight-planning computer had thrown us a curve.

Our alternate airport was on an island, and if we had to return to it, we would be landing with only 10,000 pounds of fuel. Minimum safe fuel for that routing should have had us landing with 25,000 pounds. Legally, it didn't matter that we would hardly try to find a dot in the ocean if we had a serious problem. We would, of course, go somewhere much closer and larger and less fuel consuming. But to be legal, our paperwork had to be okay.

Because of the intensity of our workload, I had not yet had a chance to point this out to Jim when our fuel man entered the cockpit and asked for the final fuel load. Jim said the flight plan fuel looked okay and asked for the engineer's concurrence. The engineer nodded. Normally we would only ask for extra fuel if bad weather were involved. I was talking on the radio getting our route clearance as the fueler started to climb down the ladder.

"Standby!" I said into my microphone. I leaned out of my seat and waved to the fueler. "Change that final fuel to 77,000 pounds," I called.

"Right, Norah. Gotcha. 77 grand," he replied, as his head disappeared down the ladder.

As I rolled my body back into my seat, my head turned past an astonished look on Jim Shreve's face. I had just countermanded his orders, and a lowly fueler had abetted my mutiny.

"I'll explain in a minute, Jim," I promised as I went back to the mike that I still held in my hand.

When I finished with the radio, I turned to Jim. He leaned over the center console, looked me in the eye, and said, "Bitch!"

I was astounded. I knew that I had temporarily usurped the captain's authority. That was serious. But I thought that Jim knew me well enough to trust my judgment and to trust that there would be a prompt and reasonable explanation for my behavior. Here I was turning to him to explain my actions, and he was preempting me with name-calling. It seemed out of character for him.

I sat, mouth slightly agape, and looked into his eyes. If I had so seriously misjudged this man, I was going to have to do some creative tap dancing to get through this moment and restore peace to our working partnership. Then I saw the unmistakable light of laughter in his eyes and the tiniest upturn to the sides of his lips. Then, big grin.

"I've been waiting for just the right moment to say that to you. The timing couldn't have been more perfect," he said. "B.I.T.C.H. is an acronym for 'Boys, I'm Taking Charge Here.' "

And I *had* just taken charge. How perfect! "Jim, I'll never get my feathers ruffled again when someone calls me bitch, now that I know it's a compliment."

*F*red Smith, founder of FedEx, asked the all-union Tiger pilots to vote out the union and give the FedEx PSP (People, Service, Profit) concept a try for a year. I was leery of this trial, not wanting to be without a union for even one day. Nevertheless, the union was voted out and the grand experiment in plantation-policy (Don't worry boys, the massah will take care of all your needs.) started. Two experiences that year permanently soured me on the idea of trusting management to stand by their employees.

The first was having management threaten to fire me when I offered suggestions about how things could be done better in Sydney and Hong Kong.

The second experience was walking through the Guaranteed Fair Treatment program. The GFT program had

263

won a national award for management wonderfulness and was one of the reasons FedEx regularly ended up on the national list of the top-ten companies to work for.

This is how the program was designed to work in four easy steps: 1. Employee has a problem with a company decision and takes that problem in writing to his immediate manager within two weeks, while invoking the GFT program. His manager has two weeks to respond. 2. If employee is not satisfied with that manager's decision, he has two weeks to take it in writing to that man's boss. That boss has two weeks to respond. 3. If employee is still not satisfied that justice has been done, he has two weeks to take it in writing to a senior vice president of his particular department. 4. If employee is still not satisfied, he can finally present the problem to a panel of his peers. This tribunal has five persons—two management and three coworkers that the employee has selected. The decision of this panel is binding. On paper this program looked exceedingly fair and well thought out.

This is how it actually worked. I received a letter from management stating that during an audit of the Flying Tiger records, it was discovered that I had been on unspecified leaves for about two years total and these leaves had not been deducted from my longevity of employment. I was, therefore, no longer a pilot with fourteen years of employment but twelve years. That reduced my hourly pay rate and number of vacation days.

I received this enlightening letter shortly after a government arbitrator had reduced my post-merger seniority number to eight years after my actual date of hire. There was nothing I could do about the arbitrator's decision to negate eight years of my working life, because when one submits things to arbitration, one also agrees to comply with whatever the arbitrator comes up with. But I could take *this* loss of longevity through the GFT process.

264

I discovered that the two years held in discrepancy were my two maternity leaves, which the Tiger contract said would not be deducted from longevity. Clearly FedEx had no right to retroactively amend my previous contract of employment. I thought that this whole matter would be easy to clear up at the first management level. It was not. FedEx did not have any "sexist" clauses in their work agreement and they did not recognize pilot maternity leaves.

I scrambled to get my second and more lengthily documented letter to manager number two in the two weeks allotted because the first manager's letter arrived at my home one day after I had departed on a ten-day trip. The second manager replied within his two weeks that he needed more time for research and would get back to me soon. Two months later, he said my case had no merit and he denied it.

Again, I scrambled to reply within my two-week allowable time and sent a long letter to manager three. Manager three invoked the management-only privilege of needing more time and took two months to get back to me. My incredulity and stress were increasing dramatically. Finally, he said my case had no merit and he shelved it.

I was all set for my panel of peers. I was sure that no one had actually read anything I had to say, so far, because I thought it was too clear and too simple to be seen as having no merit. I knew my peers would at least read my case. When I called to see how and when the panel of peers would meet, I was dismayed to be told that an employee only went on to the panel of peers if manager three thought the case had merit. The fine print on the GFT process said that management had the right to stop the process at any time.

My months of scrambling for compliance with the rules had been for nothing. I had memories of years during which all I had to do in a like situation was call my union representative and mail him the appropriate records. I was angry that this award-winning program was so management controlled and self-serving.

I started calling people in senior management and did not get beyond executive secretaries for a while. When they got sick and tired of me, they referred me to a senior vice president. He was an ex-Tiger executive, and though we were not buddies, I thought that there must be some advantage in his knowing who I was. I worked myself through that advantage in the split second it took me to say, "How dare this one-of-the-ten-best-companies-for-women not have a maternity leave! What is sexist about addressing reality?"

"Oh Norah, get off your soapbox. I refuse to listen to it. What is your immediate problem?"

I explained my experience with the GFT process. He said he could straighten it out if I could provide my pay stubs and computer pay sheets from 1984 and 1986 and the page in the Tiger contract that had the maternity leave clause. I got angry that I should be expected to keep and produce seven-year-old pay records. Fortunately, because I had a large attic I had tossed outdated file folders into, I was able to find the documents. I asked him why no other manager had talked to me or asked me for documents in the previous year. He didn't know, but he did reinstate my longevity.

Weeks later, I met a senior purple pilot in the Memphis crew room who asked how I was adjusting to the FedEx way. He unleashed my diatribe about the GFT process.

"I see," he grinned, "that you've discovered for yourself what the letters in GFT actually stand for."

"Huh? You mean guaranteed fair treatment?"

"No. GFT really stands for Get Fucked Twice—once when they screw you the first time, twice, when you spend a year in stressful frustration trying and failing to fix it."

"Oh great! I wish I had known that in the first place."

"I'm glad you didn't know. We need you Tigers to remain strongly union until the rest of our crewforce wakes up and smells the coffee. Because of your story, I have now discovered a new meaning for the GFT acronym. It may as well be Get Flying Tigers."

We long-time ALPA members and a group of purple pilots began to wage a battle to have a pilot's union on the property. I was a union organizer. One of my duties was to mix with nonunion pilots and try to facilitate union discussions in an informative and nondivisive way.

I went to the Anchorage F Street Bar early one evening looking for purple pilots to talk to. I was in battle mode with curled hair, make-up, and flattering clothes. I spotted a table of purple pilots and made eye contact with a young, hungry-looking one. He invited me to join them.

Early in the conversation I said clearly that I was a fellow FedEx pilot on a layover. This information didn't penetrate the consciousness of some of those pilots. A DC-10 captain vacated his stool for me but remained uncomfortably close. I began scrunching over to allow him room. When finally there was nowhere further to go, I addressed the man.

"I'm married. I'm not interested. Please move back."

He replied, "I have yet to meet a woman who isn't interested in a jumbo-jet captain."

Oh brother! No use trying to talk to this one. "Babe, if I dropped my drawers for every jumbo-jet pilot I met, I wouldn't have to bother putting them on in the morning. I *am* a jumbo-jet pilot."

He replied, "You don't know what you're missing."

I turned my back and concentrated on the young fellow on my other side. He confided, "You know, FedEx has the ugliest women pilots in the whole industry."

Wow. I'd thought I was beyond being astonished by male pilots' behavior, but this guy amazed me. Was he lumping me in with this "ugly" group? Or did he think that I would instinctively know he considered me to be an exception? I reminded myself that I was here to talk about a union in positive terms and now was not the time to address male/female issues, so I said, "Who cares how they look if they can fly well?"

"But they can't!" he said. "They're all incompetent."

I noted his youth and figured he couldn't possibly have flown with all of FedEx's women pilots yet. He couldn't have been an airline pilot for that long.

"Mmm," I murmured sympathetically, "so you have flown with all twenty-seven of them and they're all ugly and incompetent?"

"Well, I've flown with only three of them, but I've heard about the rest."

"I have been an airline pilot for fourteen years and I have flown with three really ugly and basically incompetent men. It never occurred to me that all 977 others were ugly and incompetent too. What an interesting conclusion. Must be male logic at work, and I'm still a neophyte at male logic."

A startled, disgusted look flashed across his face. "Oh! You're just a women's libber!"

I gave up then. I was grateful that I hadn't been able to say anything about a union yet.

*A*s the dust settled in the aftermath of the explosive merger of Tigers and FedEx, I entered the only period of popularity I have ever known. I had always evoked strong reactions. People seemed to either love me or hate me. But for a year or so, with the Tiger boys united against a common enemy, I was truly number one.

My being Tigress One started with a tactless comment in a Memphis classroom. A large group of purple pilots were seated with silver pilots during a recurrent training session, when a pilot ran in with a stack of papers.

"The list is out! The list is out!" A government mediator had spent a year deciding how the pilot seniority lists would be merged. Our positions on that list would decide the tenor of the rest of our careers—what planes we would fly, what seat we would be in, how much we would be paid, when we would vacation—important stuff. The class ended as everyone grabbed a list and looked for his name. I was merged in with pilots who had been hired eight years after I had been. Though I had been hired years before FedEx hired a woman pilot, I was now years behind their first woman on the seniority list. A FedEx woman pilot said, "I wonder if Norah knows she's not number one anymore?"

That comment pissed off a lot of people. A Tiger captain stood and said, "I don't know who you are or where you are on the list. I hope I never fly with you. It would take a lobotomy to get you okay on CRM. Norah will always have more flight time than you will. Norah will always have been an airline pilot longer than you will. Norah will always have been hired before you. **And she will always be number one with us!**"

Men who had never been warm with me before were now brotherly. They were going to protect one of their own.

I enjoyed it.

Captain Oakley Smith, Tiger's chief pilot at the time of my hiring, decided to retire a year after the merger. We saw each other in a crew room as he was preparing to depart, and he left me with this thought.

"I am really proud, Norah, that I was in command when you got hired. You were just the right woman to be our first. Whatever Tigers paid you over the years, you were worth every single penny."

Ah, acceptance. Total acceptance. At last.

32

FLYING SHAMU

1991

*I*nteracting with my children brought calm, peaceful moments that were a balm to my psyche. My marriage was no longer collaborative but divisive, tiptoeing on eggshells a constant. My children were my joy.

Shamu the whale having midair conversations with pilots brought flying alive for my son's kindergarten class. I had been doing career-day talks at high schools and colleges for fifteen years. When Bren's teacher, Mrs. Johnson, asked me to talk to her five-year-old kindergartners, I was perplexed about how to simplify my regular presentation.

Bren helped me out the night before I was to appear at his school.

"What are you going to tell my class, Mom?"

"I'm going to tell them how exciting it is to travel all over the world and see how other children live. What kinds of toys Japanese children play with; what kind of books Australian children read; about different food and customs. And how you learn all these cool things while you are at work and getting paid for it."

"Oh. What else?"

"Well, I'm going to tell them they don't have to be math whizzes or science geniuses to be pilots. I'm going to tell them that they have to go to college but they don't have to get straight As. I'm going to bring in a model of a 747 and a globe and maybe talk about how much fun it is to fly; how neat it is to see your house and town from the air; how neat it is to be like a bird."

"Oh. Anything else? Any fun stories about animals?"

"I hadn't thought of that. What do you think I ought to say?"

"I like to hear you talk about the animals you have carried. You know, Shamu and the poisonous snakes and the canaries and the dog that got covered with foam."

"I can tell all those stories. Is that what I should do?"

"Yes, Mommy, save all that boring stuff for when they grow up."

I told Bren's classmates about my most magical flight. It was giving Shamu a ride from San Diego Sea World to the Sea World in Cleveland, Ohio. Getting a DC-8 in and out of the San Diego Airport's short, obstacle-surrounded runway was the only challenging part of the trip for the pilots. Loading a huge whale and keeping him wet, breathing, and stationary en route was a complex puzzle for our loaders and cargo specialists and the Sea World veterinarians to figure out. Flying Tigers earned a worldwide reputation for being able to fly anything, anywhere, anytime. They pioneered ways to transport animals safely.

My Shamu flight also had thirty other marine mammals and fish, a veritable flying fishbowl. I had imagined some type of portable swimming pool, but it would have needed a lid to keep the water in during takeoff and landing. In fact, Shamu was traveling in a long, shallow, canvas cradle with water at the bottom. He was suspended in a huge sling in its center. Attendants coated him with a thick oily substance that retained moisture on his skin and sprayed him with water frequently.

During the flight, an animal attendant entered the cockpit to chat and mentioned that Shamu was talkative that day. He invited us to come back and visit. One by one we ducked through the fire curtain in back and approached Shamu's first class berth. His intelligent eyes tracked my

271

approach to him. I stroked his nose and talked to him. I told him I had seen him performing in San Diego. I told him thousands of people had been awakened to the possibility of his being as smart as they were and had left his show with new attitudes toward the conservation of our oceans. Every time I stopped talking, Shamu would begin to speak in his high trilling voice with variation in his sounds and his cadence. I didn't understand what he was telling me, but I had the feeling he knew what I was talking about. What a wondrous experience.

Orc Ark was later painted on the side of that plane.

My son's classmates gasped and laughed when they heard the story of the poisonous snakes that got loose on a jet. This happened to other guys, not me. Sometimes, I do get lucky.

The three-man crew of the DC-8 had a number of snakes and lizards and exotic birds on board that night, destined for a zoo in Chicago. An hour into the flight, when the engineer went to get coffee and pulled back the fire curtain that separated the flight deck and galley from the main cargo deck, he heard the birds cawing and moving in their cages more excitedly than they had earlier. Walking around looking for signs of something amiss, he discovered a large animal transport crate with a damaged corner. A two-inch-wide wedge had opened near the bottom directly adjacent to the red-lettered sign: Danger: Poisonous Snakes.

The engineer ran back to the cockpit and slammed the door shut. When he told the other two men of his discovery, they agreed with him that exploring the cargo cabin with a flashlight was not in their best interests. In fact, they decided that going to the bathroom and getting food from the galley were not good ideas, so they spent the final hours of the flight locked in the cockpit. They alerted ground to their problem, and special handlers equipped to capture the escaped snakes met their plane.

The cautious crew never did open the cockpit door but left the plane through the emergency escape windows in the cockpit, sliding down the escape tapes. Hours of searching led to the recovery of all but one of the snakes, and it was surmised that the last one had gotten out of the plane while the search was concentrated inside.

The next day, a different crew got in the cockpit to do their preflight checks for a flight to New York. As the captain checked his rudder pedals by pushing his left then right foot full forward, a large snake, disturbed from his nap behind the warm instrument panel, plopped sleepily onto the top of his feet. The captain screamed and escaped unscathed.

The night before, when the crew had locked themselves in the cockpit, stuffed a blanket against the crack under the door, gone without food or coffee and peed into Styrofoam cups, they had probably locked the snake in with them.

We often flew pallets full of baby chickens. I think they were breeding stock. Their incessant peeping could be heard above the noise of the engines. Occasionally, a few got loose. Their hopping around the cargo deck didn't produce problems, but the escape of thousands of canaries from a broken container did. The crew that flew the yellow birdcage joked afterwards that they had probably miscalculated their landing weight, because 10,000 pounds of their cargo were no longer weighting down the floor but had risen weightlessly into the air of the cabin. Had the canaries added to their plane's lift or to its drag? A larger problem presented itself when the offloaders opened the cargo door and a cloud of cacophonous canaries floated into the airspace of Chicago's busy O'Hare Airport.

The foam-covered dog event was not a Tiger story, though Tigers often transported pets and let their owners ride with them as "animal handlers." The foamy dog was a cargo-belly passenger on a Brand X passenger airline. Shortly after takeoff, the Brand X pilots had a cargo fire warning. Their checklist told them to discharge bottles of fire-retardant foam into the lower cargo space. They did that and returned to land in Chicago. Their passengers were deplaned and the belly compartment was inspected.

A baggage handler discovered Rover lying on his back, legs stiffened, body frozen with foam. As he pulled the dog's

273

body onto the ramp, he saw that Rover was, amazingly, still breathing. He pulled Rover by his leash into a less congested area and rubbed him down with rags. He pulled Rover up onto his legs to see if he could stand on his own. Not happening. Reviving Rover became the focus of the ramp activity. Finally, the plane was cleared to go and Rover, looking less death bound, was returned to his cleaned cage in the cargo hold.

Evidently, Rover survived to thrive because his owner, an elderly woman, wrote a thank you note to Brand X Airlines. She had been impressed, while waiting in the passenger terminal during the delay, to see through the window that numerous animal lovers were taking turns walking her dog around the ramp.

My son's friends also clapped when they heard about the ice cream that flew from Seattle to the Middle East and arrived still frozen for the children of Qatar. Tigers had a two-year contract with Safeway to fly 100,000 pounds of fresh and frozen meat, fresh fruits and vegetables, dairy products, and dry goods to Doha, Qatar, a wealthy Persian Gulf city. The shipment went to the newly built Doha Center, an enormous cross-shaped structure that encompassed a western-style supermarket and 80,000 square feet of shopping space. The Tiger cargo masters designed special containers for flying the frozen foods. I was dubious of Tigers' ability to get the frozen food intact from Seattle to New York to London to Doha in blistering summer heat. Although the plane landed only for fuel and crew changes, it still spent hours on melting tarmacs before it arrived at its destination.

When I flew the London-Doha leg, it was 105°F. on the ground when we landed. I watched the Doha crew offload the cargo and gasped when a faulty cargo roller jacked one of the cargo igloos off the loader. It fell 12 feet to the ground and cracked open, tumbling gallons of ice cream onto the hot ground. I ran down the stairs to help get the ice cream containers back into the igloo and was amazed to discover that they were still solidly frozen. A refrigerated truck squealed onto the ramp, and we pitched the cartons into its cool interior in a haphazard fashion. Saved them too. The children of Doha had ice cream available that afternoon.

I told the children about flying animals between zoos and racehorses to races on other continents. I told them about the loads of cattle flown from Moses Lake, Washington, to Japan for breeding (but mostly for slaughter) and the loads of workhorses flown from Seattle to Japan. (Those were for slaughter, also, but I didn't tell them that.) I told them how moisture from the animals massed together in back evaporated into the air-conditioning system and froze there at cruise altitude, then thawed out on descent into the warmer lower atmosphere. We watched yellow rivulets pour from overhead air vents onto us. There was no escaping it.

When we had to fly a load of cattle across the Pacific, we would put our uniforms into plastic trash sacks after we got airborne and spend the flight in tee shirts and sweat pants. Those urine-soaked clothes would be exchanged for the uniforms after we landed. But we stank anyway. It was on our skin and in our hair. Our suitcases would be covered in a fine yellow mist of condensation. Cattle flights were *not* volunteered for.

My worst one ever was on a DC-8 where the cockpit was on the same level as the cows. Still hours to go until Japan, the smell and noxious fumes in the air were so overpowering that we had to put on our oxygen masks. My eyes swelled almost closed, and I had a pounding headache for a day afterward. Though cows were bad, the smells of pigs and monkeys were even worse.

"Oooh, yuck. What was the worst thing you ever flew?"

Surprisingly, it was a load of strawberries. I like to eat strawberries, and when I knew I was flying 10,000 pounds of them to New York, I thought I would probably sneak back and help myself to a few of them to augment my crew mystery meal. My first step into the plane changed that idea. It was like walking into a garbage can that has spent days moldering in the sun. Millions of strawberries had a cloying, sickeningly sweet odor that made even cow pee preferable.

275

Ceiling-to-floor, stem-to-stern, roiling, barking dog fur had once been my mission to transport in the Alaskan bush. I carried the Alaskan State Champion Dog Sled team to their destination in a six-seat Cherokee. All of the seats except mine had been removed, and the dogs and their sled had been leashed to the walls. Dog snacks, large covered buckets of fish blood and entrails, had been loaded in the nose compartment of the plane to counterbalance the weight in the rear. Approaching the plane, I could not discern individual dogs. Instead, it looked as if the plane had been stuffed with fur. The whole plane was rocking on its wheels and emitting nasty threatening sounds. I thought my biggest challenge would be trying to get to the pilot's seat. Instead, my greatest difficulty was hearing the tower clearance on the radio. The dogs had no restraint in complaining about their unwillingness to fly. Once airborne, they quieted and settled into sleep. Upon landing, they resumed their howling protests. I was glad to see them out and running free.

Mrs. Johnson's kindergartners brought me back to basics in enjoyment. To hell with money and prestige. Was it fun? Did it smell good? Did it taste good? Could you do it with friends? Was it an adventure but not too scary?

Their thank-you notes told me that I had reached them, but not in a way I would have expected. I got colorful drawings of Shamu the Orca flying through the sky; no airplane; the wings were on him, and I was on his back. We had musical notes wafting from our mouths and trailing behind us. Their little hands and their pure hearts had summed up my story perfectly. Looking at their drawings, I was moved to feel the goodness of life. The remembrances of joy kept my life spark alive during difficult days of turmoil.

33

PACIFIC ISLAND INTERLUDE

1991

*A*s my marriage was inexorably falling apart, fate threw me a series of bright, funny, nurturing, happily married men to fly with. I had some big life lessons to learn about what I needed in relationships, and these men became my teachers. Jim Booth was one of them.

A lanky and handsome 6' 7" pilot, Jim was a physical cross between Clint Eastwood and Michael Crichton. He was my captain on a 747 South Pacific trip that was the envy of all the junior pilots who were still slogging between Cleveland and Chicago and Detroit. Indeed, this trip with Jim was the cream of the cream of our international flying.

Jim, Blackie Jorgenson, our engineer, and I started the trip with an evening flight from Los Angeles to Honolulu. I had flown with Blackie before and knew him to be an extremely sharp, well-muscled, darkly handsome man who was an outdoor aficionado. His mountain-man appearance hinted at a dangerousness not belied by his Vietnam experiences. I saw him being gentle and soft spoken with his wife, with children, and with animals, but it was generally agreed that he was not a man to pick a fight with.

I had not flown with Jim before, and greeted him in the LAX crew room with, "At last! A captain I don't have to lean over to dance with. Yay!" He laughed, then got down to the business of flight and fuel planning. I saw immediately that Jim was going to be a good captain to work with because he drew me into his planning, explained his thinking, and asked for my input. A captain's establishing his authority and inspiring his crew to volunteer their input is a subtle art.

We took annual classes in crew resource management (CRM). Their lessons, similar to those of basic marriage counseling, teach how to communicate with another strongly opinionated adult without alienating him. There are many "right" ways to do this and a few really wrong ones. I had experiences with some of the wrong ones—like the man who stood up in his seat and screamed, "I am the captain! Anything I say is right! Don't ever tell me I'm wrong again!"

Jim Booth had the right ways down pat. My appreciation for his right stuff grew as we sat in the cockpit before departure. Getting a 747 ready to go in the one hour allotted for preflight inspection and cockpit setup required seasoned expertise and thoroughness. One or two errors or lack of crew coordination would guarantee that the flight would take off late. On this occasion, we actually had some breathing room and time for our first cups of coffee.

We three talked, en route to Hawaii, about our plans for the two days there. Blackie was going to be with family friends, and Jim was going to rent a car to scout out locations on the north shore of Oahu for a proposed family vacation. I cadged an invitation to go with Jim, welcoming an opportunity to see something other than the beaches and stores that were within walking distance of our hotel.

All of my life, men have been disappointed in my lack of interest in cars. If cars have clean interiors, start when I want them to, have working heaters and windshield wipers, I generally don't notice anything else about them. Considering how unusual it was for me to notice a car, it is pertinent to note that I did notice the rental car Jim had selected for our island tour. As I climbed into the sporty little convertible, I saw that Jim's head was crammed against the ceiling, and the driver's seat, in full rear extension, did not give him enough room for his long legs. His knees were bent upwards against the steering wheel. I assumed that no full-size models had been available and was surprised when Jim expressed delight in his selection.

"I've really wanted to try out one of these!"

I schooled myself not to laugh when Jim pretzeled himself in and out of that car. I reminded myself that I had endured similar gyrations getting in and out of high heels and tight miniskirts. I did allow myself to laugh, though, when Jim tried to parallel park the car. I think he was used to larger cars and misjudged just how small a space this little car would fit into. Or perhaps he was just hampered by not being able to turn his head far enough to see well. It was funny to see a jumbo jet captain fumbling with a piece of comparatively tiny machinery. Jim had the self-confidence to laugh along with me. I liked that in him.

As we drove between rental properties that first day, we stopped to eat a picnic lunch at a deserted north-shore beach. What a contrast there was between the hotel-to-shore bodies on Waikiki and that peaceful expanse of sand. I swam there while Jim lazed in the lulling calm of ocean soughing and birds calling. No man-made sounds interrupted the serenity of nature.

I was reluctant to leave the beach. Life on the farm with my husband and children was chaotically full and increasingly unhappy. Scott and I had entered our sixth year of marriage counseling. I was still committed to making our marriage work but was running out of the strength to go on. I needed recharging and didn't know how to do that. I treasured moments, sometimes hours, on trips where I could be just Norah at my best.

As the sun was setting, Jim and I drove to Waimea Falls State Park and reached the entrance gate shortly before closing time. We slipped past a distracted attendant who was urging others to leave so he could lock the gates. Soon, we had the park to ourselves.

The time in the lush botanical gardens took on a fairy tale aura for me. I thought of Michener's *Tales of the South Pacific* and *Hawaii*, books read long before I had ever been anywhere tropical. I had dreamed of being in the Swiss

Family Robinson, minus the pesky kids, pirates, and wild animals. And here we were, as ancient Hawaiians might have been centuries before—no constraints, no timetables, and no worries. Just the sunset, the murmur of water in the distance, a trail of flowers through the jungle. No danger. My spirit drank it in. The opening in the wilderness that held the falls appeared before us. The pool of my fantasies. I absolutely had to be the girl of my dreams swimming under the waterfall, uninhibited, floating in paradise, bathed in the sunset rose and gold.

I tried to explain what I was feeling to Jim. I knew he was too conscientious to let me go swimming alone. My wet bathing suit lay discarded in the back of the rental car, and I could hardly just undress in front of him and swim nude. My compromise was to strip to my waist-high white cotton Jockeys and my sports bra (an unalluring but more covering ensemble than my bathing suit), and slip into the fragrant pool while Jim chose to turn his back. The fact that he did that gentlemanly act endeared him to me.

Then a shift back to the fantasy. Free in the untainted wilderness. Diving like a playful mermaid, long hair flowing behind. Laughter ringing out as I surfaced, flinging clear droplets of water from my turning head, I went to the waterfall and swam through it. A perfect moment.

We ate dinner that evening on a verandah overlooking the ocean and spoke of the stressful situation at work. The FedEx/Tigers merger was by then a year old. The changes had been monumental. We had loved Tigers and were mourning its demise while gearing up to function in a different corporate environment.

Our conversation segued into spouses and children. We pilots led double lives, parking our home problems when we went to work. Piloting required that we fly well while coordinating with two other professionals with like goals and interests. In one way it was pretty simple. We wanted to get to the same place and in one piece. If we had fun doing it, that was icing on the cake.

Home life was never that simple. An aviation career requires unique capabilities of the stay-at-home spouses. The partners have to be independent and self-sufficient. Trusting each other is imperative. Jealousy had destroyed more than one aviation marriage. Jim's wife trusted him, with good reason. My husband and I had not a jealous bone between us. However, Jim spoke of his wife with a respect and true liking that was absent in my marriage. I envied Jim and Mary for that, but I was glad for them. If I could not have a good relationship myself, I valued seeing relationships that gave me a healthy all-is-right-somewhere feeling.

Jim and Blackie and I flew on to Fiji after two days on Oahu. Watching Jim's enjoyment of the beautiful simplicity of Fiji and the Fijians allowed me to retrieve and re-experience my memories of my first trip to Fiji. I had been an engineer then and the only one on board who had not visited there. As we flew toward Fiji, I was, in my enthusiasm, peppering the men with questions about where to dive, to sail, and to swim. The captain, exasperation in his tone, finally said, "It's just another fucking Pacific Island, Norah. They're all essentially the same: They're too hot; they have too many insects; the natives are lazy; and there's nothing to do." *Wow, this guy is seriously jaded. He may as well not be alive.*

I did my first explorations of Fiji alone. A sailing trip to Treasure Island Cay brought snorkeling over an unspoiled reef and my first glimpse of a royal blue starfish. *What an unbelievable color.* I thought, at first, that it must be a man-made object, because the color was so rare in nature, other than in birds or gemstones. But those royal-sapphire-cadmium stars were abundant there. Later, I made a trip to a giant clam farm where the Fijians raised acres of huge clams with royal blue lips—otherworldly bizarre, but there to see.

I took my first windsurfing lessons in Fiji with Tom, the Sheraton Hotel Guest Entertainment Director. A huge charcoal-colored man with a laid-back manner, laughing eyes, and gentle hands, he carried my rental board to the beach for me and demonstrated its use. After three hours with him, I became what I thought of as moderately proficient in its use, meaning that I could stand on it, direct it mostly the way I wanted it to go, and manage to get it back to the shore in front of the hotel.

In Fiji with Jim Booth and Blackie, I rented a board and was self-conscious about my competence. I don't know why I had a difficult time projecting an accurate image. After all, I *was* new at windsurfing and relatively incompetent. Why not just admit it? As events unfolded, I didn't have to admit anything. My having to be rescued was clear enough.

The ride started well. I managed to stand on the board on my first attempt and to raise the sail without leaning precariously over the downwind side with my butt in the air. I sailed off, back erect, knees bent, wet hair blowing away from my body. That my wet hair was being lifted by the force of the wind should have been my first clue that I was heading toward trouble. I was too self-conscious about unimportant things to notice something vital, like this was the strongest wind I had been in, so far, and it was blowing offshore and strengthening. I knew I was picking up speed and was enjoying the thrill of it. It was like hang gliding for the first time, all rush and wind noise and speed.

When my sail-holding arms and wave-absorbing knees began to tire, I turned the board to head back to shore and saw that the beach had become a distant horizon, smudgy and indistinct. I refused to let myself get alarmed and focused on the task at hand. I had to tack against the wind, so I got on with it.

Every turning of the sail required hauling on the nylon ropes while repositioning my body. Eventually, the salt-water-soaked lines abraded the skin on my hands, and they started to bleed. *No big deal,* I thought. *What's a little pain? You're tough.* That attitude lasted about fifteen minutes, while the abrasions on my hands became deeper and the blood poured more freely. To give my hands a rest, I lowered the sail, lay on the board, and started paddling. I could see that if I kept paddling at my present rate with the drag of the sail and board, I might make the shore sometime that evening.

Calling for help was not an option because I was beyond shouting distance and there were no boats in sight. I paddled on until I began to notice that I could see my blood in the water. The extremity of my situation hit then. Sharks can smell one drop of blood in the water for miles. I flashed on the underwater scenes from the Jaws movies in which the shark silently approaches swimmers from underneath, those stupid swimmers who flopped their arms over the sides of rafts like long, white fish in their death throes. *Hell!* I yanked my arms out of the water and huddled there, pressing my bleeding hands inside my suit. While lying there, I was grateful for the warmth of the tropical water and sun. I would die of terminal stupidity before I would die of hypothermia. I didn't hear the sound of an outboard motor approaching until just before a small boat nudged my board and large hands reached out to touch my back.

"Need a ride?" Fiji Tom asked, "or would you rather just sail back?"

"Oh! A boat ride with you sounds nice, Tom. I'll just hop in!" I responded. He could see the blood on my hands but made no comment. *What a model of tact this guy is. I hope they pay him well.*

By the time we departed from Fiji the next morning, my hands were beginning to scab and didn't interfere with my flying. We had a full load of deadheads on board, an unusual circumstance for us out of Fiji, so I was I curious about them. There were eight women from Memphis, Tennessee, who worked in FedEx offices. None of them had been out of the continental U.S. before, and once I had shown my willingness to talk, they were full of questions about Australia.

Jim invited them into the cockpit, where the view is always better. Blackie instructed them about expected behavior from whoever was sitting in the cockpit for approach and landing in Sydney. They were surprised that we might allow them to be up front for the landing and held a mini lottery to see who would get the coveted seats.

It was exhilarating to re-experience the wonder of seeing a place for the first time while hearing the exclamations of the Memphis women as they caught sight of the Australian continent on the horizon. Australian ATC asked us to descend early, so our approach brought us in at low level over miles of beaches and harbors north of Sydney and in a circling arc around Sydney Harbor.

On my first trip to Sydney, I had taken a four-and-a-half-hour harbor cruise that began with the guide announcing that Sydney had the most beautiful harbor in the world. *Oh, spare me the hyperbole!* I had thought. *Doesn't this chick know that she has a boatload of world travelers here?* Australia is not easy to reach, and most veteran travelers have been to many other places before they get there. I had flown over or sailed around harbors at Rio de Janeiro, Singapore, Hong Kong, Cape Town, San Diego, and San Francisco, among others. The competition for "most beautiful" was stiff. After four hours on Sydney Harbor, I was reluctantly agreeing that perhaps our guide had not exaggerated after all. Most impressive for me was the Sydney Opera House, perched on the water's edge like a giant, multi-winged bird about to lift off. That man could dream up and build such a structure was inspirational. Sharing the first glimpse those Southern women had of the Opera House was a treat. As we deplaned, they said they had never had such a grand flight before.

Jim and Blackie and I flew from Sydney to Melbourne the next day and onward, north to Guam. On the island of Guam, Blackie received word that his wife was in the hospital in Anchorage, Alaska. Jim and I helped him throw his belongings in his bags, make reservations on one of the few departures a day from Guam to the states, and get to the airport. The company was going to have to find a replacement for our engineer, fly him across the Pacific, and give him enough time to get rested before Jim and I could fly with a full crew again. We settled in for a long wait.

The tropical island of Guam, a U.S. Territory, was not a bad place to be stuck. Our hotel, The Guam Hilton, was two years away from destruction by earthquake. There are some downsides to being on the "Rim of Fire" which refers to the volcanic nature of the Pacific Rim islands. But the negatives were not visible while Jim and I were there. We rented kayaks and explored the broad, shallow bay that most of the large hotels were built around. Some sandy tracts were so shallow that we had to maneuver around coral heads that were inches below the surface of the clear water. Swimming masks were unnecessary.

We saw a neighboring hotel that merited further exploration. The Pacific Island Beach Club was like a *Fantasy Island* set. A large waterfall cascaded down the hillside from the hotel proper into a lagoon bordered by tropical trees, vines, and flowers. The lagoon streamed around into smaller pools surrounded by chaise lounges and into canals built for swimmers and rafters. Those waterways were stocked with tropical fish, and timid snorkelers cruised there rather than in the ocean. There were water slides funneling through hidden lava rock caves and hot tubs in secluded spots. There was even a lap pool of regulation size for serious swimmers who did not want to navigate around faux coral heads and bends in the river. Jim and I explored the grounds, played a game of water volleyball, and swam up to a bar on a pool island. The seats were underwater. Yeah, Guam was not a bad place to get stuck.

Our random conversations turned to personal things—our spouses, our children, and marriage problems created by the very nature of the job, such as long absences, missing the important milestones of anniversaries and birthdays and school plays, and the opportunities for infidelity and mistrust. We spoke of communication problems between couples, and I found myself beginning to open up about Scott and my years of marriage counseling.

Scott had hit me with his fists for the first time in 1989, and I still had not told my family and friends. I was deeply ashamed that someone who had promised to love and honor me for a lifetime could beat me. What was so terribly wrong with me that my partner could do this?

I had always sworn that if a man ever hit me, I would be out the door in a flash. I had not understood why women stayed on for more of the same. But here I was, promises to myself broken, unable to even speak of my own experience. Part of me was still reeling from the shock of it, from lying on a bed immobilized by a newly set broken leg and having my husband shower blows upon my head and arms and chest while our two children and a young nanny slept in adjoining rooms. Part of me was still reeling from the unreality of the response I received when I went to counselors for

285

help later. I asked if men like this could be helped or if my staying on while he got counseling was just volunteering for manslaughter. I was told he could be helped. But no one said, "Bad boy!" to him. No one suggested that I run for the hills. No one told me that I should be telling my family and getting support. No one told me that it was mandatory that I file a police report in order to, at the very least, start a paper trail of abuse. I had given Scott the choice of jail or therapy. He picked therapy.

When counselors didn't tell him that what he had done was heinous, I began to doubt my own sanity in the whole area. Was I perhaps making a big deal out of something not so very important? Maybe my expectations for marriage and relationships were just unrealistic. I thought experienced counselors surely ought to know better than I. My career had already helped me be good at normalizing awful situations.

*I*n that tropical lagoon in Guam, feeling warmed by the sun and the safety of this solidly rational man beside me, I opened up to Jim about my marriage actually having some problems. I was incapable of telling him how engulfing some of those problems were, so I chose to tell him a story about Scott's and my communication that I could joke about, like "Ha ha, look how stupid I was to expect something here." I didn't know yet that when things got unbearable for me and I deflected my feelings with humor, I was downplaying and dishonoring them at the same time.

Early in my second pregnancy, Scott had said, with sympathy, "Is there anything I can do to help you through this pregnancy? To make it easier for you?" I had suggested that regular flowers would be helpful. I loved flowers and missed having a man send them to me. (Scott had stopped bringing me flowers after we got married, just as he had stopped giving me regular birthday and Christmas gifts.) Scott had replied that sending flowers every week was too expensive. I told him to put them on my separate credit card, and I would pay the bill. I just wanted the gesture of love from him. I also asked Scott to help me in and out of the car because I had had a difficult time getting in and out when I was pregnant with Cammie.

He never brought me flowers; he never helped me out of the car. When I asked during a counseling session why he had not brought me flowers, he said that he hated it when I ordered him around.

I turned to Jim in the pool in Guam, smiled big, and asked for some male advice. "If I don't ask for what I want or need, he says how was he supposed to know what I wanted. And if I do ask, then I'm ordering him around. So Jim, tell me how you guys really want to be communicated with."

Jim looked at me and didn't smile. Finally he said, "Norah, I can't answer that one for you."

We made plans to meet in the lobby of our hotel for dinner. As I was getting ready to leave my room, Jim called me, said he would be briefly delayed, and I should wait for him in my room.

When he knocked many minutes later, I opened my door to a bouquet of flowers. He said, "These are for you. You are a wonderful woman and you deserve flowers."

My eyes brimmed with tears when I took the flowers from Jim's arms. I cried with the pleasure of receiving flowers. I cried with the heartbreak of the dreamer who had hoped it could be this way with her husband. I cried with the sorrow of knowing that this moment would never be happening with Scott. I cried as I put those flowers in a vase. And when we flew on, I took them with me.

Jim said all the florists were closed for the evening and he'd had to enlist the help of the hotel manager. He had so convinced the manager of the urgency of his need for flowers that the manager had helped Jim raid an ornamental arrangement in the hotel's lobby. Truly a full-service hotel and a can-do Tiger.

A replacement engineer arrived and ended our lazy days just as I was falling in love with Jim. Naturally, I didn't tell anyone that. At first I beat myself up for having the feelings at all. What was I doing, a married woman, allowing myself to have these feelings for a married man? How had these feelings sneaked by my most frequently used survival tool, numbing myself? Later, I forgave myself for having the emotions. Meanwhile, I prevented myself from doing something inappropriate with them. I didn't want to replace Scott. I just wanted our relationship to be back to what it once was before the erosion of trust had truncated my caring for him. With Jim I was able to be myself, to be respected and listened to. With Jim there was an absence of fear, and I didn't guard my feelings. My marriage was dying of fear and loathing.

We flew on to Tokyo and Anchorage. I found an inscribed coffee mug in a gift store that had me hooting with laughter. Oh, how perfect for Jim. On the morning of our last day together, flying from Anchorage to San Francisco, I carried the mug to the plane in my flight bag and insisted on getting the first round of coffee from the galley. I handed the engineer his Styrofoam cup and presented the ceramic mug to Jim. A worldly looking woman on the front of the mug proclaimed, "Men are only good for one thing." The back of the mug said, "And just how important is parallel parking anyway?"

Jim laughed and said, "When I get this home, it's going to be my favorite mug."

I watched Jim walk away from me into the San Francisco parking lot; his tall frame was limned with backlight from the lights over the parked cars. He leaned into the gusting wind that blew his uniform raincoat back against his suitcase, his gait showing an eagerness to be in his car and headed home to his wife. I turned slowly away and sighed down to my toes.

I never flew with him again, but his gifts to me, of caring and flowers, are still with me.

34

ABSOLUTELY,
POSITIVELY UNEMPLOYED
1992

*P*rior to the August 1989 merging of Flying Tigers with Federal Express, FedEx founder, Fred Smith, and a management team made a series of "road shows" so they could answer employee questions about what was coming and allay fears that many workers had about their jobs being lost. Fred promised that "absolutely, positively" nobody would lose employment.

In October 1992, after FedEx decided to get out of the Military Airlift Command (MAC) business, all of the Tiger flight attendants were let go. Some were offered the opportunity to interview for other positions in the company. Some of those interviewed were hired. Out of over two-hundred flight attendants, with lengths of service up to thirty-three years, fewer than twelve were "rehired."

Gael Okicich and Betty Carver designed a tee shirt that utilized the FedEx advertising catchphrase, "Absolutely, Positively on Time." The tee shirt read, "Absolutely, Positively Unemployed" across the front, with smaller letters across the bottom reading, "Thanks Fred."

The flight attendants made their last flight from Los Angeles to St. Louis with a load of military personnel and rode the empty plane back to Los Angeles. Many knew it would be their last working flight ever, and they grabbed the opportunity to do things they hadn't been able to do before. They played music over the intercom and danced in the aisles. They rode on top of the drink carts, tossing drinks and food to other revelers, or rudely called, "Get your own drink, dammit, I'm not your servant." They videotaped each other laughing and crying and making cathartic statements to Fred Smith. After years of being in a career where personal appearance was critical, they made certain that their uniforms were not completely neat and professional.

As they buckled in for the approach to Los Angeles, one woman, no longer constrained by having to set a good example, put her tray table down, pulled her carry-on bag out from under the seat, and unbuckled her seatbelt. She jumped into the aisle and ran to the window to view the landing. She cheered up and down, arms and legs in the vees of victory, when the landing proved to be a "grease job."

A heavy drink cart, completely stocked with miniature bottles of alcohol, was liberated from the aircraft. Many remember it being laboriously lifted down the stairs. No one remembers who actually did that felonious act.

Several years later, flight attendants gathered for a going away party for senior flight attendant Judy Curtis, who had been diagnosed with terminal cancer. The purloined drink cart, still replete with miniature bottles, made a mysterious reappearance. It rolled into the party, providing the final airline catering for Judy. The Flying Tiger spirit lived on.

35

THE HORROR STARTED AT NOON

1992–93

*F*lying for a living did strongly impact my daily life in many ways that were not so obvious as being away from home for two weeks out of the month. For one, I was always on time for everything, a compulsiveness about punctuality that was irritating for my husband, whose farm-growing schedule did not involve counting the minutes until the seeds germinated. Captain Tom Cotton had advised me at the beginning of my Tiger career that if I could not be on time, be early. I took his advice literally. In my personal life, I often scheduled myself to be a little early, in case something unexpected happened. With two small children at home, the unexpected was the rule rather than the exception.

Another transference of job to home was my method of driving. I planned trips ahead of time, down to the details of where to stop for gas and food and overnights. The phone numbers of emergency services en route were ready in the glove compartment. The emergency equipment was checked before each trip, along with the oil and fluid levels and the tire pressures. My habit of always being in the exact center of my lane seemed anal retentive to some.

I learned by flying through emergencies not to let my emotions get in the way of my concentration. Being able to

291

focus was critical. I looked to my instruments and dealt with one thing at a time. I learned to think and not to feel.

A major and serious effect of my job on my personal life, and one I did not recognize until I was in my late thirties, was my inability to quit. Pilots do not quit. In an emergency they continue flying until they hit the ground. Throwing up their hands and screaming in terror was not an option. We had all heard stories about pilots who had done everything in the book when faced with an emergency, and then, because the plane was still flying and the emergency still unchecked, they got creative about new ways to try to tackle it. Some of those nonquitters had lived to tell their stories and others had died trying to save their plane.

I refused to quit on my marriage. We had started counseling during our first year of marriage and we continued to seek it throughout the next ten years of our formal union. I use "we" here, figuratively, because it finally became apparent that I was seeking counseling and he was just being dragged along. Friends later told me that Scott had made jokes about the sessions. For instance, he would say, "This week the girls are trying to get me to argue by their rules. Like I am not supposed to raise my voice, to call Norah names, to bring up anything from the past, or to try talking about more than one issue at a time. If I did it their way, I would never win! How stupid do they think I am?"

I tried to accept being screamed at on a daily basis; I even tried to learn to scream at Scott in order to diffuse the hurt I felt when he raised his voice to me. I tried for more than a decade and I failed. As the verbal abuse turned physical, I became desperate to stop the acceleration and I failed there too. I almost died trying.

One of the byproducts of living in a crazy situation was that my tolerance for insanity increased exponentially. My ability to discern what made sense and what didn't became impaired. When my husband continued to exhibit bizarre behavior, I began to question my own sanity. I was not insane. The situation was insane, and I became progressively crazy as I tried to adjust to it. I was not crazy—it was just that my situation seemed to require a crazy person.

When my marriage became physically abusive, I went through another period of questioning my sanity. The abuse itself was not the only problem, perhaps not even the biggest one. It was not only the violence to my body that was destructive but also the violence to my reality. It was like living with a Nazi who everybody else thought was Mr. Rogers.

Denial protected me from seeing things too painful to see and feeling things too overwhelming to feel. It was a shock absorber for my soul.

The horror started at noon on a clear, warm day. Sunlight filled the gazebo-like, built-in dining area at the end of my adobe-tiled kitchen. Scott and I were having lunch alone. Cammie and Bren had eaten earlier and were playing with Legos in their playroom, around a bend from the kitchen. I still don't remember what Scott and I were talking about; it was not anything that was important to me. Just chat to fill our midday hour together. I disagreed with something he said. I could see the stiffening of his face, the lengthening of his jaw, the subtle signs of impending temper. His voice rose with his reply.

I said, "You're right. I didn't think it through. You're right." His voice rose higher. My giving in so easily had not assuaged his anger. It had fanned the fire. I saw it in his eyes and was frightened. I rose, grabbing my empty plate and my half-empty Diet Coke can.

"I can see you're getting angry. I'm going out on the deck for ten minutes. When we've both cooled down, we can talk about this again." I turned my back to him and walked toward the sink with my hands full. I heard him slide across the upholstery of the bench seating and bump against the round table as he rose. I heard a low, huffing growl and knew he was coming after me. I started to run and, half turning, tossed my plate and can at him to slow him down. The safety of the door to the outside was ten strides away.

Right leg midair in the start of a sprint, arms rising to pump up my speed, I felt a knife stab of pain under my right ear and heard an echoing internal thud coming from the left side of my head. A reverberating shudder went through my left shoulder. The force of the blow from behind and the right had slammed me into the wall.

What? What? I thought, and my chin fell down my neck and down my chest, and I couldn't stop it and I could see the tiles rising to my face and I couldn't stop them from rising up to stoneslap my cheek. *What? What?* I thought, as I found my body on the floor and tried to crawl to the door, but my legs would not work, and I heard these bam bam hollow-sounding thudding noises. I heard those strange thuds going up and down my back and neck. I didn't feel them yet, I just heard them, but I knew I had to get away from them, and I squirmed and wormed my body toward the door to the outside, but my head jammed under the bottom of the cupboards by the sink. *What? What?* And I began to curve my face into my chest and cover the back of my head with my hands and pull my knees to my stomach. My skull fit into that kickspace. *Who would have thought it would fit there?* And I saw where the toes of my shoes had dulled the finish on the wood of the kickboard from all the times I had stood at the sink doing dishes. I looked at those tiny scratches and I still heard the thuds at my back. *I wonder what those noises are? Oh, oh, there are my new glasses and they're broken. Why are they under the sink? Something bad is happening. Must get away.* I tried to uncurl an arm so I could pull myself along the floor. *Maybe I could get my fingers to pull along the grout lines?* Whap. Thud. *Those bad noises. I am going to die.* I untucked my chin and moved my head so my eyes were facing the way I had to go to get out.

Then there were other sounds, a high pitched mewling from somewhere near those bad thuds. And little voices, children's voices. *Not my babies! They can't see me dying like this.* I tried to shout a warning. *Stay out!* But I could not hear my voice over those thuds and that strange whimpering noise. I saw a little pair of bare feet run into the kitchen. Even though my vision could not rise above those small feet and calves, I recognized the feet of my daughter. Those long skinny toes were miniatures of mine. Then another set of little feet ran and stood by the first. My son. *No. No!* And then the smallest little feet changed position and turned and ran out, and those little feet like mine started running toward me. They rose into the air and disappeared. *Where did they go? Where did they fly up to?* I heard a little voice far above and slapping noises by the little voice.

"Stop hurting my Mommy! Stop hurting my Mommy! Stop." Then the little feet came back; they came down in front of my face. Little hands touched my cheek. I could see my daughter's face; her eyes were wide and her mouth was wide. She turned to pound her fists at something behind me. "Bad Daddy! Bad Daddy! Go away!"

At first I could not move, then was able to crawl away. Scott left the house, taking the children with him.

I desperately needed to talk. I was, in the way of all battered wives, ashamed and embarrassed, but I was frantic to be held and comforted. I wanted to protect my parents from the awfulness, so I didn't call them. I was afraid of what would happen if I called a girlfriend in town. I wanted Bill Helbig, my best friend at Tigers. He was in a Memphis hotel. I called and cried and babbled and got hysterical and got calm and got hysterical again over the phone. I knew it was torture for him to hear it. But I knew he loved me enough to listen and comfort me and say the right words.

That beating ended our ten-year marriage. Needing emergency neurosurgery to repair my neck complicated my leaving. The chin-to-shoulder cast precluded my driving a car. As soon as I could, I bought another house in the same school district and moved. Bill called from his flight layovers and held my hand over the phone as best he was able. When I was established in my new place, Bill flew into my small town with a housewarming gift and helped me hang pictures. I cried when I took him to the airport that afternoon. I had been divorced before. I knew the nastiness of legal closure was just beginning and I was afraid for my life.

My in-laws and some of my friends began going away. It was easier for people to kill the messenger of bad news rather than deal with ugliness. My respected and much-loved father-in-law called me a liar. A sister-in-law said, "What?

295

Hit you? Not Scott."

I was sick and depressed and wounded and needy, not the ideal guest to keep on one's social calendar. I no longer fit in with acquaintances who always did things as couples. My social life faded away. My peripheral friends disappeared and my genuine friends girded themselves for helping me through the tough times ahead. Those friends were constant.

I kept a log by my phone of the friends I had called during the week, so no one would have to talk to me more than one whining session per seven days. I knew how draining it was to be there for divorcing friends and I couldn't afford to lose any more friends.

My relationship with Scott was a thief who stole something innately precious from me: my confidence that I was a person worthy of love. To be fair, being a three-time loser in marriage contributed to my feeling of unworthiness. Having three husbands crossed the line between some small mistakes and a nasty habit. It did not occur to me then that it was my partner picker that was broken, not my lovableness. Though I didn't know why my friends continued to love me, I did know that I needed their love desperately.

They held my heart gently while I struggled with learning to live again.

36

AFTERMATH
1994–96

The nightmares started the month I left
Scott. They always started with the view, from an inch off
the floor, of those little feet running. In the dreams I knew
what the thudding noises were, the pounding of workboot-
clad toes against my spine and neck, and I knew what the
strange sounds were, my own strangled, stunned cries of
pain. I felt the pain. And in my dreams I could not move;
could not stop the little feet.

My children were angry and hurt. We went to a counselor
together and separately. I found that drinking a glass of wine
before bed held off the nightmares. The one glass turned
into two, then a bottle. My drinking scared me. I went to
a twelve-step group and heard people talking about how
they were powerless over alcohol and their lives had become
unmanageable. *I'm not powerless over alcohol. I've quit
drinking lots of times. And my life isn't unmanageable, now
that I don't live with Scott.* Drinking was useful in going to
sleep; I wanted only to control the amount.

My struggles to stay dry a month were invariably followed
by a week of relapse. Because I had no problem staying dry
while working and on layovers, I blamed my relapsing on
the legal process of divorce. The combination of living in a

state where wife beating doesn't abrogate parental rights and my having a job that kept me away for two weeks a month resulted in my not receiving sole custody of my children. I felt helpless to protect them.

After hearing the joint-custody decision, I drove home to calm down. Dropping my keys after I unlocked the door, I bent to retrieve them and fell to my knees. Pain stabbed through my gut and circled upward. I gasped for breath and a howl emerged. I started to sob, then cry, and crumpled flat. I keened and clawed at the rug. *No, no, God!*

My children needing a ride home from school motivated me to cling to a wall and pull myself off the floor. I washed my face, breathed deep, and walked to my car.

To escape for a few days, I planned a ski trip with women friends. On the first day, acute back pain forced me off the hill. The kicking injuries to my back precluded my skiing.

"Were you kicked by a horse?" the doctor asked as he bound me in a back brace. "Not quite," I replied.

The prescribed painkiller dulled my senses but didn't take away the pain, so I reverted to my drug of choice, alcohol. During a month of physical therapy, I observed Scott entering a serious romance and becoming relatively mellow. I was glad for our children's sake but wondered why I remained too emotionally distraught to date. *Why is it that hurters always get a life sooner than hurtees?*

*A*fter returning to flying, I encountered a captain who was regaling my crew with a story of what I was like in bed. I didn't even know him. I called the union's professional standards representative and made a formal complaint. *I don't have to take this shit anymore.* I received a written apology but was surprised by how energy-depleting the experience was.

I was running out of gas.

37

HOW MANY BLONDES DOES IT TAKE TO FLY A JUMBO JET?

1996–97

*1*996 brought huge changes for the last of the Tiger 747 pilots, many of them unfortunate. The remaining Tiger 747s were sold. I took my last flight on my beloved fat lady in the summer of 1996, accompanied by two of my favorite crewmembers, Dick Crawford and Cliff Call. Dick was slated to retire after that flight. Cliff and I, both forty-six, were scheduled to be trained in September on the MD-11, the jumbo that would replace the 747.

The last of the Tiger bases was closed, and I was given the choice of being based in Anchorage or Memphis. I looked at the potential schedules and realized that if I commuted to either new base, I would lose two days off for every trip I flew and would spend three weeks a month on the road. I could no longer live in the small farming community with little air service and successfully commute to work. I had a huge dilemma.

I had joint custody of my children but couldn't take them out of the state. Was it going to be good for them to go to a new city and be left with a nanny for two weeks out of the month? I could move to Anchorage or Memphis and leave them behind with Scott and his new wife, or I could just quit being an airline pilot.

Something elemental had gone awry, a parent keeping a child safe. I had wanted to be able to say, as my mom always had, "Come home to me, you'll always be welcome and taken care of here." I couldn't offer my children the house they'd grown up in, with Mommy and Daddy under one roof waiting to grandparent. I couldn't offer them what I couldn't give myself, safety from physical harm and emotional trauma, or assurance that some things, however intangible, would always remain the same.

I decided to leave my children where they had been born and raised, where they were surrounded by aunts, uncles, grandparents, and friends, and where they would have two parents to come home to every night.

The decision broke my heart.

The pilots who had attended the MD-11 school said it was the toughest they had ever been in. It became a career killer for many 747 crewmembers. Men with thirty years of airline experience, the last twenty as jumbo-jet captains, were failing the school. Guys who had never busted a checkride before were failing the type-rating ride on the MD-11.

The consequences for those failed rides were extreme. The "failed" captains were not allowed to retrain and retake the ride a few weeks later, nor were they allowed to be bumped into the copilot's seat to fly the plane from there. Those 747 drivers who flunked after spending two months away from home in school were then faced with more months away from home in another airplane school (usually the DC-10). FedEx rules said that these men had to fly copilot on the DC-10 for two years before they could return to the captain's seat on any plane.

We pilots waiting for training to start heard stories about highly skilled and respected men busting their checrides and facing ending their careers in the copilot's seat. If they were fifty-five or older, they had only a few years left, and making reduced copilot's pay for those years impacted their retirement income. But reduced income for the rest of their lives was the less chilling aspect of flunking MD-11 school. Much worse was the fact that their spirits were being broken. Pilots without healthy self-esteem do not fly well; they cannot make command decisions in split seconds. I watched once-proud aviators slink out of the MD-11 simulator with their tails dragging, licking their wounds. MD-11 school in 1996 was a bloodbath.

I entered MD-11 school knowing that some pilots were passing; I was determined to be one of them. I had never flunked a checkride before. *I am not going to flunk now.*

Overhearing a conversation in a restaurant between two purple-pilot instructors briefly daunted me. They talked about those whining, incompetent Tigers and how much fun it was to see them flunk. After all, the Tigers were mostly too old and too stupid to be trained on a new generation of glass-cockpit jets. These instructors were doing aviation a favor by getting us dinosaurs out of the skies.

"I'm going to see how many I can personally put out to pasture," one said. He laughed, a nasty sound of inhumanity. I got lucky. I never saw those Memphis-based men again.

I made it through the school bent, but not broken. Because I passed the captain's simulator type-rating ride and the captain's initial-operating-experience testing before I flunked a captain's standards ride, I was allowed to fly copilot for six months before returning to the captain's seat. At the time, I was so relieved to be out of training that I didn't care what seat I was in. *Just let me fly again.* Shortly thereafter, the FAA shut down the MD-11 school temporarily, correctly ascertaining that the large flunk rate indicated a problem with the school. I moved to Anchorage. My first trip as copilot on the MD-11 was memorable.

Streaking through the dark sky, out from the night-jeweled twinkling of Hong Kong toward the sculpted snow of Anchorage's mountains, I looked for the Hale-Bopp Comet. It was March of 1997 and I knew I should be able to see the comet sometime during the eleven-hour flight. When a blur of not-sparkling, not-circular light appeared in my windscreen, I wondered. It was unusual. It might have been man-made. An hour of its rising in my window and growing larger had me sitting on the edge of my seat. *Was that it? Yes.* Its tail, miles of trailing ice particles, became distinctly V-shaped. Its head wavered in shape. It flew through the sky, outlined by the aurora borealis to the north and bright stars to the south. I watched it for hours until it faded from sight with the dawn.

I contemplated a phrase I'd heard, that life was not measured by the number of breaths one took but by the moments that took one's breath away. I thought of the other marvelous things I had viewed from the cockpit. These were God's gifts to pilots: snow crawling down the Rockies, sunrise over the Grand Canyon, the vast green mat of the Amazon jungle, the twisting silver road of the Mississippi, and the top of Everest—a cone 10,000 feet below. I had seen the Great Wall of China curving below, the harbor at Rio, the starkness of the Australian Outback, the towering plume of Mt. Saint Helen's ash, the curvature of the earth at the North Pole, the deep blue of the stratosphere. I had crossed the equator, awed by sunstreaked evenings, dappled earth, velvet night, and spun-silver clouds. I flew inside God's weather; saw horizontal rain and contrails. One night over the north slope of Alaska, I turned off my small plane's lights and flew, just a dark spot against the starry skies, into the green and yellow and pink of the dancing of the Aurora Borealis.

The ocean and sky had always been more church to me than the centuries-old buildings humans had rites in. The ocean and sky were my sanctuaries. They signified something primal and wild but simple, straightforward, and safe. They were the only proof I ever needed that there was a God. In touching them, I had touched God's face. The pervasive feeling of wonder in the cockpit that night was a memory I treasured as life began to turn black in the coming months.

A break in worsening depression came, one month later, when I flew with a woman captain for the first time. In my forties, as my bright coppery red hair grayed out to a muted strawberry blond, people stopped telling blonde jokes around me. Being deprived of blonde jokes was insulting until I met Captain Janis Skliar.

In the Anchorage crew room, I watched a tall, athletically slender, patrician-faced woman stride in. A flowing mane of blonde hair topped her head-turning figure. I noted the captain's stripes on her shoulder epaulets and approached her with my hand outstretched.

"I'm Norah O'Neill. I believe I'm your copilot for this trip. I'm new on this plane. This will be my second copilot's trip on the MD-11."

"I'm Janis Skliar. I'm a new captain on this plane. This will be my second trip too." She paused. "Are you scared yet?" she asked with a hint of smile crinkles around her eyes.

"No. I can see we'll get along just fine."

We were a good team. Most of our seven-day trip was spent alone in the cockpit with no jumpseaters catching a ride. Janis was bright, funny, and a talented pilot. What an incredible package. Our cockpit conversations were a mix of straight airplane business and pure woman talk. We were experienced women from different backgrounds; she flew in the military, I was enough older than she to have not had that option. She was newly married and secure in that relationship. We talked men, with a minimum of male bashing. We talked about feelings. *This is an amazing experience. There are no undertones. All I have to do is be me and do a good job. Why did being the first woman out here have to be so hard? This could have been so easy.*

Janis was a font of blonde jokes. Throughout her career, blonde jokes had been slipped to her anonymously and overtly. She collected them. I told Janis about one of my favorite blondes, Anita, a cinematic technical director whom I had met in Mexico. Anita and her four male companions had just wrapped a film and were vacationing together to celebrate. As we lounged by the pool one afternoon discussing possible plans, Anita said the marlin fishing of the previous day had left her so aching that she was just going to lie around. A film editor suggested that she perhaps lie around in a beauty parlor chair and let a beautician do something about her half-inch-long dark roots.

Anita sat up in her chaise lounge and huffed out, "I'll have you know that I had my roots done the day before we left!" An uncomfortable silence ensued. *She paid someone for those dark brown roots and platinum hair?* Into that void, Anita threw her punch line.

"Do you know how expensive it is and how much work it is to have to go in to have my roots dyed dark?" she said, fluffing her fingers through her short brown and white spiked do. "I wouldn't want anyone at work to think I was a *real* blonde."

*I*n Singapore, Janis and I rolled a high-tech jumbo jet into its parking stall and shut her down for the night. When we exited the plane and hopped into the waiting crew bus, the driver waited a long time to put it in gear. He finally asked, "When are the pilots who flew the plane going to be coming out?"

We laughed

"Hey Janis, how many blondes does it take to safely fly a two-man jumbo jet across the Pacific Ocean?"

"Two."

38

CRASH LANDING

1997–2000

*I*n the fall of 1997, my personal life finally spiraled down into a crash landing. It was my spirit dying. I had walked through some traumatic events; I had walked through depression; I had walked through chaos; and I could not walk through anything any longer.

I was a woman with a stainless steel exterior concealing a marshmallow center, which was doing a meltdown. The molten mess was beginning to crack its casing. My life had become a gray tunnel with a black hole at the end of it. I had to force myself to get out of bed in the morning.

I was without my children in the cold and dark and aloneness of Anchorage. I knew what was required to make a new life in a new place—joining a gym, joining a church, doing volunteer work, getting out, and being seen. I did none of it. I was so tired. Nightmares awakened me nightly. I descended into a waking hell of hopelessness.

Flying was my last refuge, but my flight time was curtailed when most of my trips were bought for someone else's training. I stayed home and sank into an abyss. I thought if I stopped drinking again, the blackness of my fading existence would recede and I would want to live again. Really live. Not drinking was a start, not the answer.

I had been good at stuffing my emotions and deflecting my pain with psychic Band-Aids. My favorites were humor, relationships, busyness, and alcohol, but they stopped working. The pain and the rage festered into a boiling eruption that imploded.

I should have wept when a husband ran off with another woman. I should have wept when a husband beat me. I should have wept when men I worked with said, "Fuck me or I'll get you fired." Instead, I had called on all the coping skills I had learned as a military brat. I breathed deep, put my shoulders back, held my head high, looked straight ahead, and walked on.

I should have wept.

Finally, it was my love of flying that led me to get help. I knew I was sick. I could not bear the thought of taking my sickness into a plane. And that year I loved planes more than I loved myself.

I flew my last flight on September 1, 1997, though I didn't know it would be the last. How could the grand passion of my adult life go away without my even having a hint? I should have felt some premonition, some nuance of soul flicker. I did not. Later, I would grieve that not knowing. Unlike pilots who know they are retiring and bring along the video camera to record the last landing and fire trucks spraying a saluting arch to taxi under to their final parking, I flew my last leg without even taking a mental snapshot.

Lady Diana had just died in France. Mike Linden and I met at San Francisco International Airport to prepare for our flight to Anchorage. We did our flight planning under clear skies and somberly talked about Diana's life. I wished that she'd had more joy and less anguish.

We reached Anchorage after dark and were instructed to make a visual approach to Runway 32. This was unusual because the approach to Runway 32 was noise sensitive and was used only when the wind direction and velocity mandated it for safety. The visual approach to 32 was also unusual for the MD-11, since it was one of the few approaches in our flight system that a pilot could not set up for the plane to fly totally on autopilot. We ex-747 drivers hated having to let "Auto" always fly the approaches and landings and we celebrated the rare times that we were able to fly the fun parts ourselves.

That night, I entered the downwind leg visually, with all of the cockpit magic video screens painting pink lines that I could follow and use for backup information. The stars were bright; we could see the mountains with their first dusting of snow and the water of Cook Inlet black below us. Coastline inbound, turning final, gear down, winds burbling bumpily over dark low hills on final approach; I flew the MD-11 to a smooth touchdown.

Flying was all over for me, and I didn't have a clue.

I went home that night determined to quit drinking. I was shocked to discover that I couldn't stop. The twelve-steppers had predicted it; had said the day would come when I wouldn't be able to stop. I hadn't believed them. After a week of drinking over that discovery, I called Sandy Donnelly, who had worked on the union committee established to help alcoholics. Within the hour, Tiger pilot Sheri Laurie took me to the emergency room. Sandy flew from Arizona to Anchorage. When I was released, Sandy and Sheri helped me pack for 30 days at a treatment center. Sandy held my hand when I flew there and waited to see me safely checked in.

It was my own brain that undid me. The keen intellect that was a gift from God at birth; that blend of genetics that allowed me to be a courageous adventurer; that same brain that produced those phenomena also produced a disabling disease that ended the life I treasured.

I received a letter from the FAA a week after I started treatment. They noted that I should not be flying in my condition and asked me to mail them my airman's medical certificate. It was ironic that they didn't trust me to stay on the ground. After all, I was the one who had told them I had a problem. I cried when I got the letter. My not being able to fly was there in black and white. The enormity of the reality was sinking in.

At first I equated my stay in a treatment center with going for a master's degree in radical lifestyle changes at a nasty boarding school—if I got As, I got to leave. If I got Fs,

I died. Unlike my previous experiences with school, I didn't get As and I didn't graduate. The flawed neurotransmitters that were the root of my alcoholism used my IQ against me to send deviously evil thoughts. I had a long-toothed, long-clawed rodent living in my head. He spun his caged-squirrel wheel faster and faster as my disease raced, cranking out sick messages to my psyche.

Captain Bob Poindexter called. "Norah, Sandy gave me this number. I'm shocked. We've flown together often, and I've never seen you drunk. I know life has been hard for you lately, but alcoholism? Are you sure? I always thought alcoholism was an excuse for people with no willpower or backbone or moral fiber. Clearly this isn't the case with you. Please educate me."

"Oh Bob, I'm embarrassed. I feel like such a failure because all my best thinking and willpower led me here. They're telling me willpower is useless when it comes to alcoholism. I'm having a difficult time understanding that. What else do I have?" I started to cry.

"What can I do to help?" Bob asked.

"Write to me. Call me. I feel like I've been transported to an alien planet."

Only temporarily released from the grip of mood-altering and brain-fogging alcohol, I had to face my nightmares and flashbacks without self-administered anesthesia. Released after ninety days in the treatment center, I drank again. I returned and was punished for relapsing by being forced to wear a sign that said "Ghost" and warned people not to communicate with me in any way. Counselors said they were trying a therapeutic tool to force me inside of myself. I sat in the corner and wasn't allowed to speak or participate in group therapy. With no outlet, my disease raged and I lived in a constant nightmare. After forty-five days, I was asked to leave because I was "hopeless."

Because I was too ill to go home, FedEx sent me to a trauma treatment center in Santa Fe, New Mexico. I was diagnosed with post traumatic stress disorder and spent forty-five days grappling with it. Part of my therapy was imagining myself in a safe place and recalling traumas at a distance until

I could think about them without reliving them. My safe place was with dolphins. I spent hours swimming between two dolphins across the ceilings of rooms in my memory. The flashbacks stopped; the nightmares lessened.

I went home but realized that I still saw my life as a gray tunnel, though now there was light at the end of it. Some days I felt as if I were walking on the bottom of the ocean, with movements slowed and the surface unreachable miles above. My sleep was still broken, now by dreams of drowning, clawing toward the surface sunlight. Not being able to breathe awakened me. A half-year passed of struggling to surface. Years of being depressed had changed my brain chemistry, and I needed help to restore it to normalcy.

Faint hopes of flying again in the future had to be given up. I had to become willing to take medication for the rest of my life in order to be well. Pilots cannot fly on antidepressants. I was told that the acid test for clinical depression was whether or not the medication worked. It worked on me. I handled the news by drinking.

The FedEx rule was two strikes and you're out. I was called to the chief pilot's office after the second relapse. A kind man, Fred Peters said he didn't want to fire me after twenty-two years of exemplary service, so he offered to let me resign. Because I was crying too hard to be able to type, he said he would write the letter for me. While he was typing, his computer screen went blank. A computer technician repaired it. Fred resumed typing and the screen went blank again. He went to his secretary's computer, began typing, and *her* screen went blank. He said, "The universe is conspiring against your resigning."

I wasn't forced to resign, but was given an unpaid medical leave.

Slowly, imperceptibly, on a day-to-day basis, the complex layers of my illness were peeled back and explored, much like the patient peeling of an onion. I got help from counseling and twelve-step groups one day at a time.

Financial reality captured my attention during the slow days of the healing process. How was I going to pay for groceries? My disability-insurance carrier found a loophole through which to deny me disability payments. My regular retirement funds would not be available until age sixty.

I turned forty-nine, wondering what I was going to do for a living. I cycled through a panic-stricken period. My parents flew to Anchorage to offer support. We began our days having coffee on the deck of my penthouse condo. We made lists while overlooking the Westchester Lagoon Bird Sanctuary, Cook Inlet, and Sleeping Lady Mountain.

What should have been an exhilarating view was marred by the constant intrusion of low-flying jets on approach to Anchorage International Airport. Every time I saw a plane fly by, I cried. When I was indoors and heard a plane, I cried.

Dad and I went to the public library to research the writing of a current resume. We detailed my minimum monthly expenses. My health insurance was refusing to pay some of my ongoing medical expenses, my condo fees were rising, and my liquid cash was disappearing at an alarming rate. Clearly, I needed to go to work. But doing what? I lined up interviews for waitress jobs, housekeeping work, temporary office help, and ground transportation. Dad and Mom went back home to San Diego while I was still filling out applications.

The next two months were demoralizing. My interview for a waitress position at my formerly favorite restaurant was typical of my experiences.

"Let's see, Miss, ah, O'Neill, now where did you waitress before and why did you leave there?"

"Well, sir, it was on Kodiak Island in 1973, and I left to pursue a flying career."

"Yes, I see here that you have been working as a commercial pilot for twenty-four years. Why aren't you flying now?"

"I lost my Airman's Medical Certificate. I'm taking a medication that I can't fly on, though it doesn't impact anything I do on the ground."

"Ah. Don't you think you're a little overqualified for this job?"

"No, sir. I want to work hard in a place that is uplifting to be in. I want to be around people. I know what good service in a fine restaurant looks like. I could do an excellent job for you."

"But wouldn't you just leave as soon as you could get your pilot's license back? We like to get employees who look upon waitressing as a career."

"Sir, it does not look like I'll ever get my license back. But if I did, at some point in the distant future, go back to flying, all that would happen is that you'd lose an excellent employee and regain a good customer. This is the restaurant I have always brought my Alaskan visitors to, and I can no longer afford to eat here."

"Well, Miss, ah, O'Neill, I'll get back to you if we have a job opening."

I learned that I didn't have enough experience to be considered for office work. A taxi company wanted to know why FedEx wasn't letting me drive one of their trucks if I was such a valuable employee. I was hired, finally, to clean houses, but the work was part-time. I started to drum up more house-cleaning business by calling Tiger pilots who had crash pads in Anchorage. I found myself working six days a week and not being able to pay my property taxes and fire insurance. I cashed in an annuity and gained financial breathing room. But I desperately missed my children and couldn't afford the airfare to go see them. I no longer had airline-employee reduced-rate fares or jumpseating privileges.

My parents were alarmed at my descending spirits and suggested that I come home for a visit. (Actually, my seventy-nine-year-old father told me if I didn't get on a plane to San Diego soon, he would fly up and drag me onto a southbound plane. I got the hint.) I went for a two-week visit and stayed two months. While I was there, I put my fully-paid-for condominium on the market. It sold. I decided that I needed to relocate to an area where I was within driving distance of my children.

311

In January 1999, I moved to Seattle, put my house money in the stock market, and began to search for work that was meaningful to me. I interviewed for a job teaching 747s in a simulator. I had both flight and ground instructor licenses and 16 years of experience on the plane. I wasn't hired. Months later, at a gym, a woman told me why. I had more actual "heavy metal" time than any of the men had. They didn't want a woman who knew more than they did. I decided it might be better for me to build a new life without any contact with airplanes.

I couldn't bear the thought. Powerless to stop, I began my final swirl down the sewer drain of alcoholism. I despaired. When death began looking like a viable way out, I called for a ride to a hospital. Despite no longer believing that anyone could help me, I checked myself into another treatment center.

Against expectations, the counselors didn't punish me or add to my shame and self-loathing. Their treatment embodied loving me until I could love myself. When they said I had to change everything, I asked where to start. Becoming completely honest, totally open, and 100 percent willing was how it worked for me.

A counselor asked, "What is the most important thing in the world for you, Norah?"

"My children," I replied. "I feel so guilty about spending months away from them at treatment centers."

"Norah, you're a warrior in a battle to save their mother's life. Someday, they'll thank you for taking the time. But, if you put your children first, you're going to lose them. Anything you put before staying sober will be lost."

When I grasped that concept, I was released back into the world. I did everything that was suggested, and I got sober. Getting sober is the hardest thing I've ever done. It was more painful then childbirth and more complex than flying a jumbo jet. I couldn't do it alone. I asked for, and received, continuous help. I still do.

Living sober allowed me to tap into a part of myself that had lain dormant for years. Having lived life at Mach .84 for most of adulthood had blown me by anything time-consumingly creative. For the first time since college, I had time to paint. I began to write again. Some of my paintings sold. The stock market boomed. I saw my children frequently and became a day-to-day mother again. I expanded my network of support groups.

My children decided that I had been living alone for too long and brought me two farm kittens for company. I started to garden again and searched vainly for flowers that my cats would not think were a new version of cat salad. I began to build a life different from any life I had ever imagined. Ten years ago, if I had been told that I would one day become one of those old women living alone with a house full of cats, I would have been horrified. Not anymore. With no more stress or chaos or leaping from one adrenaline rush to another, I was at peace.

I found that the courage to go on is just fear that has said its prayers.

39

FREE
FLIGHT

2001

Not being able to fly continued to bring tears until three years after losing my airman's medical.

While driving south on Seattle's crowded I-5 one rainy night, I saw a glimmer in the clouds and the belly of a plane emerge. For a second it flashed red and green and white against the clouds around it then plunged back into the broken overcast. Though swallowed whole into the whiteness, its lights still glowed through.

I knew what those pilots had just seen. One would have had his head lowered, eyes intent on the instruments in front of him. The other would have been looking out the window, waiting to call out his first sighting of the ground. When they flew out of that cloud, he would have said, "Ground contact." And then he would have looked ahead and seen the cloud they were about to enter. He would have watched it race toward him and then braced slightly for impact.

I had always tensed, though I knew the white wall would offer no resistance. But it always looked so solid. And then it would just enfold me. I always smiled when it did—this man-made, metal-winged tube meeting the elements and joining in perfect symbiosis. Flying. I pulled my car off the freeway and cried.

That was the last time I cried over losing flying. Soon afterward, I saw a plane and was only grateful that I'd had the great good fortune to fly for so many years. Many people never got that opportunity. I found that I could talk about some of my flight experiences again and laugh over them or marvel that I had survived them. I found that feeling grateful rather than deprived led to a deeper level of healing. The grieving cycle was over. I awakened every morning, glad that I was alive, glad that I had healthy and vastly entertaining children, glad that I had marvelous parents, glad that I had loyal friends, and glad that I had learned how to just be.

When I finally surrendered myself totally to God and the twelve-step program that saved my life and gave me a daily reprieve from alcoholism, I discovered in a simple prayer the solution to a lifetime of struggling.

How did a woman with my strengths get victimized? Bad things do happen to good people. Sometimes the good people have no part in it except to have gotten up and gone to work. But sometimes they do have a part, in not having done the things they needed to do.

The Serenity Prayer reduced the complex solution to a few lines. God grant me the serenity to accept the things I cannot change, the courage to change the things I can, and the wisdom to know the difference.

I have always had courage and the willingness to make changes. What I lacked was the wisdom to know the difference between what was possible for me to do and what was impossible. I have learned to accept people exactly as they are. If I don't like the way they are, I stop relating to them—as simple as that.

I don't have any fatally-flawed men in my life now. I don't have friendships with people who are emotionally unavailable. I don't try to relate to people who have different morals than I do. Either people are honest and open and willing to take risks and be vulnerable, or I am not with them.

I no longer bang my head against brick walls. I know how to quit. I have learned that sometimes surrendering *is* winning. I will never be a victim again. I have learned to live my life on life's terms and to accept the things that I cannot change.

I thought being *fulfilled* meant having a career and marriage and children. Those were important desires, but they did not *fill* a deep aching emptiness inside of me. I could fill that need only by looking within and aligning myself with a power greater than myself. Now I am *filled* with faith and hope and the grace to be the best me I can be.

*E*very morning I sit on my front deck with my first cup of coffee, a book of daily reflections, pots of flowers, and two orange cats. I look over the water of Puget Sound toward Vashon Island and the mountains of the Olympic Peninsula while I say my morning prayers. There is always the roil of water over the rocks of the shore, sometimes gurgling, sometimes crashing. Even in the worst weather, there are people on the water—tankers, container ships, naval vessels, sailboats, motor boats, and kayaks. I have seen seals and gray whales and orcas and dolphins.

One misty morning, there was a pod of orcas swimming south, their spume glimmering in shafts of sunlight as they surfaced. I ran to the beach so I could watch them swim with my view unobstructed by neighboring houses. I was careful to avoid tromping on the bed of sand dollars nestled in a long triangle of rock-bound sand in front of my building. I was aware of the spitting of water from clams, the scuttling of crabs, the bite of the barnacles into the rubber soles of my shoes and the slipperiness of the lime green seaweed. The gray cloud ceiling was broken and moving. I was cool in the cloud shadow. Then rays of light broke through above me, and I was limned in their warming glow. Spotlighted on the shore, I felt intensely alive. My senses hummed. I was immersed in the moment.

Another conversation with God. My happiness lies within me. The most difficult of circumstances won't keep it from me when I tap into the source. Life is a gift granted to me moment by moment. I am in awe of the wonder in it. I revel in it. I marvel at creation and realize how special I am to be a participant. I smile inside. I smile outside.

Grounded by the ocean that still offers me serenity, I watch the seabirds fly. In my heart, I can fly with them. When my soul was freed, it grew wings.

EPILOGUE

2002

My love affair with flying became like a love affair with a fickle, inappropriate man. I loved him and gave him my all, but he left me. Just when I healed to the point where I accepted that he was gone and realized that I could live well without him, he came back. Was I nuts enough to take him back and volunteer to possibly go through the whole process again?

One month after completing *Flying Tigress*, my good-bye love letter to flying, I regained my FAA Medical Certificate in April 2001. What I had thought would be a totally joyous occasion was not. I was scared to know the desire again, frightened of what it could bring. Could I go back to the jet-lagged, stress-filled, rarely-at-home vagabond life and remain sober and at peace with myself?

My decision to fly again was fueled by my faith that if I were getting the opportunity to do it, perhaps I was meant to do so, and by my pressing need to have a decent income again because my children were approaching college age. I thought if the pressure became too crazy, I could always quit. After all, I had learned to live without flying.

Retraining after almost five years was brutal. I seemed to remember nothing useful about the MD-11 and was at kindergarten level again. I became grateful that prayer was an active part of my life. Sometimes, praying for strength and a functional memory was the only way I could get myself to face another four hours of humiliation in the simulator.

In September of 2002, I left on an around-the-world flight with Richard Redditt. It was the final phase of my training and the first in the actual plane rather then the flight simulator. My check airman, Rich, was an ex-Tiger pilot, tall and athletically fit. His thinning hair was graying, and a beak of a nose dominated his pleasant, bushy-eyebrowed, craggy face. He knew my history.

As we left Memphis for Paris at 2 a.m., he said, "Relax, Norah. I know you're a good pilot. Just have fun and do whatever you want to do this leg. I won't nitpick or quiz you until after you've gotten comfortable. We have two weeks to get you up to speed and we're going to have fun doing it."

I felt the stiffness in my neck relax and my grip on the wheel ease, and I got on with flying rather than worrying. I smiled at Rich and noticed that he had grown taller and better looking in the last few hours, that wonderful transformation that happens when the good person within shines through. I saw the earth fall away and the stars come closer and I flew east through the night, cocooned in my beloved cockpit. I had come home again.

Rich and I flew from Paris across Europe and Asia to Subic Bay in the Philippines, departing Paris at one in the morning. Because of the thirteen-hour length of the flight, we had another captain and copilot on board to take over the controls when we rested. The relief captain was Dick Rothstein, my first study partner at Tigers. It was the first time in the twenty-six years since we had been hired that we actually operated together. I was awash with sweet memories of our pairing and hoped that my performance would be good. It was not particularly good, nor was it downright scary. Dick called out the worst of my errors and I corrected them. I reminded myself that that was what cockpit teamwork was supposed to be like.

Once we were safely settled in cruise, the three men went one by one to the small room behind the cockpit that held

319

our galley and bunk beds and changed into more comfortable clothing. Shortly before leaving Memphis, I had dinner with Tom Witts, my original 1996 MD-11 instructor. He advised me to bring pajamas on the trip with Rich; he said all the guys changed into them en route. I didn't own any pajamas so I ran to the local department store to purchase a pair. I chose roomy blue flannel ones covered with a playing kitten motif. When the three men returned to the cockpit in sweatpants and tee shirts, it became apparent that I was going to be the only one in real pajamas.

I brazened through my return to the cockpit saying, "I thought the occasion deserved the 'cat's pajamas' so here they are." *I am going to kill Tom Witts.* Once Rich quit laughing at my appearance and heard the story behind the cat's pajamas, he said, "I'm going to buy Tom dinner as a thank-you." Dick unpacked his camera.

We worked out a crew-sleeping schedule. Ribald cockpit humor arose. *Let's see, which one of you do I want to sleep with? And do I prefer being on top or on the bottom? Or should you start on top and finish on the bottom?*

After I napped through Eastern Europe and part of China, I crawled back into my seat still wearing the cat's pajamas and watched the sun come up over the Himalayas. I felt a crystalline moment of perfect joy—I could see the earth curve and our highest mountains slowly emerge on the horizon, outlined by the peach and rose glow of a sunrise spearing through their jagged crags. I was doing something I loved with people I liked and respected. All was right with my world.

AVIATION TERMS
AND DEFINITIONS

ADF Automatic Direction Finder: an instrument with an arrow-shaped pointer. The arrow points to a radio beacon.

ALPA Airline Pilots' Association, the largest union of airline pilots in the United States

APU Auxiliary Power Unit: a small jet engine, often in the tail of a large jet, used to produce electrical power and/or air on the ground for air-conditioning or engine starts

ATC Air Traffic Control

Bug Adjustable yellow pointer on an instrument in the cockpit, most often used on airspeed indicators and altimeters

CFI Certified Flight Instructor

Crosswind Wind not blowing directly down the runway

CSD Constant Speed Drive

CRM Crew Resource Management: FAA required course for airline pilots that teaches how to communicate well and safely in the cockpit

D.F. Steering Direction Finding instructions: sometimes given by air traffic control to a "lost" pilot they can see on radar; sometimes given by a controller who has an instrument that homes in on a lost pilot's radio.

Deadhead An airline employee who is catching a ride without paying for a ticket or actively working the flight he is on

Downwind leg   The part of the rectangular landing-traffic pattern around an airport that runs parallel to the runway and opposite the direction of landing

Duty time limits   The hours that pilots are legally allowed to work. They can be decided by FAA regulations or by company contracts.

EPR   Engine Pressure Ratio: shown on a dial in the cockpit and often used to decide a throttle setting for a desired amount of power

FAA   Federal Aviation Administration

FAR   Federal Aviation Regulation

GCR   Generator Control Relay

GFR   Generator Field Relay

GR   Generator Relay

Hydroplaning   To skim along like a hydroplane boat. In jets it means that the wheels are contacting the water on the surface of a runway, not the actual pavement itself. Hydroplaning often results in reduced braking ability and a loss of aircraft directional control.

IFR   Instrument Flight Rules

IGS   Instrument Ground-Guidance System

ILS   Instrument Landing System: a precise system that utilizes radio beacons for height above the ground (glideslope) and distance from the runway centerline (localizer)

INS   Inertial Navigation System: onboard navigational computer that does not rely on data from outside the aircraft.

ISA   International Society of Women Airline Pilots, founded in 1978

Leg   A section of a flight that includes one takeoff and one landing. A flight number might include several legs during the same duty period for the pilots.

Line of time   A pilot's monthly schedule, comprised of pairings of flights. A pilot receives his schedule of routes, destinations, and days off based on his seniority number.

Minimums   The lowest altitude to which a pilot can legally descend on an approach to an airport or on a published airway (highway in the sky). Or the least visibility or lowest ceiling of clouds that a pilot can legally shoot in an approach to an airport.

NATRACK North Atlantic Track: published routing for air traffic over the North Atlantic Ocean

Navaid Aid to navigation

NDB Non Directional (radio) Beacon

NOTAMS Notices to airmen, usually about data critical to aviation safety, including runway construction, navaid outage, navaid variations, restricted areas, and long-term changes in airport areas

TRACON Terminal area control (by radar)

Trim An adjusting of an aircraft's controls that allows the plane to continue at the same speed and angle without the pilot's input. Trimming is done using manual trim knobs or electronic tabs in the cockpit.

TRU Transformer Rectifier Unit

Type-rated Licensed by the FAA to fly a particular large aircraft

Vee speeds Speeds calculated for every takeoff and landing in a heavy jet, predicated on weight, wind, temperature, atmospheric pressure, length and condition of useable runway, and condition of the components of the aircraft. V1 is a go/no go speed; once it is reached, the airplane can no longer stop in the runway distance remaining. It is a maximum speed in the takeoff at which the pilot must take the first action to stop the plane within the accelerate-stop distance. If a takeoff is rejected after V1, the aircraft will most likely slide off the end before stopping. VR is the speed to rotate the nose of the plane to its initial takeoff attitude. V2 is a speed computed for flying in the event of the loss of power on an engine or for some other abnormal situation.

Vertigo A sensation of dizziness or whirling

VFR Visual Flight Rules

VOR Variable Omni Receiver: a navigational aid

Windshear A rapid and large change in direction of the wind

CHAPTER PHOTOS

1. Me, Steve, and Monica running on virgin snow, Mt. McKinley. *Photo credit: John Terence Turner*
2. In kindergarten, I was already asking, "Why can only boys do it?"
3. Flying over Alaska, 1973
4. A WWII-vintage C-46 that I flew with Paul Haggland on charter flights
5. In front of a Chieftain in an Alaskan Pipeline camp on the North Slope, 1974
6. Me with Paul Haggland and Alaskan governor Richard Egan on a flight that changed the rules about women flying into pipeline camps
7. Tigers: warm, welcoming, and frightening
8. A pilot's view of a glacier and mountains north of Anchorage
9. Dick Rothstein, me, and instructor, Mike White, during initial operating experience on the DC-8, January 1977
10. Tigers' DC-8. *Photo credit: John Beatty*
11. With my beloved fat lady, the 747. This photo was taken at the time I was the only woman in the world flying the 747.
12. Tiger crewmembers' luggage tag
13. Jean Haley Harper, president; Norah, vice president, Sharon Hilgers Krask, secretary, and Judy Lee, treasurer. ISA officers 1980-82
14. Jim Vinson, known for his humor and difficult union work, displayed fairness that was a blessing for early women copilots.
15. A sad, reflective moment. *Photo credit: James Collison*
16. While biking around the island of Moorea, Karen Kahn and I stopped at a hut where an English artist sold hand-painted clothing. Karen took this photo in the artist's front yard, and the dress remained my favorite for many years until my daughter inherited it.
17. Shiny, new Tigers' 747

18. Captain Ron Burson dubbed my post-swimming hair arrangement the Norse-goddess hairdo.
19. Reunited with Hayward Evans on an Anchorage layover
20. Getting angry was more effective and satisfying than being hurt.
21. Skiing in Sun Valley *Photo credit: James Collison*

INDEX

ABOUT THE AUTHOR

Norah O'Neill was a commercial pilot for thirty years, first in the Alaskan bush and then with the airlines, Flying Tigers and Federal Express. Hired as the first woman pilot for Flying Tigers, she set many milestones for women in commercial aviation. She continues to promote careers for women in aviation as a speaker to elementary, high school, and college students and at aviation conferences.

Norah majored in journalism at the University of California at Santa Barbara and at San Diego State University. She holds a BS in Professional Aeronautics from Embry Riddle Aeronautical University.

The mother of a son and a daughter, Norah lives in the Pacific Northwest. She is currently writing a novel.

Photo credit: Tara Gimmer